DETENTION CASTLES
OF STONE AND STEEL

DETENTION CASTLES
OF STONE AND STEEL

Landscape, Labor, and the Urban Penitentiary

James C. Garman

The University of Tennessee Press • Knoxville

Garman, James C.
Detention castles of stone and steel : landscape, labor, and the urban
penitentiary / James C. Garman.— 1st ed.
    p. cm.
Includes bibliographical references and index.
ISBN 1-57233-354-5 (hardcover)
 1. Rhode Island State Prison (Providence, R.I.)
 2. Prisons—Rhode Island—History—19th century.
 3. Imprisonment—Rhode Island—History—19th century.
 4. Prison industries—Rhode Island—History—19th century.
 I. Title.
HV9475.R62R564 2005
365'.9745'09034—dc22   2004018398

I ask, therefore, in this brighter day than the days that have gone, can not these detention castles of stone and steel be viewed more as clinical hospitals, and can not as great a study of these cases be made as is made of those in the hospitals devoted entirely to physical ills?

—Henry A. Jones, n.d.

Discipline is a political anatomy of detail.

—Michel Foucault, 1979

CONTENTS

ILLUSTRATIONS

TABLES

ACKNOWLEDGMENTS

I have accumulated many debts on my travels through the world of the nineteenth-century prison. Portions of this book originated as components of archaeological reports; others developed as my dissertation in the Department of Anthropology at the University of Massachusetts, Amherst; and still others came to light as the dissertation was revised into manuscript form. Along the way I was privileged to work with numerous individuals who were unstinting with their assistance.

Archaeological data recovery of the Rhode Island State Prison was undertaken when I was employed by PAL, a private not-for-profit cultural management resource firm in Pawtucket, Rhode Island. Kirk Van Dyke's talents for surveying the holdings of local archives and for recording the smallest details of the prison infrastructure were both greatly appreciated. Dana Richardi prepared the archaeological plans that illustrate this volume and Gail Van Dyke the map showing the proposals for the prison. Stephen Olausen, director of PAL, generously provided permission to reproduce these images. Staff of the Rhode Island Historical Preservation and Heritage Commission, including Paul Robinson, Richard Greenwood, and Charlotte Taylor, all provided helpful review on earlier components of the project. I would be especially remiss if I did not thank the owners' representatives of the developers whose projects engendered archaeological fieldwork at the Rhode Island State Prison and the Smithfield Town Farm, including Rick Duggan of the Providence Place Group and Andrew St. John of Fidelity Corporate Real Estate.

At the University of Massachusetts, Amherst, I was fortunate to have a perceptive and generous committee consisting of H. Martin Wobst as chair and members Stephen Mrozowski (University of Massachusetts, Boston), Roland Chilton (Department of Sociology, University of Massachusetts, Amherst), and Leo Carroll (Department of Sociology and Anthropology, University of Rhode Island), all of whom were patient, thorough, and above all insightful. I am also grateful to Robert Paynter, who always had encouraging words for an overwhelmed graduate student.

Rhode Island's skillful archivists and curators helped me navigate the maze of documentation pertaining to the prison. Thanks to the hard work of the state archivist Gwen Stearne and the archivist Kenneth S. Carlson, I was able to work through the fifty or so boxes of prison material at the Rhode Island State Archives. Ken proved especially obliging as the project developed, both by keeping a sharp eye out for prison material in other collections at the archives and by compiling an invaluable database with baseline information concerning Inmates Nos. 1 through 1,000 of the Rhode Island State Prison. Rick Stattler and Dana Signe K. Munroe of the Rhode Island Historical Society provided generous assistance with manuscripts and photographs, respectively. Susan Hay, curator of costumes and textiles at the Museum of Art, Rhode Island School of Design, shared her observations on the museum's delightful collection of fans painted in the prison. Melody Ennis of the museum kindly arranged for photography of the fans.

My colleagues at Salve Regina University have been kind enough to read portions of this manuscript as it progressed. Thanks to Debra Curtis, Linda Crawford, Donna Harrington-Lueker, and Elaine MacMillan for their critical comments on chapter 4 of this book. I am especially grateful to Debra for her keen observations of Stuart Hall's reading of Foucault. Grants from the University's Faculty Small Grants and Faculty Travel committees, both chaired by Johnelle Luciani, RSM, were instrumental in allowing me to augment existing research and develop the manuscript more fully.

A fellowship from the John Nicholas Brown Center for the Study of American Civilization provided access to resources I might not have been able to obtain otherwise; I thank the director Joyce Botelho for her support of the project. Aspects of the documentary and archaeological research discussed here were presented at a variety of conferences and seminars. The most inspiring of these was the 1996 George Meany Memorial Archives symposium "Building History and Labor History." Conversations with Paul Shackel and Michael Nassaney at the symposium were enormously helpful in developing the theoretical model used here. Other friends and fellow archaeologists have also been patient and encouraging, demonstrating a kind ability to humor my obsession with the nineteenth-century penitentiary. Thanks especially to Paul A. Russo, who supervised the day-to-day work of excavating the prison; Lauren J. Cook, who introduced me to the prose of B. Traven; Ronald J. Onorato, who helped me come to terms with the differences between the architectural vocabulary of John Haviland and that of Thomas A. Tefft; and Daniel P. Lynch, with whom I shared many stimulating conversations about material culture and the prison. David Cornelius, an expert in the architecture of the Eastern State Penitentiary, was kind enough to send pertinent citations on the Rhode Island State Prison from his extensive database of Haviland's papers.

It has been a great pleasure to work with the University of Tennessee Press. Scot Danforth is an editor as encouraging and thoughtful as any writer could hope to have. Randall McGuire, Christopher Matthews, and one anonymous reviewer provided a wide range of perceptive commentaries on an earlier draft.

From my parents I have acquired two skills relevant to this project: from my father, James E. Garman, the importance of fine-grained historical research in obscure repositories; and from my mother, Dorothy A. Garman, the importance of maintaining a sense of humor about the enterprise. My greatest debt is to Evelyn S. Sterne, who never ceased encouraging me along the way. This book is dedicated to her, with the greatest appreciation, affection, and love.

ACKNOWLEDGMENTS

CHAPTER 1

"In Limbo's Patrimony"

Theoretical Approaches to the Social Reform Institution

On a gloomy February evening in 1867, Thomas Casey sat in his solitary-confinement cell in the Rhode Island State Prison and tried to organize his disparate thoughts. A two-time loser, Casey was nearing the end of his second term in the prison. As a seventeen-year-old in 1854, he had been charged and convicted of an assault on one Mary E. Hicks; the stern indictment charged that Casey had "beaten, bruised, wounded and ill treated" Mary Hicks before proceeding "feloniously to ravish & carnally know her . . . against the peace & dignity of the State" (Rhode Island Judicial Court Archives [RIJCA] *State v. Thomas Casey*, Docket 606). In 1858, three years after his release, Casey landed back in prison on a conviction of assault with a dangerous weapon. He had been there ever since. That was a long time ago, nearly half my life, thought Casey, who gnawed the stub of a pencil as he composed a letter to Governor Ambrose Burnside. Due to the limited supply of paper issued to inmates, he was forced to use the reverse side of a letter his mother had written him in 1863. As he sat in the glow of a single gas jet, he took up the pencil and began to write laboriously. Don't want to sound *too* desperate, he thought as he slowly formed the letters on the page: "Sir = I am in limbo's Patrimony I.E. State Prison. now. I am 9 Years. and my health is so Poor from its affect, that I Have hardly any holpes to Weather the Storm But so far I have clung to hope But hope deferd, makes the Heart Sick: yet, I am one of These boys Who never says die" (General Treasurer's Records C

1184, 47C:1, Rhode Island State Archives [RISA]). Knowing full well that acknowledgment of the crime was an essential component of the petition, Casey then turned to the particular circumstances of his case. The ritual of the pardon letter demanded an admission of guilt. It was a fine line, though. Admit too much and they might keep him in there forever: "My Crime was, an, A Tempt to Kill. Under the Affects of the, fiend: Rum I am Partly Guilty = But not So Much as duffy: Who turned States Evidence and got off. I am now A Christian I hope: Tom Casey" (General Treasurer's Records C 1184, 47C:1, RISA). Reviewing the letter, Casey decided that it needed something else, something to demonstrate his sincerity and his newly found faith in religion. He found a second scrap of paper and added a postscript:

> and if God has Granted me marcy: Why Not my fellow man
> Resemble him: it is more Blessed to give then to receive—and,
> Blessed ar the mercifull for they Shall Receive mercy . . . and
> now my dear friend I state to you a fact— . . . If I had not a firm
> Resolve to live in the face of G[od] the Rest of my life: I would
> Not Trouble you at all. . . . God Bless, thee, fare thee well
>
> Thomas H Casey
> (General Treasurer's Records C 1184, 47C:1, RISA)

That will do, Casey decided, and just in time too. He could hear the steady tread of the underkeeper's boots on the flagstones of the hall, the bawl of "Lights Out!," and the slow hiss of the gas jets shutting down for the night. As he stretched out on the straw-stuffed mattress, listening to the Saturday-night parade of revelers howling on Gaspee Street, he thought, it won't be much longer. It won't be long at all.

The next morning General Nelson Viall, warden of the Rhode Island State Prison, scanned Casey's letter over the breakfast table. Born in 1827 in Plainfield, Connecticut, Viall had enjoyed an unusual career. He had gone to work in Providence as a molder in an iron foundry at the age of nineteen. After a successful stint in the Mexican War, his travels had taken him to Brazil, where he managed a failing iron foundry for four years. He had then found his way back to Providence, where he joined the United Train of Artillery, a local militia band (Bartlett 1867, 339).

The Civil War had proved opportune for Viall. He started the war as a lieutenant in the Rhode Island Artillery and was quickly promoted to captain. Three weeks after the Union disaster at Bull Run, he was promoted a second time to the rank of major. A diligent and meticulous quartermaster,

2

he had organized the Fourteenth Regiment, Rhode Island Heavy Artillery, which was made up of African American recruits. Just before the war ended, President Lincoln had made him a brigadier general. Viall had returned to Rhode Island triumphant to parades, testimonials, and other honors (Bartlett 1867, 340).

The new post as warden of the Rhode Island State Prison had seemed a perfect fit for the former quartermaster. He had not predicted the mind-numbing minutiae required to oversee the state's most heinous offenders. Now reading the scrawled letter before him, Viall thought with a smile, Tom Casey again. Last week he had sent him to the Dark Cell for twenty-four hours for talking in the prison workshop. Put it in the docket with the others, he told his clerk, and let Burnside deal with the matter.

Governor Burnside, preoccupied with composing his memoirs of the war, later rolled his eyes when he saw the formidable packet on his desk. Engrossed in telling his version of the disaster at Petersburg, Burnside had no time for trivialities such as requests for pardons. He was still brooding over Lincoln's offhand remark about that horrifying July afternoon. "Only Burnside could have managed such a coup," Lincoln had commented acidly, "wringing one last spectacular defeat from the jaws of victory." Easy enough for Lincoln to say, thought Burnside, who had watched in horror as the Confederate sharpshooters, stunned by the explosion under their lines, had regrouped and meticulously shot down his men floundering in the smoking desolation of the crater. His reverie ended long enough for him to summon his attorney general, Horatio Rogers Jr. Burnside gave the bundle of letters to Rogers, stared out his window at the grimy city, and went back to work on his manuscript.

Rogers too did not have time for such trivialities. He had been terminally ill for nearly two years, and his time was short. He dropped the packet on the desk of one of his clerks, known only as Fitzgerald, who skimmed the petitions and composed standard form letters back to Warden Viall, asking for comments on the inmates in question. The letter he wrote for Casey does not survive, but based on other examples from the period, it must have contained a series of questions concerning Casey's attitude under the conditions of imprisonment. Was he well behaved; was his conduct appropriate? Did he participate in work willingly? Did he engage in the mandatory weekly religious services held in the prison chapel? Rogers may have been mildly interested in Casey, who had steadfastly maintained his innocence for nearly a decade and, while politically unconnected, was perhaps not entirely unknown to the attorney general's informal network of Irish and Irish American residents of Providence.

Viall, for his part, had little time to waste on the specifics in the matter of Thomas Casey. He was preoccupied with conducting the annual inventory of prison goods and negotiating a new contract for the labor of his charges. He did not bother to respond to Fitzgerald's letter until June 21, 1867, when he scrawled a hasty note:

My dear Fitzgerald

I return the Note of Thos. Casy a Convict in this prison, and would Say that there is no good reason *that I know* of why Casy should not Stay his time out—he has aped the Christian up to the rising of the Gen. Assembly when he forwarded to the Religious Instructor a Note Saying that he should withdraw from the Sabbath School and worship on the Sabbath in consequence of the partiality of that body. his ill health is from the habit of self abuse.

Very Truly yours,
Nelson Viall Warden
(General Treasurer's Records C 1184, 47C:1, RISA)

So much for Thomas Casey, thought Fitzgerald as he scanned the note. He gathered up all the documents pertaining to the case and bound them with a red ribbon. He placed the bundle in a folder marked "Prisoner Petitions (1867)—Not Granted" and gave the folder to his clerk to file in the basement of the State House, in a drawer jammed with similar requests that had been denied.

More than 130 years after Thomas Casey scrawled his letter to Governor Burnside, punishment and the proper means of rehabilitating and reforming society's transgressors stand at the forefront of public concern. The complexities of this debate, which continue to baffle government authorities, taxpayers, victims of crime, and criminals, lie deeply rooted in Jacksonian-era arguments about the means of "curing the problem" of deviant behavior. Precisely what constitutes punishment and what role labor plays as a corrective, rehabilitative, or punitive force are the subjects of continued scrutiny.

I intend to examine the historical precedents of the modern debate by considering power, work, and the manner in which they were negotiated within the landscape and built environment of the nineteenth-century reform institution. The primary case study derives from historical archaeological investigations of Rhode Island's first state prison in Providence.

Constructed in 1838, the prison was enlarged and rebuilt in several phases before its abandonment in 1877 and its demolition in 1893. Other case studies include the Smithfield (Rhode Island) Town Farm and Asylum (1834–70), established to meet the local need for poor relief, and the various orphanages, asylums, and juvenile reform structures at the state farm in Howard, Rhode Island (ca. 1870–90). Archaeological and architectural analyses of these complexes address different aspects of the questions raised here about the relationship between landscape and labor in the milieu of industrial capitalism.

The interwoven stories of Thomas Casey, Nelson Viall, Horatio Rogers Jr., "Fitzgerald," Ambrose Burnside, and myriad other individuals survive only as water-stained documents filed in the Rhode Island State Archives. The arena where their stories took place—the first Rhode Island State Prison—is now the site of a $450 million upscale retail mall and movie theater complex. Public memory of the prison as a focal point of the nineteenth-century Providence skyline, briefly revived during an archaeological excavation, has vanished. My objective is to consider documents (the state-sanctioned, archived component of the material world) and artifacts (the accidental survivals of the material world) to reconstitute the inner workings of the nineteenth-century prison.

Why Should We Care about the History of Imprisonment?

The notion of the nineteenth-century social reform institution commands the power to conjure distinctive images in our minds: forbidding granite walls, a Dickensian workhouse, keepers and wardens and watchers of gleefully sadistic mien. As an adolescent growing up in Rhode Island, I was warned constantly that forgetting to turn down the heat would lead our family to the poor farm, or that misbehavior would start me down the pathway to Sockanosset, the home for the state's juvenile offenders. These references to the deep past bore no relation to the present circumstance: Portsmouth, Rhode Island, had closed the doors of its poor farm and workhouse in the 1920s, and Sockanosset had long since become a modern facility with a staff of psychologists and social workers. The point is that the oral tradition and associated memories of institutions were still sufficiently powerful to terrify and compel better behavior from miscreant youths.

Visit a correctional facility today and you will find few visual parallels with our mental images of the grim fortresses of the nineteenth century.

Contemporary institutions are designed to meet federal mandates for light, space, and air circulation. Correctional officers are thoroughly trained, polite, and efficient; many have university degrees in the administration of justice. Even the Orwellian language of corrections, emphasizing "intake centers" and "campus life," stands in stark contrast to jangling nineteenth-century terms such as "penitentiary," "cell blocks," and "warden."

Given the disparity between past and present conditions, the reader might ask why citizens of the presumably more enlightened twenty-first century should trouble themselves with considerations of the nineteenth-century prison. Surely the disciplinary regimes of nearly two centuries ago have little to tell us about the way we live our lives today. We could wish this to be true, but that imprisonment has become a part of everyday life in America is an inescapable conclusion. In my hometown one of every fifteen men is on probation. Your hometown is likely no different. You may well know someone who has flirted with prison time, spent time in prison, or will be sentenced to prison in the future.

Had you been a citizen of the new nation in 1838, the year the Rhode Island State Prison opened its doors, the odds of your knowing an inmate of the state would have been slim indeed. At that time the American experimentation in imprisonment had just begun, with states and territories vying to outdo one another by constructing massive granite-walled complexes as laboratories for the carefully controlled reform of malefactors. The difference between then and now is that we have become a punitive society seeking retribution against criminals; the discourse of reform is now secondary to the discourse of retribution, and we are largely content to lock away offenders in warehouses run increasingly by private contractors.

State documents bear out these assertions. In the new nation period Americans firmly believed that they stood at the forefront of a bold experiment aimed at "curing" the problem of criminality in society. "No government can be presumed to be activated by that spirit of revenge," wrote a Rhode Island committee meant to consider the feasibility of a state prison in 1834. "The penalties annexed to these laws have for their object the prevention of crime by reforming the delinquent and by detaining others from like courses" (John Brown Francis Papers, Box 5, F 86, Rhode Island Historical Society [RIHS]). Precisely one hundred years later a committee appointed to examine the state of prison industry in Rhode Island noted that prisoners had only two rights: the right to regular food and the right to religious worship. "All things else," the committee added, "are only privileges granted to him as a matter of courtesy by the Warden as a reward for good behavior or meritorious accomplishment" (Preliminary

Report of the Committee on Prison Industries 1934, 2). Within the span of a century a process with the high purpose of reform became a process whereby food and opportunities for religious worship were guaranteed and everything else was a matter of privilege extended at the discretion of a state officer. Thus, in thinking and writing about the nineteenth-century prison, my initial questions concern the historical trajectory of change: How was the stated purpose of "reforming the delinquent" transformed to a doctrine of punishment? Why did notions of social reform give way to notions of punitive action? What changed, both within the walls of the institutions and within the sprawling boundaries of American capitalism?

The answers to questions about what underlies the transformation of attitudes toward reform in the United States are inseparable from all-encompassing changes in ideological context. Born in a spirit of post-Enlightenment democracy, an agrarian era of reform and republicanism, the prison is now a razor-wired bastion of industrial liberal capitalism (Melossi and Pavarini 1981). So integrated is the notion of punishment into everyday life that until recently a billboard hanging over a busy highway outside Boston's Suffolk County House of Corrections informed harried commuters, "If you committed a crime, you'd be home now." Unlike our Jacksonian forebears, we rarely interrogate the idea of imprisonment as society's mechanism for punishing the deviant; we look instead for ways to make it cheaper, more efficient, and more effective in meeting its primary goal of separating criminals from society.

To separate criminals from their liberty is, next to the death penalty, the most formidable exercise of state power against the individual. This, then, is a book about power and the way power is deployed and contested in the context of institutional confinement. It is necessarily a book about power because within the walls of the penal institution power is ubiquitous, inescapable, and enveloping. It has physical representation in walls, cell blocks, bars, locks, and keys; and it has metaphysical representation in documents of commitment, internal reports, and statements from the keepers to the public. Virtually everything pertaining to the prison and to "prisonness" constitutes this context of power. Anthony Giddens (1984, 161) has described such contexts as *locales*, or "power containers," noting that they "refer to the use of space to provide the 'settings' of interaction, these settings in turn being seen as essential to specifying the 'contextuality' of action—in time and space—in a fully sociological way."

From the forbidding, fortresslike exterior of the facility to the cramped and crowded conditions of individual cells, the stern expression of nineteenth-century society's disapproval of criminal and deviant behavior

7

was inescapable. Yet at the beginning of this process, respectable society was by no means unified in its approach to punishment. Competing trends in corrections have been present from the beginning of the experiment. Foucault (1979, 234) cautions those who would see the prison as a static, monolithic entity disturbed by occasional waves of reform: "One should also recall that the movement for reforming the prisons, for controlling their functioning, is not a recent phenomenon. . . . Prison 'reform' is virtually contemporary with the prison itself: it constitutes, as it were, its programme."

This notion of state power as a dynamic *process*, not a static object or thing wielded by one group over another, is central to understanding institutional practices in the milieu of capitalism. In discussing the prison, I hope not to fall into the trap of trying to sort out dominant and subordinate ideologies at work within the matrix of confinement (cf. Abercrombie, Hill, and Turner 1980). To equate the prison with state power, as deployed by dominant groups, is too simple. The narrative of the prison is about more than the power of the evolved capitalist state; it is about the complexities of power, and its dissolution and decentralization and contestation by the various stakeholders in the ongoing process of punishment.

Central to that analysis is an appreciation for the ways in which inmates such as Thomas Casey tried to develop and wield their own small measures of power. As Paynter and McGuire (1991, 6) state clearly, "If power is heterogeneous, then it is not limited to a single area of society." Do prisoners of the state have power? In the sense that they live lives of confinement, structured by imposed patterns of work, worship, and sporadic, state-approved recreation, they do not. Yet to the extent that they can individually or collectively contest the coercive and repressive disciplining of the state, they do indeed possess this "power" (Paynter and McGuire 1991, 6).

Historical archaeology is well suited to the task of studying the complexities of power relationships. Established during the cold war as a means of studying the material world of presidents, generals, and other male, white leaders of democracy, the discipline has come of age through its practitioners' more recent efforts to study the lives of the enslaved, the insane, and the poor (cf. Mayne and Murray 2001). Strikers at a Colorado mining camp (Saitta, McGuire, and Duke 1999), Japanese American inmates of a "relocation camp" (Burton 1996), and prostitutes in the famed New Orleans Storyville (Powell 2002) are all considered subjects worthy of archaeological scrutiny. Whether or not the stated purpose of these studies is to critique liberalism, these are archaeologies of capitalism, studies that seek to inform us of where we have come from and where we are going

(Mrozowski, Delle, and Paynter 2000, xiv–xvii). This study follows in that trajectory, situating the nineteenth-century prison and prison subjectivity as a primary site of resistance to the imperative of capitalist discipline.

Landscape, Labor, and Power

Concerning the relevance of nineteenth-century institutions to critiques of the present, three related fields of inquiry should be considered. The first is the landscape of social experimentation in Jacksonian America. Although Americans in no way "invented" the prison, the sweeping nationwide project of prison construction in the 1820s and 1830s was the first of its kind in the world. The architectural configurations of institutions, and their associated archaeological landscapes, can inform the modern observer of the ways in which humans built, maintained, expanded, and revised a reform project that had never previously been tested.

In particular, the *cultural landscape* of the prison will be considered in an effort to trace the dichotomy of reform and punishment in the nineteenth century. By *cultural landscape* I mean a definition that is more broadly constituted than a passive stage setting to human activity. Following Marquardt and Crumley (1987, 1), I consider landscape to be the wide range of material manifestation of relationships between humans and the environment, a range that actively structures human relations. A set of stairs added to an existing building is part of this landscape, as is a line of rough board fencing, a walkway, or an alley between buildings that allows a view beyond the walls of the institution. These examples speak to the ability of space to shape movement and therefore human activity (McGuire 1992, 105).

Historical archaeology, defined as the study of capitalism through consideration of the material world, is the methodological approach used here (Johnson 1996; Leone 1988, 1995; Mrozowski, Ziesing, and Beaudry 1996; Nassaney and Abel 1993, 2000; Paynter 1988, 1989; Paynter and McGuire 1991; Shackel 2000). Within this definition I consider the material world to include all precedents and products of human activity, including built environments, landscapes, artifacts, and documents. By bringing to bear an ever more inclusive definition of material culture—one incorporating relict landscapes, viewsheds, and unrealized visions committed to paper but never built—the archaeologist can gain some measure of access to interpretive spaces, especially when the extensive documentary record pertaining

9

to the institution is used to interrogate and reinterrogate the material remnants identified through archaeological excavation.

My second area of inquiry concerns *labor* and specifically the complex web of social relations surrounding the labor process in the nineteenth-century institution. Labor was absolutely essential to the corrective regime of the nineteenth-century institution. In all of the accounts I have examined I have not found a single case of a prison, town farm, or state farm that did not at least nominally require its inmates to work. This requirement fostered a peculiar form of corporate capitalism, especially when set against the backdrop of industrialization in nineteenth-century New England (Faler 1981; Gross 1993; Mrozowski, Ziesing, and Beaudry 1996; Shackel 2000; Siracusa 1979). Prisons maintained an astonishing diversity of entrepreneurial enterprises as part of the regime of forced labor. In Rhode Island alone examples ranged from unskilled tasks (rag-picking and oakum production) to those requiring more complex operations (the preparation and painting of decorative fans). The motivations for these enterprises were complex and worthy of scrutiny.

To equate labor with work in an institutional environment is to overlook the web of relationships engendered by the labor process. At the Rhode Island State Prison labor constituted an arena of struggle between the state, prison authorities, and convicts forced to perform tasks in the institution's workshops. Those in charge of the prison work program faced many of the same challenges as did their private-sector counterparts: unruly workers, lack of markets for their products, and competition with other manufacturers of similar goods. There was, of course, an important difference: although the private sector's reaction to dissenting workers was to fire them, blackballing them from further employment in the city or region, the prison's only recourse to problems with its recalcitrant and unwilling labor force was to punish it physically, and at times brutally. Prisoners developed a remarkable range of resistive responses to forced labor, including malingering, feigning incompetence, sabotage, and arson. Questions about the *ideology* of forced labor then become important. Where were the origins of the program of coerced labor used in nineteenth-century Rhode Island? To what extent did this program resemble or deviate from the industrial order imposed by mill owners and other manufacturers on labor in the private sector? How can success or failure of a labor program be measured within the context of coercion?

The issue binding landscape with labor, and the principal area of inquiry pursued in this book, is that of *power* contested on multiple levels.

The prison is one of the most physical expressions of the state's power to dominate and terrorize. Yet if we consider the prison as a metaphor for the state, we will see that the prison, like the state, is composed of institutions with competing resources and agendas (McGuire 1992, 164). Close reading of the institution's records supports this notion. Of even greater importance than the complexity of power is its interpretation as a "relational quality that results from human action" (McGuire 1992, 165), rather than an absolute or fixed quantity. Both these ideas speak clearly to the necessity of developing a more complex understanding of the material manifestations of state power and its interplay with the allegedly powerless—in this case, those who were sentenced to a year or five years or ten years or life behind the walls of the Rhode Island State Prison.

Landscape

We cannot know much about what went on behind the walls of the nineteenth-century institution until we have a complete notion of what the space behind those walls looked like. Thus interpretations of the penitentiary's cultural landscape and its change over time offer the first avenue toward interpreting the lives of the dispossessed. *Cultural landscape* is a term that almost defies definition. Environmental archaeologists, cultural geographers, historians, and others have all adapted the term to suit disciplinary needs. For this study the emphasis is placed on interpretations that counter traditional archaeological notions of landscapes as stage settings or backdrops to human activity by emphasizing their inextricable links to culture. "First, we assume that human understanding of the environment is cultural, that humans collectively define and redefine their surroundings," write Marquardt and Crumley (1987, 5). "Not only is all human reality culturally comprehended (cognized), but it is in constant flux, as people in groups, acting on the basis of vested interests . . . expend energy in ways that, in turn, affect and come into conflict with the results of past social actions, energy expenditures, and perceptions." Henri Lefebvre (1991) offers a perspective that is similar, but with a more explicit emphasis on power as the defining element in "spatial architectonics": *"(Social) space is a (social) product"* (Lefebvre 1991, 26; italics and parentheses in original). His definition of "produced space" could well describe the historical trajectory of the first Rhode Island State Prison:

11

the space thus produced also serves as a tool of thought and of action; that in addition to being a means of production, it is also a means of control, and hence of domination, of power; yet that, as such, it escapes in part from those who would make use of it. The social and political (state) forces which engendered this space now seek, but fail, to master it completely; the very agency that has forced spatial reality towards a sort of uncontrolled autonomy now strives to run it into the ground, then shackle and enslave it.

(Lefebvre 1991, 26)

For Lefebvre, space is not an object created and left alone, with occasional updates or modifications; space is a social process, one which competing interests with different levels and kinds of power are continually contesting and recontesting. Thus what is especially interesting about the prison is not its spatial configuration but the role of the complex in mediating different sets of relationships between prisoners, guards, keepers, and the public. From this perspective, space assumes a much more dynamic role, subject to continuous contestation by competing interests; externally it takes on aspects of *legitimation* and *intersubjectivity* in its mediation between criminals and respectable society.

Such interpretations are by no means new to historical archaeology. One of the best-known cases is the Paca Garden in Annapolis, Maryland (Leone 1984). In studying the formal garden of an elite eighteenth-century planter, Leone (1984) argues that the planter's garden was a deliberate and conscious justification of his status as a loyal member of the mercantile elite. This interpretation has been scrutinized to different ends. Ian Hodder (1986), for example, cites the possible intersubjectivity of the landscape-artifact (that is, its ability to be read in different ways by different sectors of society) and suggests that textual ambiguity might cloud the issue of whether the garden deliberately marked Paca's membership in the elite or masked it except to those who were already in the know. Conversely, Paynter and McGuire (1991, 15) describe the Paca Garden study as an exercise in interpreting the legitimating power of landscape: "Discipline has a material dimension in the creation of the modern working class."

In this vein, Michael S. Nassaney and Robert Paynter (1995, 1) have developed three propositions underpinning archaeologies of space. Their first proposition, drawing on the work of Lefebvre (1991), is that powerful individuals manipulate spatiality explicitly and implicitly, and that space is a social process, a means rather than an end. Their second proposition revolves around the continuous restructuring of landscape "through a dialectical process to produce a pattern that better serves the changing goals and motivations of human action" (Nassaney and Paynter 1995, 2). The third and final proposition concerns the abilities of the built environment to reify inequality through architectural symbolism (Nassaney and Paynter 1995, 2; cf. Harvey 1989; Zukin 1991). This perspective is especially compelling—and appropriate for the world of the nineteenth-century institution—because it explicitly examines the relationship between power and both diachronic and synchronic change in the material world.

To see the possibilities of legitimating power in archaeological landscapes, archaeologists have to look beyond the individual artifacts in their screens and consider the broader cultural landscape. For the Rhode Island State Prison, this concept might be imagined as a funnel; forming the mouth of the funnel is the state's monumental built environment of confinement: cell blocks, keeper's house, and workshops. At the middle level are landscape elements that mesh with the built environment: fence lines, points of entry and exit, drainage patterns, and heating systems. At the bottom of the funnel are artifacts, the material residue of everyday life. Although intriguing, this view tends to privilege the perspective of the archaeologist, who carefully sifts through the rubble, draws plans and profiles of what she sees, and files carefully labeled polyethylene bags of artifacts away in a climate-controlled storeroom.

A more holistic cultural landscape paradigm encompasses all the disparate elements that are part of the formation of sites. In a state-run reform institution, one of the most important categories of analysis is that of the "what-might-have-beens": that is, plans, specifications, official documents, written suggestions, and other material representing plans for projects that were deeply desired but never executed. In the vast archive pertaining to the Rhode Island State Prison are numerous examples of "wish lists" from the board of inspectors: a new wall, an iron gate, an air-circulating system, a proper chapel for Sunday worship. Although never actually built, these buildings on paper speak to the desire of authorities to get things right and are almost as important as what was actually built. Thus in addition to its material components, cultural landscape has an abstract dimension in that what people thought about the prison and the ways in which they imagined it could be improved are as important as what actually took material form.

The process of imagining what might have been is a firm reminder to consider the institution's intersubjectivity, which I define as its ability to be

13

read in different ways by different individuals, including state legislators, prison authorities, inmates, and the public. The internal landscape of the prison is by nature more difficult to interpret than the external. Of the twelve nineteenth-century renditions of the complex identified in local archives, eleven are front exterior views; the twelfth is a rear elevation obscured by the perimeter fence, with only the roofs visible above the line of wooden planks. Mid- to late nineteenth-century panoramic views of the cityscape deliberately exclude the prison, indicating that its presence had become less an object of civic pride and more an embarrassment to city boosters (fig. 1). No interior view of the prison has been located. Archaeology represents virtually the only way to experience the structure's internal configuration and to interpret the lives of the confined.

As compelling as the problem of internal landscape may be, it would be misguided to privilege its interpretation at the expense of the facility's external articulation with the rapidly expanding built environment of nineteenth-century Providence. During its term of operation the prison served as a direct statement to the outside world of several important aspects of life: order, morality, and above all, the state's separation of "deviants" from respectable society. The siting of the prison within downtown Providence embraced a dramatic contradiction: the boardwalk of the city's principal public park, the Cove Promenade, ran directly in front of the institution. Deviance was immediately barred from nondeviance by walls and fences, yet wholly integrated into the larger cityscape of the burgeoning metropolis.

A paradigm emphasizing the legitimating powers of landscape, as well as the landscape's intersubjectivity, provides detailed insight into the ideology of the institution and its authorities. Christopher Tilley (1990, 309), in his review of Foucault, has pointed out that the spatial characteristics of institutions have been studied at length: "Techniques of social control become increasingly invested in varied institutional architectural forms: hospitals, prisons, factories, schools, office buildings. . . . The aim in all these institutions is to create a space for surveillance." Although the need for surveillance is indisputable, these institutions surely had other aims. In the case of the prison, some that come to mind immediately include punishment of criminals, deterrence, separation of convicts from respectable society, moral and religious instruction of those considered immoral, and rudimentary vocational training. Yet surveillance pervades all of these aims and requires construction of a landscape sufficiently flexible to permit change and sufficiently formidable to help constitute, convey, and reinforce the power of the state. Randall McGuire (1992, 102–3) notes,

14

Fig. 1 — The Rhode Island State Prison, barely visible through the trees toward the left edge of the photograph, bordered by the Cove Foundry and Machine Company and other industrial buildings to the east. Undated silver gelatin print by an unknown photographer. Author's collection.

"Material culture entails the social relations that are the conditions for its existence. It is both a product of these relations and part of the structure of these relations. Material culture both limits and enables action, and therein lies the key to its interpretation."

The principle of panopticism underlies many architectural designs of institutions requiring surveillance. Jeremy Bentham, the late eighteenth-century English reformer, has been credited with developing the architectural configuration of the Panopticon; its constituent elements generally include a central dome or octagon, with cells lining the interior spaces. At the center of the dome is a watchtower or central observation point. Through techniques of backlighting, the observed are obscured from the observer; the idea is that, from the central point, the monitor can observe individuals without their cognizance. The theoretical principles of panopticism, which originated in prison construction, spread through almshouses, hospitals, schools, and factories, all of which appeared to their designers to require some level of inmate monitoring. Bentham's theatrical Panopticism, however, with its emphases on lighting, sound, and even costumes, never

15

emerged in its fullest form; to the contrary, few American prisons were built in accordance with even the most basic Benthamite principles (Johnston 2000).

But panopticism is more than an architectural style; even when institutions were not built in compliance with Bentham's prescriptions, panopticism served as a way of ordering the world and imparting instructive lessons of reform. Surveillance goes beyond simply observation; the overriding goal of surveillance is for individuals to become aware that they are being watched, and to thus become monitors of their own behavior before incurring authoritarian disapproval (Leone 1995). It is a technique that combines discipline and self-discipline, one that attempts to force individuals to reform themselves; it is also a strategy that depends on controlling the most essential aspects of human action, including movement and communication. The body of literature relating to the architectural configuration of the penal institution is substantial (Evans 1982; Foucault 1979; Ignatieff 1978; Johnston 2000; Melossi and Pavarini 1981; Rothman 1971; Semple 1993; Spens 1994; Upton 1992). Dell Upton's discussion of Philadelphia's Eastern State Penitentiary, a thoughtful reflection on early nineteenth-century ideas of body and self, is part of a larger effort to reinterpret urban space of the new nation as "repressive urbanism . . . whose enunciated ideal was the humming city, but which used silence and architecture to create a new, mute, inner-directed citizen" (1992, 71). Drawing on John Haviland's design for the Eastern State Penitentiary, he demonstrates the importance of the built environment to the larger proposition of corrections. Among the aspects of confinement designed to reduce communication among inmates were vaults meant to muffle sound, the hooding of prisoners to prevent nonverbal communication, and thick walls that eliminated the opportunity for prisoners to tap coded messages to one another (Upton 1992, 66).

The reconstruction of the prison's cultural landscape through the methods of historical archaeology forms the entry point into the analysis of discipline. Within this domain the single most important reform strategy, outweighing education or religious instruction, was daily work, viewed as the ultimate means of curing reprobates and guiding them back to the ways of respectable citizens. Requirements of labor, and the ways in which they were conceived, deployed, and contested, offer means of bridging the axes of landscape and power in the reform institution.

Labor

Convicts forced to work in the prison workshops faced a range of options between two extremes. At one end of the spectrum, they could comply with issued directives of their overseers, conduct themselves in an exemplary manner, and ultimately win release at an earlier date. At the other end of the spectrum, they could resist the requirement of labor in occasionally spectacular fashion. The responses, framed in a dialectical and recursive relationship against directives from above, spanned the spectrum between these two options and ranged from small-scale, almost invisible actions to outright confrontation. These actions ultimately reverberated up and then back down the hierarchy and reshaped social relations within the institution. Before examining these reverberations, it is necessary to review the ideological and economic bases that justified prison labor.

Work formed the backbone of all efforts to reform criminals (as well as the indigent and insane) in the nineteenth century. "Work is neither an addition nor a corrective to the regime of detention: whether it is a question of forced labour, reclusion, or imprisonment, it is conceived, by the legislator himself, as necessarily accompanying it" (Foucault 1979, 240). Three distinct trends of thought exist concerning the nature of prison labor in the nineteenth century. These include the institutional ideology of the time, which held that work was a necessary corrective to the evil habits of the criminal and an indispensable component of the institution's sustainability; the interpretation of Michel Foucault (1979, 240), who argues that the work carried out by prisoners was devoid of meaning, purpose, or potential profit and that it simply served to reinforce relationships of power between authorities and the confined; and an explicitly Marxist perspective, suggested by Rosalind P. Petchesky (1993), that prison labor was the ultimate exploitation of a confined workforce.

Prison labor as an agent of reform. The rationale for work as an agent of reform was straightforward: those caught in the clutches of idleness needed to reform their habits to incorporate daily and repetitive work if they were expected to become productive, nonrecidivist citizens of capitalist society. Institutional records also suggest that authorities believed that imprisonment could be made self-sufficient. From the outset, the General Assembly of Rhode Island and the prison authorities expressed hope that the labor of the convicts would pay for the maintenance of the institution, and thus avoid a drain on the taxpayer-supported general fund. The first report of prison labor in Rhode Island (*Acts and Resolves of the Rhode Island General*

17

Assembly [ARRIGA] October 1839, 25) summarizes the issue aptly: "After procuring all the information in their power as to the kind of mechanical labor practicable with solitary confinement, not injurious to health, easily learned and carried on, and likely to be made profitable, or least liable to loss, the inspectors decided upon that of manufacturing shoes and boots." After the construction of a communal workshop, prison authorities in their report of 1849 expressed continued optimism that prison labor would create a self-sustaining institution: "and from the ready sale of the articles manufactured, the undersigned have no hesitancy in saying that if the accommodations of the workshop could be enlarged, so that all the prisoners could be put to labor, it would not be many years before this department would nearly, if not quite, pay for its own expenses" (*ARRIGA* October 1849, 78). These expectations, if sincere, were certainly naive. Authorities were under tremendous pressure to comply with public expectations that prisoners would work while confined, and that work would be employed as a reformatory agent. In reality, the prison work program lost staggering sums of money from the time of its establishment until the early 1850s. An eventual solution to the problem was innovative and evocative of modern sensibilities: prison authorities privatized the work program, establishing contracts with outside firms for convict labor. By 1877 the prison held agreements with a shoemaker, the Providence Cotton Tie Company, and a wire-goods manufacturer; authorities were also in the unique position of writing themselves a contract for prison laborers to build the furnishings for the new house of correction in Cranston. These agreements stemmed the fiscal hemorrhaging of the prison but put aside permanently any idealistic notions of work as a vocational method or reformative agent.

Improvement efforts within the walls of the prison were directed toward moral reform and education. The prison's extensive library provided a range of approved inspirational reading material for the semiliterate and the educated. In contrast, the labor program was only peripherally vocational; most tasks were unskilled or semiskilled and could rarely have provided a parolee with a trade. In reading nineteenth-century documents, one is struck by the importance of the *routine* of the work regime, and of the instillation of the habit of daily work—aspects of labor that Foucault (1979) developed in his analysis of institutional power.

Prison labor as an enforcement of power relations. Those who choose to study nineteenth-century institutions must inevitably reckon with the ideas of Foucault, as articulated in *Discipline and Punish* (1979 [1978]) and, to a lesser extent, in *Madness and Civilization* (1964). In both works

IN LIMBO'S PATRIMONY

Foucault is primarily concerned with the notion of *discourse*, or the ways in which a dominant group inscribes normative behavior on subordinate groups. Inmates in institutions constitute a population of "docile bodies"; execution of a system of discipline could, in Foucault's reading of the nineteenth century, create obedient, self-monitoring workers from these bodies. Here the penitentiary's architectural environment and everyday efforts at discipline may be linked to the *homo oeconomicus*, the developing Enlightenment sensibility that hard work should be the cure for all of society's ills. Within the institution, individual work in solitary confinement cells was more than a daily routine of tasks; the role of labor was to create obedient, self-monitoring workers out of criminals. This principle ultimately applied to inmates of almshouses, workhouses, hospitals, and insane asylums as well (Rothman 1971).

Yet even Foucault (1979, 139) found the range of reform institutions overwhelming: "There can be no question here of writing the history of the different disciplinary institutions, with all their individual differences," he notes. "I simply intend to map on a series of examples some of the most essential techniques that most easily spread from one to another." Thus Foucault's concept of *discipline*, in which the state attempts to produce respectable citizen-workers out of the poor, the insane, and the criminally minded, becomes a leitmotif linking the primary issues examined here: landscape, labor, and contestation over power within carefully planned environments. Foucault has argued that eighteenth- and nineteenth-century prison labor cannot be seen as vocational in the sense of teaching inmates practical trades. Furthermore, he divests the labor process from any meaningful or productive result to the individual or to the state: "What, then, is the use of prison labor?" he writes. "Not profit; nor even the formation of a useful skill; but the constitution of a power relation, an empty economic form, a schema of individual submission and of adjustment to a production apparatus" (Foucault 1979, 243).

That many aspects of prison labor revolved around menial, unskilled tasks having the larger goal of infusing prison routine with regularity is indisputable. The problem with interpreting prison labor as merely a reinforcement or reminder of power relations is that it ignores a real economic goal underlying the state's agenda: that is, to make penal institutions at least self-sustaining, if not actually profitable. Whether or not that agenda succeeded was largely dependent on the institution, the type of labor performed, and the level of surveillance in the labor program. Thus power *and* profitability are inextricably linked, as the works of Petchesky (1993) and others (Adamson 1984a,1984b; Conley 1980, 1981, 1982) demonstrate.

Prison labor as production. Petchesky (1993), approaching the problem from a Marxian perspective, views work as the exploitation of the labor power of the confined. "Prison labor was both highly productive and highly profitable," she writes, "[and] its productivity is inseparable from its ideological functions of enforcing discipline and the work ethic" (Petchesky 1993, 595). Citing nineteenth-century evidence from the New York State Prison at Auburn, she frames the progression from solitary confinement and labor within cells (known as the Pennsylvania system of imprisonment) to solitary confinement with daily labor in congregate workshops (the Auburn plan of imprisonment) not in terms of moral debate but rather in terms of labor process, arguing that "social conditions are more conducive to productivity than is solitude—an idea that capitalism itself embodied" (Petchesky 1993, 600). The eventual development of a contract system, in which private contractors bid for the privilege of prison labor, was a natural extension of the state's efforts to discipline convict-workers and turn a profit on the institution. The tactic of using convict contract labor, Petchesky argues, is no different from other nineteenth-century strategies that sought to increase profits by reduction of wages. Her interpretation is satisfying in that it bridges nineteenth-century ideas and contemporary anthropological theory concerning power and the use of power. Although admitting that prison labor has a programmatic goal of disciplining workers, she explores its role in accumulation of wealth for the state and for the industrial capitalists who used inmate labor.

Prison labor, then, cannot be written off as a mere disciplinary strategy; in addition to its role as a tool of reform, it was important for the maintenance and financial well-being of the institution as well as the training of future citizens. The nature of the workforce, and the means of disciplining it, will be increasingly important here.

The means of training and discipline. Bowles and Edwards (1985, 176–82) have defined three distinct dimensions of control in the workplace. These include *simple control*, which relies on the use of supervisors to "bully, charm, cajole, motivate, or drive workers to work hard" (179); *technical control*, in which the pace of machinery dictates shop-floor activity; and *bureaucratic control*, a variant on the carrot-and-stick approach, in which management employs a strategy of incentives in order to accomplish its goals of production. To a greater or lesser extent these three aspects of control were crucial to the development of New England's industrial order in the nineteenth century (cf. Beaudry and Mrozowski 1987a, 1987b, 1989; Gross 1993; Nassaney and Abel 1993; Prude 1983). Industrialization involved the reinvention of the work day, the mechanization of production, and the retraining of agricultural and craft laborers into industrial workers. For example, Jonathan Prude (1983, 112) reviews some of the aspects of factory discipline in central Massachusetts: "'Rules and regulations' varied from mill to mill. But generally speaking, Yankee factories of this period . . . demanded that during working hours operatives display the traits of punctuality, temperance, 'industriousness,' 'steadiness' and obedience to mill authorities." Kathleen Bond's (1989) study of mill owners' responses to post–Civil War labor disturbances at the Boott Mills in Lowell goes one step further, identifying the means of social control over operatives who were off the time clock. These included strict regulation of living conditions in the company-owned boardinghouses, prohibitions against drunkenness, and strict control of employee wages and debts.

None of these measures has direct correlates within the prison because nineteenth-century convicts had little or no control of their living conditions, no legitimate access to alcohol, and no means of accumulating wages or debt. The sole incentive for nineteenth-century prisoners to work was avoidance of punishment. No wage incentives were offered; furthermore, the concept of "time off for good behavior" does not appear to have been established in Rhode Island until the third quarter of the nineteenth century. Thus the problem of finding parallels between a private-sector industry and an institutional setting remains a real one.

Comparison with other state and local institutions offers a way to approach the interpretation of labor in a confined setting. An extensive body of literature addresses prison life from a variety of themes, including racism (Carroll 1988; Cleaver 1968; Jackson 1970), institutional organization (Cressey 1961; Etzioni 1961), and gender (Giallombardo 1966; Ward and Kassebaum 1965). However, relatively few prisons have been studied archaeologically (Cotter et al. 1988). More promising case studies have been provided with almshouses and poor farms. Two Massachusetts examples are Cook's (1991) study of patterns of work at the Uxbridge Almshouse and Bell's (1993) summary of excavations at the Hudson Poor Farm Cemetery. More recent examples include Huey's (2001) review of almshouse establishment in upstate New York and Baugher's (2001) exploration of the material symbolism underlying the New York City Municipal Almshouse complex. Investigations at all of these sites suggest that labor was an instrumental aspect of the institutional regime, one that was required of all inmates.

The necessity of work as a means of disciplining convicts and making the institution self-sustaining has been established. The question then becomes one of complicity in the disciplinary process. To what extent did

21

prisoners allow authorities to make use of their labor power? And in what ways did they directly or indirectly comply with, co-opt, or resist the requirement of work? Answers to these questions depend on an explicit consideration of the nature of power as well as the nature of resistance.

Power

Landscape and the built environment ostensibly represent the state's efforts to control a subordinate group. Labor may well have been an arena where the confined had some measure of control over the conditions of their imprisonment. A clear understanding of the deployment, maintenance, and resistance to power is necessary to bridge the gap between landscape and labor and to create a fine-grained ethnography of nineteenth-century prison life.

Foucault's meditations on the nature of power are intriguing. His notion of discourse—the relationship between power and knowledge—deliberately rejects the interpretation of power as a physical property. For Foucault, power is a dynamic process, one comprised of "dispositions, manoeuvres, tactics, techniques, [and] functionings" (Foucault 1979, 26). This notion of power redistributes it from the state and transforms its essence. We are encouraged to see the web of relations engendered by power, relations that are always active, always in a state of tension with one another, rather than a property handed down from above. The production of the modern subject and the notion of power/knowledge regimes are Foucault's most revolutionary contributions to understanding power; they have come to serve as a conceptual tool for many anthropologists (Escobar 1995; Ong 1987).

Like Foucault, Pierre Bourdieu is interested in the ways in which discourse authorizes reality—that which is otherwise unnameable. Bourdieu sees certain "authorized language(s) invested with the authority of a group" (Bourdieu 1977, 170). These languages are not only authorized but also legitimated and naturalized through discourse. The similarities between the two men on this particular subject end here. Foucault takes an extreme position by arguing that there is no escape from the power/knowledge configuration. We see this as he challenges the role of the human sciences, particularly anthropology, calling for an end of the study of humans (Foucault 1970). Foucault interprets the human sciences as effectively engendering technologies of social control and insists that social scientists "abandon a whole tradition that allows us to imagine that knowledge can exist only where the power relations are suspended and that knowledge can develop only outside its injunctions, its demands and its interests" (Bourdieu 1977, 27).

Such critiques are radical responses to the dominant ideology thesis (cf. Abercrombie, Hill, and Turner 1980), which positions power as a force that originates in the dominant sectors of society and trickles down through subordinate sectors. Most critiques of this thesis raise similar charges, including the problem of the ultimate origins of the dominant ideology, the effect of the dominant ideology on dominant and subordinate groups, and the vague means of the dominant ideology's transmittal from dominant to subordinate groups (Larsen 1994). Others point out that the dominant ideology is notoriously difficult to define because it is always under attack by opposing beliefs and is therefore a "work in progress" (Paynter and McGuire 1991, 13).

Despite Foucault's innovative notion of decentralization, there are moments, especially when considering the state's ability to deprive individuals of their liberty, when we must acknowledge that power originates in the state and is deployed through its myriad institutions. Furthermore, the origins of resistance and the relationship of resistance to power are left ambiguous. "[W]here there is power, there is resistance," writes Foucault (1978, 95). "Consequently, this resistance is never in a position of exteriority." If power is everywhere, then resistance is too, and the difference between the two is negligible. This is a notion that has disturbed some critics, particularly Said (1978, 1983), who criticizes Foucault's "unwillingness to take seriously his own ideas about resistance to power" (Said 1983, 246). How can resistance (or points of resistance, as Foucault prefers to call them) be both an "adversarial alternative to power and a dependent function of it" (Said 1983, 246)? Said rejects the idea that all resistance is dependent on power and that all resistance is "morally equal to power" (Said 1983, 246). He reminds us that we rely on forms of resistance such as emergent movements, counter-hegemonic forces, and historical blocs that work outside systems of domination, making social change possible. Said insists that Foucault's notion of dispersed power fails to account for these political processes (Said 1983, 246–47).

Along similar lines Sangren (1995) argues that Foucault neglects to distinguish between the effects of power and its producers. By disassociating power from individuals, by disavowing agency and intention, power "comes to occupy the position of transcendence in Foucault's cosmology" (Sangren 1995, 26). Stuart Hall's critique echoes Said's and Sangren's. He insists that Foucault needs to account for the multiplicity of regimes of truth or else run the risk of conflating his notions with the older, more conventional reading of dominant ideology (Hall 1986, 49). This is a complicated aspect of Hall's critique because although Foucault does conceptualize power as a "multiplicity of force relations" (Foucault 1978, 92), he generally sees each society as having a regime of truth or "general politics of truth" (Foucault 1980, 131). For Hall, this is not adequate. Hall's theory of articulation reconfigures the problem of ideology. By rejecting a simple correspondence between class and ideology, Hall recognizes the contradictory effects of ideology by acknowledging its polysemic nature, that "ideology does not say the same things to the same people at the same time" (Fiske 1996, 218). By opening up ideology (Fiske 1996), Hall is better able to account for the complex processes—the social movements, subjectivities, and oppositional politics—involved in cultural production. Foucault's failure to account for the interconnectedness or, in Hall's words, the "relations of force" (Hall 1986, 49) that organize the social structure marks his failure to theorize social formation and cultural reproduction, thus demonstrating his unwillingness to recognize the crucial fact that power is unequally distributed within and across cultures.

The extent to which ideology figures into the discussion of power is of central importance to this book. Specifically, *who* used different aspects of the built environment to express ideology and resistance to that ideology? How did different groups make their competing versions visible in the material and documentary records of the institution? And how exactly did individuals create, maintain, and subvert power within the material confines of the system?

Here the essential issue is the *dyadic problematique*: "How does A get B to do something?" and, conversely, "How does B prevent A from getting B to do something?" (Paynter and McGuire 1991, 5). For archaeologists of capitalism, power is a dynamic concept relying on three constituent elements: power as a heterogeneous force, power as requiring the use of discipline, and power as "the result of the interplay of dominance and resistance" (Paynter and McGuire 1991, 5). All three of these elements necessarily underlie the interpretation of human relations within the reform institution.

My intent is to examine the exercise of power by interpreting relationships between those ultimately in charge of reform institutions, those responsible for daily operations, and inmates. The complex matrix of social, cultural, and economic relationships offers a means of interpreting the contestation of power within the walls of the institution. On one level, those in charge of the daily operation of the prison were answerable directly to the state for the successful maintenance of the facility and for the prison's ability to pay for itself. On a second level, the prison staff, particularly the underkeepers (or guards), were answerable directly to the keeper in charge of the facility for maintaining security within its fortresslike walls. On a third level, inmates forced to labor in the workshops of the institution were directly answerable to their supervisors, including the underkeepers, work overseers, and outside contractors, for the successful completion of assigned tasks. To what extent those supervising the daily operations of the prison were able to negotiate the directives of the state is as important as the extent to which those confined in the prison were able to contest the directives of the prison staff. These issues of agency and contestation of power are visible at the Rhode Island State Prison and the other institutions studied here.

Prison subjectivity and cultures of resistance. Prison authorities faced the unenviable task of converting criminals into productive and reformed citizen-workers. The myriad difficulties encountered in this process may be a testament more to collective and individual action at multiple levels than to any structural deficiencies in the prison or its cultural landscape. Interpreting this contestation of power is critical to understanding the four-way dialectical relationship between different stakeholders in the prison system: state authorities, prison officials, guards and deputies, and convicts. Interpreting this relationship requires an approach dependent on interpreting the "heterogeneity of power" as expressed by Paynter and McGuire (1991, 7). This approach, which defines domination as "the exercise of power through control of resources" (Paynter and McGuire 1991, 10), emphasizes social relations that organize human activity at every level, not just at that of elites. "Control of resources" has a range of meanings for the different levels within the institutional hierarchy. For prison authorities, it means the threat of curtailment of state funds or legislative support for the prison program; for prison staff, it means threats to job security and safe working conditions; for prisoners, at the bottom end of the kicking order, it means threats of violence, longer confinement, denial of access to fresh air, and prevention of human contact. Ways in which individuals from all of these groups were able to combat threats from all directions—above, below, and sideways—will be explored through concepts relating to power struggle.

Everyday resistance in the prison. There is a question of how to define resistance and its attributes; more important is the question of how to use notions of resistance to study human activity in a coercive and repressive institution. The literature concerning resistance has become increasingly extensive as anthropologists and labor historians take a more dynamic view of the *dyadic problematique*. Anthropological studies of resistance have focused on ritual resistance among the Tshidi of South Africa (Comaroff 1985), maintenance of traditional religious practices in the face of Christianity (Taussig 1980), and large-scale peasant rebellions and revolutions (Wolf 1982). Paynter (1988, 386) notes that studies of utopian communities, including the Mormons and the Shakers (Leone 1973; Starbuck 1984), show the "systematic opting out" of large, organized groups from capitalist North American society.

The concept of resistance used here is that articulated by James Scott (1985, 29) in his discussion of "everyday resistance." Careful to distinguish between evasion and outright defiance, Scott (1985, 32) defines everyday resistance as "intended to mitigate or deny claims made by superordinate classes or to advance claims vis-à-vis those superordinate classes." Drawing on the extensive literature concerning slavery in the United States, he rightly points out that acts such as foot dragging, feigning illness, production slowdowns, and other forms of goldbricking usually have a material basis in struggles between classes. Some southern planters, unable even to imagine enslaved African Americans deploying resistive tactics, wrote off these activities as laziness; the more creative ones imagined that Africans had "by nature" a different work ethic, one that was vastly inferior to their own, Protestant-oriented discipline (Genovese 1976 [1974], 295–324).

Acts of everyday resistance often have their roots in consciousness, if not in explicit intentionality (Scott 1985, 37). People may not have a well-defined agenda underlying their acts of resistance because they are so enveloped in the conditions of their repression that it becomes part of their daily behavior. Scott returns, circuitously, to one of the critiques of the dominant ideology thesis: he is concerned with the "extent to which elites are able to impose their own image of a just social order, not simply on the behavior of non-elites, *but on their consciousness as well*" (Scott 1985, 38–39; emphasis added).

Numerous problems face the anthropologist who would interpret resistance. These include the nature of the deed (solitary versus collective action); the motivations and intentions underlying the particular deed (self-interest versus "real" revolutionary intent); the consequences of the deed (self-gain versus revolutionary change); and the ontological theme of the deed, or whether the act "embodies ideas or intentions that negate the basis of domination itself" (Scott 1985, 292). These complexities stress the notion that interpreting resistance is indeed an act of reading human activity, one that stresses the relationship between the contemporary "reader" and the historical act.

Up to this point I have discussed individual acts of resistance. Yet collective everyday resistance must surely have been part of the prison culture as well. In his ethnography of a British vocational school, Paul Willis (1977) finds important parallels between the school and the "shop-floor culture" of the iron foundry in which the students' fathers worked. Willis describes resistance in the iron foundry as "the massive attempt to gain informal control of the work process," adding that "limitation of output of 'systematic soldiering' and 'gold bricking' have been observed from Taylor onwards, but there is evidence now of a much more concerted—though still informal—attempt to gain control" (Willis 1977, 53). In addition to this struggle for control, resistive activity in the workplace has an obvious aspect of "getting back at the boss," a phenomenon described by Bowles and Edwards (1985, 179) as having innumerable manifestations in the contemporary American workplace: feigning illness, foot dragging, using controlled substances on the job. The authors trace this sentiment back to the workers' sense that they are exploited, and that these are the only means they have to counter this exploitation.

Prisoners could have been engaged in fighting for control in several arenas; the most obvious parallels with Willis's study are the prison workshops, where convicts labored ten hours a day, six days a week. Close examination of the records shows prisoners asserting themselves to slow down the work process. But is this "systematic soldiering" merely loafing or is it resistive activity? For Scott (1985), the act and the intent are indistinguishable: "When there is strong evidence for the intention behind the act, the case for resistance is correspondingly strengthened. The insistence that acts of resistance must be *shown* to be intended, however, creates enormous difficulties. What are we to call the poor man in Sedaka who 'appropriates' a gunny sack of paddy from a rich man's field: a thief, *tout court*, or a resister as well?" (Scott 1985, 290; emphasis in original). Whether or not the prisoners' resistive activities were intentional, whether or not they were aware that they would be punished brutally, and whether they intended revolutionary action or just a break from the shop floor, their transgressions against the code of prison life must be read in the context of a dialectical relationship of domination and resistance. Precisely how those relationships became manifest, and how they affected the social structure of the institution and larger schemes of criminal reform, must be examined closely through the documentary and archaeological records of the Rhode Island State Prison.

Creating Discipline through Architecture and Hard Labor

Within the context of the penitentiary, the creation of discipline encompassed the twin projects of moral reformation through architecture and the transformation of criminal into worker. The theoretical framework for this study interprets contests over power within the prison by examining first the cultural landscape and then labor as key components of institutional life. The previous discussion has shown, however, that there may not have been consensus throughout the hierarchy about what constituted proper discipline and how different aspects of the prison's cultural landscape should be read.

This absence of consensus is by no means unusual in the context of institutionalization, and it represents the norm rather than a deviation from the norm. The project of imprisonment reached a fever pitch in Jacksonian America, with numerous ministers, philanthropists, financiers, and cranks all espousing various theories of punishment and reform. Before considering the planning process underlying the first Rhode Island State Prison, it will be necessary to trace the evolution of imprisonment, with particular emphasis on the emergence of the penitentiary in an age of Enlightenment rationality.

CHAPTER 2

"By Reforming the Delinquent and Deterring Others from Like Courses"

Rhode Island's Struggle for a State Prison

The origins of imprisonment as a reform strategy and the relationship between prisons and broader historical, cultural, and economic processes of change have been the subjects of extensive theoretical debate. Pieter Spierenburg (1987, 1991) notes that the beginning of this debate in the 1970s coincided with a sharp break in the historiography of imprisonment. Earlier studies tended to accept the written and material legacies of eighteenth- and nineteenth-century reformers at face value, and interpreted "the rise of the prison simply as the result of the benevolent endeavors of humanitarian reformers" (Spierenburg 1987, 439). Within the last thirty years scholars have approached the problem from the opposite perspective, with the construction of prisons and penitentiaries interpreted as a direct measure of oppressive control and the instillation of discipline. Despite the complete reversal of perspectives and what he views as a concomitant inattention to subtleties and empirical data, Spierenburg (1987, 439) allows that the post-1970s "revisionist" approach has nonetheless been beneficial to the historiography; its progenitors were among the first to situate imprisonment within local, regional, and global histories and economic contexts, rather than as an inevitable step in a Spencerian march from primeval cruelty to modern reform (Foucault 1979; Ignatieff 1978; Rothman 1971).

The most hotly contested issue has been the extent to which the development of the penitentiary hinged on the shift from mercantile to industrial capitalism, and whether incarceration embodied an explicit ideology of disciplining wage-earning classes in industrial society. This debate is between "process-oriented" historical perspectives versus those (like Foucault) who favor a "modernization-oriented" approach (Spierenburg 1991, 3). Process-oriented writers, who view the early nineteenth-century prison as an outcome that developed from experiments in early modern European states, see a steady evolution in incarceration as a strategy of punishment and reform (McGowen 1986, 1987, 1995; Peters 1995). Spierenburg (1991, 3), while also expressing this view, goes even further; he has little patience for the popular notion that "something entirely new was created from about 1800 on." His nuanced reading of archival data associates the development of incarceration in different times and places with the centralization of the state and the state's acquisition of a monopoly on violence and repression. Using a *mentalities* approach, Spierenburg methodically demolishes myth after myth about the development of the prison in early modern Europe.

The major competing body of theory finds a direct association between the creation of what is now recognized as the modern penitentiary and the advent of industrialization, with imprisonment used to instill discipline and to generate profit for the state (Adamson 1984a, 1984b; Conley 1980, 1981, 1982; Foucault 1979; Melossi and Pavarini 1981; Petchesky 1993; Rusche and Kirchheimer 1968 [1939]). The peculiar case of the United States, and its incredibly rapid postrevolutionary transition from a society embracing corporal and capital punishment to one extolling the virtues of the penitentiary, troubles some writers. Even Spierenburg (1991, 3) is forced to admit that "a relatively condensed tradition did take place in America, due to the particular circumstances of its development."

This theoretical debate has great significance for understanding the issues faced by the promoters of the first Rhode Island State Prison during the first thirty years of the nineteenth century. As one of the last states or territories to establish a prison, Rhode Island was able to watch the development of the Jacksonian-era national debate over reform, a debate that engendered an endless series of tracts and pamphlets issued by adherents of the Pennsylvania and Auburn plans of imprisonment. Interpreting the faltering series of decisions made by a series of legislative committees—a process that unfolded over nearly four decades—requires a brief review of trends in incarceration in continental Europe and England during the eighteenth century. Where were the roots of imprisonment as an agent of social reformation? How did North American colonists adopt and reject elements of European modes of punishment? Most important, what was the relationship between the larger, theoretical argument concerning punishment plans and bottom-line considerations of self-sufficiency and profitability in the new penitentiaries?

This chapter reviews some of the seventeenth- and eighteenth-century predecessors of the nineteenth-century penal institutions, with close attention to the question of the origins of the penitentiary and framing the review in terms of current historiography. Then political discourse concerning the construction of the Rhode Island State Prison is situated within prevalent American trends of social reform in the nineteenth century. The chapter concludes with a discussion of the pervasive influence of financial expediency in the selection of a system of punishment, a construction plan, and a building site and the results of that influence on reformers' efforts to transform criminals into nonrecidivist and productive citizens of the new nation.

European Experiments in Punishment

Incarceration has been used sporadically as punishment since biblical times. The revival of Roman law among European nation-states in the twelfth and thirteenth centuries and the implementation of civil and ecclesiastical confinement show that penal servitude was by no means a nineteenth-century invention (Peters 1995, 32–33). Although many forms of medieval punishment focused on the body, numerous city-states and religious groups practiced forms of imprisonment. Monasteries, for example, contained prisons for religious offenders, who were sometimes confined for life in solitary cells (Johnston 2000, 21–24). The Châtelet prison in Paris served as a site of "close confinement" for nobles and commoners convicted of noncapital offenses (Peters 1995, 39). These efforts at incarceration lacked most of the constituent components of the nineteenth-century penitentiary: classification of prisoners by offense, regimes of labor, religious instruction, and the strict regulation of everyday life.

Process-oriented scholars note the steady evolution of incarceration in postmedieval Europe. "Far from representing a radical change in the penal system," writes Spierenburg (1995, 64), "the proliferation of penitentiaries in Europe after 1800 was the product of gradual development during the preceding centuries." In addition to well-documented and occasionally spectacular forms of capital punishment, early modern European nations practiced at least four distinct forms of penal bondage: sentence to the galleys, labor at public works, imprisonment, and transportation to colonies (Spierenburg 1995, 66). Confinement in city houses of correction, with a component of mandatory labor, became a mode of punishment distinct from the relief practices of almshouses and asylums.

These houses of correction, or prison workhouses, initially were designed to control the poor and vagrant, rather than criminal offenders, as traditional medieval-based forms of relief (hospitals maintained by Christian orders, for example) gave way to state-organized institutions. They first appeared in England in the mid-sixteenth century but spread quickly to other northern European countries in the succeeding fifty years. One of the most important of these early establishments was Amsterdam's *tuchtzuis* (literally "workhouse"), which later became better known as the Rasphuis (fig. 2). Established in 1596 to house beggars and vagrants, the Rasphuis became, by the 1650s, a prison workshop for males convicted of noncapital crimes. A related institution, the Spinhuis, was established for female offenders shortly after the conversion of the Rasphuis to a penal institution. Thorsten Sellin (1944) believes that the burghers of Amsterdam saw their newly won economic prosperity threatened by the class of wage-laboring poor in rural and urban districts. "The gradual migration to the towns," he writes, "caused by the breakdown of the feudal system and the growth of urban industries, was giving rise to a proletariat, dependent for their livelihood on the sale of their labor, suffering from each unfavorable fluctuation in employment" (Sellen 1944, 9). The Rasphuis, then, the most important postmedieval development in incarceration, stemmed from responses not to crime and civil disorder but rather to poverty and economic displacement.

Renewed interest in classical learning, including the revival of Plato's works among elites, informed the search for appropriate models of social control. Enmeshed in this humanistic impulse was widespread recognition that work was the cure for the idle. The regime of mandatory labor was central to the ideology of the Rasphuis as a means of personal transformation for society's offenders. Inmates pulverized and grated wood logs imported from the East Indies, the West Indies, and South America to make powder for cloth dyes. Sellin (1944, 17) attributes the requirement of work to the keen Dutch sense of Calvinist-inspired mercantile capitalism: "Under these circumstances, one can understand more easily the willingness of the thrifty burghers of Amsterdam to experiment with *labor* as a penalty for the shiftless and vagrant gentry of the city who against their will might be made to contribute their share to the economic life of the community and acquire skills which could later be used to the profit of themselves and their masters." Yet in addition to labor, life in the Rasphuis incorporated other elements foreshadowing inmate life in nineteenth-century prisons: a strict

32

FIG. 2 — *The gate of the Amsterdam Rasphuis with the motto "Castigatio" ("Correction") prominently displayed under the seal of the city. Photograph by the author.*

timetable governing daily routine; the possibility of sentence reduction through good behavior; and prohibitions against personal visits by friends and families, effectively cutting off offenders from potential sources of moral contamination. Foucault (1979, 121) agrees with Sellin's emphasis on the importance of the Rasphuis for later developments, calling the institution the link between the theory of postmedieval individual transformation and Enlightenment-inspired reform techniques. Others caution against seeing the Rasphuis as a direct antecedent of the penitentiary (Spierenburg 1987, 448).

In an important essay Spierenburg (1987) dismisses the notion that any particular form of capitalism was the single underlying factor in the development of imprisonment. The Rasphuis had developed during Amsterdam's embrace of mercantile capitalism, while the nineteenth-century penitentiary developed under industrialization. Equally significant, he notes, was the failure of the elite in the New World colony of New Amsterdam to establish an institution similar to the Rasphuis. Surely the leaders of New Amsterdam were familiar with the Rasphuis and its efficacy at controlling deviance. Yet they chose not to build one, preferring to punish offenders through the use of corporal and capital punishment, banishment, and fines. Through this comparison Spierenburg (1987, 453) concludes that capitalism was not the driving force behind imprisonment. What is needed, he argues, is an interpretation focusing on state power, particularly the centralization of the state and its monopoly on violence and repression: "If economic processes do not provide the primary explanation, the next step is to inquire whether my argument about state formation processes, developed from the European evidence, can also be valid for America." Spierenburg's attempt to divorce the rise of imprisonment from large-scale economic forces seems somewhat disingenuous in its differentiation of state formation from the development of capitalism. Braudel (1992 [1979]) and Wolf (1982) demonstrate clearly that the crystallization of European states in the early modern era was a process emerging from first mercantile and then industrial capitalism. The state does not form in an economic vacuum; it gradually centralizes authority, record keeping, and police forces as part of its evolution to industrial capitalism. Thus on its own merits, "state formation," although a useful heuristic, is ultimately unsatisfying as an explanation for the rise of imprisonment. A close review of English and European experiments in penal reform considerably strengthens the case for the association of imprisonment with industrial capitalism.

Eighteenth-century English and European Experiments

One of the earliest Enlightenment experiments in penal reform occurred in Ghent during the third quarter of the eighteenth century. The Maison de Force was perhaps the first institution to distance punishment completely from the medieval notion of bodily punishment and squarely into the realm of capitalist discipline. Like the Rasphuis, the Maison was a combination workhouse/poorhouse/reformatory in which all occupants were forced to labor. This system reaffirmed the Enlightenment sensibility that individuals could be transformed through labor and religious instruction, countering the Calvinist notion that deviants were predestined to vagrancy and evil, and could only be useful to society through their labor. Foucault (1979, 121) termed the Maison system "the universal pedagogy of work," noting its

34

clear advantages over fines and corporal punishment. In particular, confinement at labor "would create a mass of new workers" for the state. A second point of importance concerning the Maison is its architectural configuration. The Maison was the first complex in which reformers consciously used the built environment as a strategy for reform. The construction of subunits comprising an octagon, for example, permitted the segregation of offenders by class, a novelty soon undermined by increased commitments and assignment of multiple felons to cells meant for individuals (Johnston 2000, 39).

In England similar efforts were under way in the third and fourth quarters of the eighteenth century. Randall McGowen (1986, 1987, 1995) has thoroughly traced the history of imprisonment in England through all its attendant permutations. The English house of correction, or "Bridewell," had appeared in the middle of the sixteenth century for petty offenders, especially vagrants. But seventeenth-century incarceration was by no means a product of state centralization in England. McGowen (1995, 81) emphasizes the wide range of levels of confinement in the first half of the eighteenth century: borough and manorial jails, for example, and ecclesiastical prisons. County jails were subject to widespread fraud on the part of keepers, and conditions in these institutions varied widely depending on the number of debtors and their families confined within their walls.

Transportation to the American colonies was as important as confinement and capital punishment, with more than thirty thousand individuals transported to America between 1718 and 1775. Despite the popularity of the measure among legislators for its cost-effectiveness, it began to fall from favor by mid-century. One of the most important reasons for the failure of transportation was the persistent rumor that many of those transported prospered rather than suffered in the New World. Not long after mid-century, when the outbreak of hostilities with the American colonies closed the door to transportation, British legislators found themselves struggling with issues of penal reform and imprisonment.

Perhaps the most important leader in the penal reform movement was the Nonconformist John Howard, whose *The State of the Prisons in England and Wales* (1777) required copious original research. Howard's political appointment as sheriff of Bedfordshire inspired his interest in prisons; unlike his lazy predecessors, Howard actually visited the jail for which he was responsible and was thoroughly shocked by the conditions he found there. He then set off on a two-year tour of the prisons of Great Britain, compiling copious empirical data about the number of prisoners, the number of felons in relationship to the number of debtors, the number of individuals confined to a cell, and the costs of boarding prisoners. What he saw in the prisons so disturbed Howard that he became a lobbyist for penal reform, using his widely read book as a cornerstone toward that goal.

The effective end of transportation to the American colonies combined with Howard's efforts resulted in the approval of the Penitentiary Act of 1779, written by Blackstone and Eden. The act, which set standards for imprisonment in England, called for the construction of two national prisons, segregated by sex. Within the institutions prisoners would wear standard uniforms, labor, and earn time off for good conduct. Yet from a standpoint of practice, the full promise of the Penitentiary Act was never realized. Numerous factors contributed to the ultimate shelving of the plan: disagreements over the location of the new prisons, doubts over the wisdom of centralizing imprisonment, and above all, the cost of the seemingly endless war with France. The system of dispersed confinement in a variety of local and county institutions thus persisted until at least 1800.

Following the death of John Howard while visiting prisons in Russia, Sir George Onesiphorous Paul became the leading proponent of English penal reform (McGowen 1995, 91). Paul promoted construction of the new Gloucester County Prison, built between 1785 and 1792 under the architectural direction of William Blackburn. At Gloucester inmates spent the first third of their sentences in solitary confinement. For the duration of their sentences inmates were cut off from social contact, instructed in daily labor, and supervised by a new, professional class of jailers, often drawn from the ranks of former military officials. This last development was most important because the jail superintendent drew a salary and reported to a board of inspectors, effectively ending the system whereby jailers profited by supplying prosperous inmates with better food and living accommodations.

Foucault (1979, 122) cites the initial isolation of Gloucester prisoners in solitary confinement as the primary English contribution to philosophies of penal reform. "The cell, that technique of Christian monasticism, which had survived only in Catholic countries, becomes in this Protestant society the instrument by which one may reconstitute both *homo oeconomicus* and the religious conscience" (Foucault 1979, 123). Developments at Gloucester did not presage every aspect of the nineteenth-century penitentiary. For example, only the most heinous offenders were kept in isolation for the duration of their sentences, with less dangerous criminals practicing communal work by day and confinement at night. Nevertheless it is clear that by the end of the eighteenth century, experimentation with solitary confinement, mandatory labor, and religious instruction were all in place in

England and on the Continent. Superintendence of prisons was slowly becoming professionalized along with systems of record keeping, inspection, and accountability. But neither England nor the European continent would provide the next major stimulus to incarceration; the newest (and arguably most important) innovations would derive from the former North American colonies, particularly Pennsylvania and New York.

Punishment in Eighteenth-century New England

Prisons as reform institutions were unknown in the American colonies of the seventeenth and eighteenth centuries. Houses of correction, which had proved so desirable in northern Europe, were rarely established in the Dutch and English colonies before the early eighteenth century. Those that were set up tended to be places of temporary refuge for the indigent, rather than the formal, structured institutions of the Dutch republic.

In New England punishment was almost exclusively a local administrative affair, with small-scale jails (rather than colony-wide prisons) constructed and administered primarily by towns. These jails had two primary purposes: the confinement of debtors and the holdover of criminals awaiting punishment or execution. Often the construction of a jail was among the first acts carried out by newly established town governments, a testimony to their deep-seated fears of social deviancy (Thompson 1986). Based in the British criminal codes, punishment of prisoners, rather than rehabilitation or reformation, prevailed throughout the seventeenth and eighteenth centuries. Both corporal and capital punishment, including the whipping, branding, and hanging of malefactors, were used extensively, but perhaps not as extensively as we have been led to believe (Colvin 1997, 34). A perpetual labor shortage in the colonies led to an increased emphasis on monetary punishment rather than forms of discipline that would necessarily hinder or reduce the labor force (Colvin 1997, 34).

A strong correlation exists between punishment in London, where property crimes were treated as capital offenses, and punishment in New England. London's elite deliberately employed the death penalty for property crimes that might not have been considered capital offenses in rural or less urbanized areas (Linebaugh 1992). The use of the death penalty for offenses against personal property was part of a larger strategy to drive home the message of private property's sanctity to the urban proletariat: "Most of those hanged had offended against the laws of property," writes

Linebaugh (1992, xx), "and at the heart of the 'social contract' was respect for private property." Such an interpretation is in line with that of Bukharin and Preobrazhensky (1969 [1922]), who view the subjugation of offenders against property as a consequence inherent in the development of the capitalist state. "The *administration of justice* in the bourgeois state is a means of self-defence for the bourgeois class," they write. "Above all, it is employed to settle with those who infringe the rights of capitalist property or interfere with the capitalist system" (Bukharin and Preobrazhensky 1969 [1922], 86–87; emphasis in original). Although the "thanatocracy" Linebaugh describes in London never established itself in New England, the deployment of the death penalty was by no means unknown throughout the pre–Revolutionary War period. Given the extreme mobility of individuals in the region and the absence of centralized record keeping, consistency in justice was difficult to administer. Rothman (1971), citing the case of Isaac Frasier, notes how random the road to the scaffold could be in colonial New England. Frasier, a lifelong thief, passed from town to town in Connecticut receiving at first only relatively light punishments for his many crimes: "Suddenly, one day, his reputation caught up with him, and a Connecticut court, fully informed of his history, passed the death sentence. Frasier's life in crime aptly demonstrated the fragility of eighteenth-century law enforcement. The criminal went undetected . . . until abruptly he ended up on the gallows" (Rothman 1971, 52). The penal code of Massachusetts attempted to provide some small measure of gradualism by prescribing a series of escalating punishments: for the first offense, a fine or whipping; for the second offense, a triple fine, an hour sitting on the scaffold with a noose around one's neck, and a whipping of thirty stripes; and for the third offense, hanging (Rothman 1971). Again, the absence of systematic and centralized records of punishments and offenders hindered efforts at judicial consistency; individuals were much more likely to move on after receiving punishment, rather than risk the penalties for second and third offenses.

As was the case in most colonies, Rhode Island's penal code of 1647 encompassed a wide range of capital offenses: high treason, petit treason, murder, manslaughter, witchcraft, burglary, robbery, arson, rape, crimes against nature, and "the malicious burning of a barn having corn in it" (Staples 1853, 3–5). A wide range of fines was employed to punish adulterers, embezzlers, forgers, vandals, and trespassers. By 1835 the death penalty had been eliminated for high and petit treason, witchcraft (dropped in 1767), crimes against nature, and barn burning, leaving the state with six capital crimes on its books. Construction of the state prison would spark a revision in the criminal code that left the death penalty for only one crime, that of murder (Staples 1853, 11).

Such conditions prevailed throughout the colonies until the end of the American Revolution. Between 1780 and 1830 increasing awareness of the European experiments, combined with spirited republicanism, engendered an extended debate concerning the nature of crime and the most appropriate philosophies of dealing with it. Rothman (1971, 59) concludes that patriotic sentiment forced a reexamination of colonial criminal codes: "established in the days of oppression and ignorance, the laws reflected British insistence on severe and cruel punishments." The link between nationalist pride and new efforts at social reform was striking: "Old theories and methods of punishment had been swept aside," writes McKelvey (1977, 31). "The penitentiary and its associated institutions were as legitimate offsprings of the age as the young democracies themselves." Reformers in many states targeted the death penalty, resulting in the rewriting of numerous penal codes to reserve hanging only for murder and a handful of other grave offenses. Incarceration, with an emphasis on reforming the criminal and returning him or her to society, would become the standard in the new nation. In a search for models that would carry out this idealistic goal, individual states and territories turned not to Europe but to Philadelphia, the city most deeply associated with the American Revolution and the subsequent embrace of republicanism and all its attendant components.

The Walnut Street Model

Elements of the Rasphuis, Gloucester, and other English and European experiments all crystallized in material form at Philadelphia's Walnut Street Prison. Opened as a city and county jail in 1773, Walnut Street was an American and British military prison during each army's occupation of the city. In 1786 a revision of the colony's penal codes established imprisonment as the punishment for all crimes except murder and arson. One year later the Philadelphia Society for Alleviating the Miseries of Public Prisons, the first organization of its kind, convinced the legislature to designate Walnut Street as a temporary colony-wide prison.

In many ways Walnut Street can be seen as the predecessor of *both* the Pennsylvania and Auburn plans of punishment. As in the Gloucester

County Jail, only the most dangerous criminals were kept in solitary confinement; others labored in workshops and slept in communal cells. The reformers' influence included the adoption of several innovative aspects to penal confinement. For the first time the American punishment process was hidden from the American public (Foucault 1979, 125). Retribution thus became a matter between keeper and prisoner, and the intended transformation from criminal to reformed citizen occurred in isolation rather than on a scaffold in a public square. Perhaps more significantly, the offender was treated as an individual. Particular knowledge of an individual, crimes committed, and life circumstances prior to punishment led to an almost Linnaean classification of convicts: those explicitly condemned to solitary confinement; recidivists, or repeat offenders; those not likely to become recidivists; and a probationary class of new prisoners (Foucault 1979, 125). As perhaps the first American experiment in penitentiary construction, Walnut Street has come to be seen as the embodiment of Enlightenment rationale and American republicanism. American folklore would have it viewed as a splendid Quaker endeavor supporting repeal of the death penalty. More ominously Walnut Street, as the inspiration for other state prisons, may represent the first manifestation of "the concept of a centralized state apparatus" in the New World (Takagi 1993, 542). From this perspective the transformation of Walnut Street from a local jail to a state institution mirrors the larger struggle of the individual states to form a republic: "The demand for a strong centralized government was to guarantee the development of a new economic order on the one hand, and on the other, to solve the problem of law and order" (Takagi 1993, 537). This view draws heavily on the emergent conflict between industrialist and agrarian classes in the new republic; the labor power of the inmates served to reassure powerful agrarian interests, who feared that industrialization would seriously affect the availability of farm labor. Workhouses and prisons would feed the demand for industrial labor by centralizing a class of urban poor dependent on industrial wages to stay out of the institutions.

Out of the Walnut Street experiment arose two competing plans of punishment that have attracted a great deal of attention in the historiography of imprisonment: the Pennsylvania, or separate, plan; and the Auburn, or congregate, plan. A consideration of the elements of these plans, as well as their relationships to state formation and industrial capitalism, brings the debate about imprisonment into early nineteenth-century Rhode Island.

The Pennsylvania and Auburn Plans

Social reform and its potential salutary effects on criminals, the poor, and the insane dominated American popular discourse in the Jacksonian era. Rothman (1971) meticulously traces roots of this zeal for reform, noting the shift from the Calvinist sense that deviants were irredeemably evil to the Enlightenment-based notion that society could transform them into productive citizens. Republican rejection of European and explicitly British ideals was central to this sentiment. "The rhetoric of the revolution had prepared Americans to fulfill a grand mission, and now they would demonstrate how to uplift one part of mankind, the criminal class" (Rothman 1971, 70). The rise of progressive social policies during the presidency of Andrew Jackson (1829–37), including an emphasis on the scientific management of criminals and the insane, fostered the association of Jackson's name with these reforms.

Such a notion did not occur in a metaphysical vacuum or simply as a direct consequence of Enlightenment rationality. Some argue that social reform was linked inextricably to the rise of industrial capitalism and the disciplining of the wage-earning class (Foucault 1979); others argue even more explicitly that this disciplining process was bound up with labor. Colvin (1997, 112), for example, situates the debate within the broader economic context of industrialization; within this interpretive scheme, the transition from a subsistence/mercantile economy to an industrial order resulted in cycles of indebtedness, property loss, and an overall reorientation from community-based principles to intense competition. Within the immediate context of punishment the discipline of immigrants, homeless persons, and the unemployed sharpens its focus through an emphasis on "productive work" (Melossi and Pavarini 1981, 129).

This interpretation has not been popular with those who have looked closely at the long-term evolution of incarceration in America. Rothman, for example, voices a strong belief in the sincerity of the nineteenth-century reformers and criticized Foucault's argument as ahistorical and cynical. "But this perspective is too narrow. It makes every spokesman and leader of this movement a tool, conscious or not, of the economic system; rhetoric and perceptions not fitting a production-oriented explanation are ignored " (Rothman 1971, xvi). Was the Jacksonian-era belief in reformation tied to notions of industrial production and worker discipline? To answer this question it is necessary to look closely at the two competing philosophies and the arguments marshaled by supporters in favor of both plans (Lewis 1967; McKelvey 1977; Rothman 1971; Teeters 1955; Teeters and Shearer 1957).

Reformers in Pennsylvania developed the *separate plan* (later known as the Pennsylvania system), put into force at the Eastern State Penitentiary in Philadelphia in 1829. Eastern State was built at the staggering cost of $772,000 (Johnston 1994, 109). Designed by John Haviland, who was clearly influenced by recently completed English penitentiaries, Eastern State was built on a radial plan, with seven cell block wings extending from a central rotunda. The prison was surrounded by a wall with a single opening; de Beaumont and de Tocqueville (1979 [1833], 103–4), citing the great expense of construction, noted that much effort had been wasted on "gigantic walls" and "gothic towers" serving no purpose but to mimic European castles. Convicts at Pennsylvania-system institutions reflected on the enormity of their crimes in complete isolation. Kept in solitary confinement at all times and hooded when they were brought out into corridors, prisoners ate, worked, and slept out of sight of any other human being. They were not permitted to speak with or even see their keepers, and the discipline of silence reigned throughout the walls of the institutions. Visits were limited to a strictly controlled list of morally certain prison officials and members of the Philadelphia Prison Society (Colvin 1997, 87). Solitary confinement cells were equipped with outside walled exercise yards, thus extending the solitary experience to the external world. The idea was to cut off the prisoner completely from any source of contamination that would engender a return to a former life of deviance.

The psychological impact of these measures was formidable. On entering the institution the prisoner was kept in complete isolation from all distractions. Gradually authorities introduced tools and materials to establish a daily regime of labor. As Rothman (1971, 86) notes, "Labor would become not an oppressive task for punishment, but a welcome diversion, a delight rather than a burden." Pennsylvania-plan reformers also instituted a direct correlation between behavior in prison and length of sentence, an innovation later duplicated by other state governments.

Foucault has discussed the Pennsylvania system at length. "This was," he writes, "no doubt the most famous because it was associated in people's minds with the political innovations of the American plan and also because it was not . . . doomed to immediate failure and abandonment" (Foucault 1979, 123). The idea was to "partition life" under the strictest of timetables. "Each moment of the day was devoted to a particular type of activity, and brought with it its own obligations and prohibitions" (Foucault 1979, 124).

Furthermore, the explicit purpose of the plan was to remove the prisoner from all possible sources of contamination. The terror of the plan derived neither from the lash nor the scaffold but from isolation and the metaphysical confrontation between criminal and crime. "Thrown into solitude he reflects," wrote de Beaumont and de Tocqueville (1979 [1833], 55); "placed alone, in view of his crime, he learns to hate it, and if his soul be not yet surfeited with crime . . . it is in solitude where remorse will come to assail him."

An added advantage of the Pennsylvania plan—which its supporters emphasized—was its relative cost efficiency for initial construction. Cells in these prisons tended to be larger than those in Auburn-plan institutions because they served as the inmate's domestic and work space. However, there was no need to construct large, communal workshops; better still, guards could be less well trained since contact with inmates would be minimal. Advocates of the congregate or Auburn system responded that revenues from labor programs could never offset the initial costs of the Pennsylvania-system prisons. Even the French visitors concurred: "The prisons, constructed on the Auburn plan, are infinitely cheaper" (de Beaumont and de Tocqueville 1979 [1833], 104). They certainly would have recognized in the Auburn-plan prisons most of the elements of the Rasphuis, an innovation with which they had been familiar for more than two centuries (Spierenburg 1987, 455).

The *congregate plan* developed in New York, first at the New York State Penitentiary at Auburn in 1819 and then at the New York State Penitentiary at Ossining (Sing-Sing) in 1823 (Rothman 1971). Convicts at Auburn were housed in solitary confinement at night but worked communally (albeit silently) in specially designed workshops. They were permitted daily supervised exercise in the prison yard and were allowed time for Bible reading and other activities meeting with the moral approval of their keepers. Because the rule of silence still prevailed, the major difference in the two plans lay in the Auburn convicts' ability to at least encounter other human beings, a phenomenon that the Pennsylvanians found contrary to all ideas of reform.

The key difference between the two systems lay in the way labor was organized: solitary labor in individual cells in the Pennsylvania system, and factory-like conditions in the Auburn system penitentiaries. Most of the debate concerning the role of the penitentiary in disciplining marginal classes originated around this crucial difference. "Thus the originality of this new system," write Melossi and Pavarini (1981, 129), "lay essentially in the introduction of work structured in the same way as the dominant form of factory work." Their argument, echoed by Foucault and rejected by process-oriented scholars, is that the ability of a convicted criminal to be transformed into a disciplined worker would constitute the basis of reform. "Going beyond the ideological screen which purported that treatment was of a re-educative nature, the real judgment of good character was based on working ability" (Melossi and Pavarini 1981, 129). Elam Lynds, warden of the Auburn penitentiary, described the system's explicit purpose as transforming the reprobate into "a silent and insulated working machine" (Lewis 1967, 88). To that end the accoutrements of reform—moral instruction, education, and other components of improvement—formed a backdrop to the real intention of creating worker-citizens.

Partisans of the Auburn plan, like the adherents of the Pennsylvania plan, trumpeted anecdotal data supporting their contention that their system was actually more cost-effective than that of their competitors. Although Auburn-plan prisons required a higher initial financial outlay for workshops, chapels, and hospital cells, communal labor in large workshops was more conducive to institutional profitability, and the cost of constructing the workshops more than offset the cost of constructing larger cells in the Pennsylvania-plan prisons. The experience of building the Eastern State Penitentiary bore out these contentions over costs. "By 1825," writes McKelvey (1977, 21), "Auburn prison was a smooth-running industrial plant, and it was not long before this prison and those at Wethersfield, Charlestown, and Baltimore were realizing small surpluses over and above their expenses—an irrefutable economic argument in support of the system."

Most American states and territories, lured by dreams of potential profitability, adopted the Auburn plan. The spate of prison construction increased steadily throughout the early 1830s. By 1835 Auburn-plan prisons included Auburn (with 770 cells); Sing-Sing (1,000); Wethersfield, Connecticut (232); Charlestown, Massachusetts (304); Windsor, Vermont (136); Concord, New Hampshire (120); Washington, D.C. (214); Baltimore, Maryland (320); Richmond, Virginia (168); and Frankfort, Kentucky (100). Pennsylvania's Eastern and Western State Penitentiaries, along with the New Jersey State Prison in Trenton, were the only examples of Pennsylvania-plan prisons. In New England only Rhode Island lacked a state penitentiary. The absence of a prison in Rhode Island was by no means attributable to an absence of discussion; as we shall see, the process of investigating and planning a penitentiary occupied nearly a half-century of legislators' time.

44

Planning a Prison in Rhode Island

How did the broader nineteenth-century debate over penal systems affect Rhode Islanders' efforts to develop and implement a prison or penitentiary? Certainly the citizens of the colony and then the state shared the views of other Americans concerning the need to control deviancy. From the time of Euro-American settlement in the 1630s through the 1750s, a series of five different jails had been erected in Providence. Jails had also been established in the seats of Bristol, Kent, Newport, and Washington throughout the same time period. By the 1820s, when penal reform swept the United States, these local facilities still served as Rhode Island's only institutions for incarceration. Languishing within the jail walls was a diverse group of inmates: debtors, trial witnesses deemed likely to flee, those awaiting trial and punishment, and those under sentence of death.

In Pennsylvania and other colonies, the end of the American Revolution had fostered debate over the employment of medieval forms of corporal punishment. After the departure of occupying British and Hessian forces from Rhode Island in 1779, the Providence jail became a de facto colony-wide jail for society's most heinous offenders, a status it maintained for more than fifty years. Nonetheless, branding and other disfiguring forms of punishment were still in use throughout the early nineteenth century. Greene (1963, 1–2) has noted an especially gruesome incident of branding in Newport as late as 1832. The gradual decrease in corporal punishment cases and the consequent increase in imposition of unpayable fines heightened the pressure on decrepit jail facilities. In some cases Rhode Island simply banished criminals, a practice to which neighboring colonies naturally objected.

Discussion of a state penitentiary began as early as 1794, when the General Assembly of Rhode Island, having only considered the matter in haste, ordered the condemnation of the existing Providence jail and the construction of a new state prison and adjoining Providence County Jail. This set off a three-year controversy in the assembly, with a three-person committee appointed to come up with a plan for such a structure. In May 1797 this committee reported that the institution could be built on the existing jail lot for approximately twelve thousand dollars. This proposal was rejected in January 1798 in favor of rebuilding the Providence County Jail, which was never done.

Between 1818 and 1834 at least nine different committees were appointed to consider different aspects of the prison question. In January 1818 the first committee recommended "confinement at hard labor"

(Greene 1963, 93) as the plan of punishment, a vague recommendation at best. The second committee, appointed at the same session "to consider and report on the expense of erecting a State Prison," returned in November 1818 to inform the assembly that the state prison, originally estimated at twelve thousand dollars, would now cost twenty thousand dollars to build and five hundred dollars per annum to maintain. Five years later a third committee was appointed to determine the costs of a state prison. That committee appears to have been active until May 1826, when it was dismissed and a fourth committee appointed.

In 1828 a fifth committee appointed to review existing conditions at the Providence jail found conditions at the decaying facility entirely inappropriate in light of the contemporary debate (Staples 1853, 12). Prisoners were caged in large, communal cells, and keepers augmented their paltry salaries by providing extra provisions and other perquisites to prisoners who could pay for them. Despite these observations, one historian of Rhode Island noted acidly, "The result achieved [by the fifth committee] was that intended by the opposition. Nothing was done" (Field 1902, 458). This committee inspired a sixth committee "to fix on a site for a new jail." The sixth committee made a full report, recommending Great Point on the northern edge of the city as its chosen locale. A seventh committee, appointed in January 1832 to carry out negotiations for the land with the city of Providence, was discharged in January 1833, as was the eighth committee, appointed in June 1833 for the same purpose.

The ninth committee, appointed in October 1833, finally was able to force the issue of revising the penal code in favor of imprisonment. This committee, which included Governor John Brown Francis, unleashed additional controversy among the more reactionary political forces seated in the General Assembly of Rhode Island. It is worth examining this committee's report in some detail, especially because the sentiments expressed in that document reflect the national debate over reform.

The Ninth Committee Makes Its Report (1834)

In January 1834 the "Committee Appointed upon the Subject of a State Prison" issued its report on the state of punishment in Rhode Island. The manuscript copy of this document is in the Rhode Island State Archives (General Treasurer's Records, C 0490; Box 70:B). Consisting of eight pages bound with a red ribbon, it is more than a mere committee report; it is a scathing indictment of the existing methods of punishment in Rhode Island, an overview of systems at work in other states, and a well-reasoned but ultimately flawed argument for the adaptation of a state penitentiary modeled on the Pennsylvania plan.

The report opens with two rhetorical, philosophical questions that the committee took as its theme for the discussion: "Is any alteration in the penal code of the State, necessary; also, in the present pecuniary situation of the State, can an effectual alteration be made?" (General Treasurer's Records C 0490, Box 70:B, RISA; *Report of the Committee Appointed upon the Subject of a State Prison [RCASSP]* 1834, 1). Thus in establishing the terms and conditions of the debate, financial considerations were at the forefront. How much would the project of social reform cost the taxpayers of Rhode Island? Could incarceration be made financially feasible in the state?

There were, the committee noted, two types of punishment in place in Rhode Island: corporal punishment and fines. Corporal punishment, still occasionally practiced, consisted of "cropping, branding, and whipping." The committee's opinion of corporal punishment's efficacy was succinct: "He [the criminal] is made to bear on his person the indelible marks of disgrace. A subsequent life of perfect innocence cannot obliterate them. No tears of penitence can blot them out. No change of residence will enable him to conceal them. . . . Such punishments are indeed a relic of a barbarous age" (*RCASSP* 1834, 1). Fines were no better since those most likely to be punished—the poor—could scarcely afford the fines and languished in county jails under little supervision. In such an environment moral reform was impossible. "In these Jails all the convicts are confined without employment, and without Instruction of any kind. The intercourse between them is free and uninterrupted. Is this calculated to reform the prisoner? In the absence of all moral and religious instruction, in the absence of that solitude & silence which harrows up the conscience by unbidden recollection of crime . . . what change for the better can be reasonably hoped for, in the moral character of any prisoner?" (*RCASSP* 1834, 2).

In addition to the poor state of discipline and reform, the county jails constituted a serious drain on the state's financial resources. The committee noted that the state spent nearly two thousand dollars per annum on feeding, clothing, and housing these prisoners, not including confined witnesses and those merely awaiting trial. Furthermore, random sentencing by arrogant local justices led to other stresses in the political system. Prisoners with well-connected and powerful friends presented a seemingly endless series of petitions at the biannual sessions of the General

47

Assembly of Rhode Island, tying up the legislators' time in attempts to win much-coveted pardons for their patrons. Surely the state could obtain better value for its money by abandoning its random and decentralized system of punishment.

The committee then considered total solitary confinement without labor and the "penitentiary system as at first adopted," neither of which correlate directly to the Pennsylvania or Auburn plan. Total solitary confinement without labor was rejected out of hand because of its effects on the psychological health of prisoners. Yet the committee found that Walnut Street and Newgate, where inmates were confined in communal cells at night, were "schools of vice and iniquity . . . highly expensive to the States that established them." The Auburn and Pennsylvania plans were seen as compromise solutions, "a midway course" bridging the need for solitary confinement and the requirement of labor.

Communication, which had never been fully eradicated in Auburn-plan prisons, was an impediment to successful reform of inmates. Citing the constant communication between prisoners that had led to the recent murder of the keeper of the Wethersfield, Connecticut, prison, the committee rejected such a plan for Rhode Island. It was the Pennsylvania plan, and particularly the Eastern State Penitentiary, that impressed the committee: "This institution has been in operation a number of years with success. In it, no prisoner knows who besides himself are its inmates. He sees no human face except his keeper's & his instructor's, he hears no voice except that which is urging him to the formation of habits of industry & respect for the laws. He applies himself to his labor, as a recreation, & in hours of rest is left to communicate with his own heart" (*RCASSP* 1834, 5). Thus almost by a process of elimination the committee chose solitary confinement at labor as the state's best solution. Although the cells would have to be larger than those constructed on the Auburn plan, the long-term savings on the larger complex would be significant because the direct cost of supervision of prisoners permanently confined to cells would be relatively low. For an Auburn-plan prison with fifty cells, the state would require approximately twenty-five thousand dollars, including the building site; for a Pennsylvania-plan prison, the estimate was closer to thirty-five thousand dollars. The proximity of the site to sources of raw material, especially quarries, would reduce the projected costs. Furthermore, the committee noted, fifty cells might not be necessary; perhaps the state could construct half that number and add to the complex as financial conditions permitted. In any event, the committee was convinced that the institution would ultimately pay for itself. Committee members concluded, "The prospect that the adoption of a modified system of penitentiary punishment will relieve the State from the future support of convicts and ~~will~~ [*sic*] may produce a moral reformation . . . induces your committee to hope that the Subject will receive the immediate attention of the Legislature" (*RCASSP* 1834, 7–8). The strikeout in the original document is indicative of the committee's more realistic expectations concerning the social aspects of the project of reform.

One key paragraph—a broad, sweeping statement about the purpose of punishment—did not make it into the final version of the report. It survives only in a manuscript version of an earlier draft in the John Brown Francis Papers (Box 5, RIHS). The excised paragraph displays the marked influence of Quaker philosophy underlying the committee's struggle to define state punishment. The committee members wrote: "The only legitimate end of human punishment, is the prevention of crime. The sole objects of penal laws, are to prohibit the doing of certain acts, and to enforce the performance of certain others, the doing and omission of which acts are essential to the safety or happiness of the community." Possibly such a reasoned, Enlightenment-based approach was seen as potentially unpopular with more conservative, rural legislators, many of whom continued to favor approaches to punishment that focused on the body. Whatever the reason, by deleting the paragraph the committee lost its opportunity to make its most reasoned argument for imprisonment. "The penalties annexed to these laws," they concluded, "have for their object the prevention of crime by reforming the delinquent and deterring others from like courses." Sacrificing the broader issue of punishment theory for the specific method to be employed, the committee set the tone for decades of debate over the financial aspects of reform, rather than its theoretical basis.

The Taxpayers Agree to a Prison

Noticeably absent from the committee's report is a specific consideration of the sources of funding for the prison, as well as a source for its maintenance, upkeep, and repair. Yet notations on the reverse of the document indicate that it was read into the state house record on January 29, communicated to the state senate on January 30, referred to committees on January 31, and approved by both chambers on February 1. The speed with which the report cleared the general assembly is indicative of the legislature's enthusiasm to get on with the business of reforming the plan of punishment in the state.

As expected, financial considerations occupied a significant portion of the assembly's review of the proposed project. Between February and April 1834 a political struggle erupted in the assembly over the cost and source of funding for the project. This controversy may be interpreted as a dispute between agrarian interests south of the geographic center of the state, who were opposed to the cost of the prison, and their more industrialized contemporaries in the state's northern portion (Greene 1963). Representatives of agricultural districts knew that their constituents would pay more than their fair share of the project costs. In Rhode Island ratable property was limited to land and permanent infrastructure. The revenue-producing components of textile mills—looms, for example—were considered the mill owner's personal property and not subject to taxation. A tax on the state's ratable property would inevitably cause the large landowners of the rural southern area to pay proportionally far more of the costs than the mill owners and capitalists in the industrialized center of the state paid.

Despite the cantankerous debate at the highest level of state government, support for the project was strong among ratepayers across the state. A series of printed petitions favoring the prison contains more than sixteen hundred signatures. Evidently the idealism of Jacksonian reform had spread even to the most rural districts of Rhode Island. In April 1834 a general referendum was held on the question "Shall a State Prison be built, to be paid for by a tax on the ratable polls and estates?" Ratepayers, who voted on the question in their annual town meetings, approved the measure by an overwhelming vote of 4,433 to 502 (Staples 1853, 13).

Thus after fifty years of delay, Rhode Island had finally chosen a system of punishment and a means of raising funds for the prison within the space of four months. The rush toward constructing the facility continued with the selection of John Haviland of Philadelphia as the architect for the complex (Jordy and Monkhouse 1982). No evidence survives of a solicitation for designs; it is likely that Haviland was chosen on the basis of his expertise. By 1834 he had already built the two purpose-built Pennsylvania-plan prisons in operation: the Eastern State Penitentiary in Philadelphia and the New Jersey State Prison in Trenton (fig. 3).

The process of architectural design in the 1830s bore little resemblance to today's practices. It is unlikely that Haviland even visited Providence to meet with the building committee or to review any of the sites under consideration. The strongest link associating him with the Rhode Island State Prison is found in his own papers, where on October 24, 1834, he recorded receipt of $150 "for drawings and specifications of a prison for

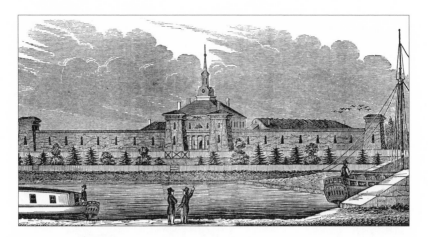

FIG. 3 — *John Haviland's massive Egyptian-revival New Jersey State Prison at Trenton, with cell blocks extending in lines from the keeper's house at the center. Undated line engraving. Author's collection.*

the State of Rhode Island" (Haviland Papers, Vol. 4, 315). The building committee may have simply written to him and requested specifications for building a small prison. These documents were eventually distributed to local contractors requested to bid on the largest public undertaking in state history.

Proposals for the New Prison

With the approval of the ratepayers secured and the specifications in hand, the General Assembly of Rhode Island appointed a new committee "to advertise for proposals for erecting the same, and to select a location for the same" (*Report of the Committee to Draw Up a Specification . . . for a State Prison* [*RCDUASSP*], General Treasurer's Records C 0490, 70:B, Folder 2, RISA; proposals for the new prison are all contained in Folder 2, RISA). The committee received six proposals from six contractors offering a total of seven sites distributed throughout the state. The proposals, which range from cursory to extremely detailed, provide further evidence of the state's emphasis on the economic viability—indeed, on the potential profit—of a state prison (table 1).

The sites for the prison varied greatly, depending on the location of suitable land (fig. 4). David Melville and William Vars proposed Hope

TABLE 1

Proposals for the First Rhode Island State Prison, 1834

Contractor	Location	Cost
Melville & Vars	Hope Island	$42,000.00
Henry Bailey	Warren	$47,700.00
Welcome Matteson	Coventry	$48,000.00
Stephen Eddy	North Providence	$35,000.00
James Lewis	Providence/Cranston	$42,867.65
James Lewis	North Providence	$41,817.65
James Lewis	North Providence	$41,817.65
James Lewis	North Providence	$38,060.00
Nathaniel F. Potter	North Providence	$39,650.00
Nathaniel F. Potter	North Providence	$38,650.00
Nathaniel F. Potter	Great Point	$39,500.00

Island, located in the geographic center of Narragansett Bay. In addition to unparalleled security, Melville and Vars noted, "the quarries on this Island are so extensive, that they could always be worked to advantage by the State, and a ready market always found for their product" (*RCDUASSP*, 2).

Welcome Matteson of Scituate selected Netmug (Nipmuck) Hill in Coventry for similar reasons. In addition to convenient nearby granite quarries, Matteson noted the location's proximity to the new mill villages lining the Pawtuxet River: "Four [miles] from the Hope, Fiskville, Jackson, and Arkwright factories—Five from Washington factory, six from Phenix and Coventry factories, one from Central factory and ten from Natick factory" (*RCDUASSP*, 3). Matteson may have cannily anticipated that most of the inmates would be drawn from the mill villages (an anticipation that would prove correct over the next fifty years); more likely, he was considering the need for prison industry and the eventual solution of selling convict labor to private contractors.

Neither Matteson's proposal nor that of Melville and Vars was entertained seriously. Similarly, Henry Bailey's proposal for Warren, a small commercial town in the East Bay, was rejected as inappropriate. The committee only inspected sites in the greater Providence metropolitan area, indicating their desire to have the structure in the capital city rather than an island, a small town, or the rural hinterland. Such thinking was not unusual for a public building, even a prison. Many of the Jacksonian-era prisons were built on the margins of capital cities. Haviland was building the New Jersey State Prison at the edge of Trenton, for example, and Charles Bulfinch had designed the imposing Massachusetts State

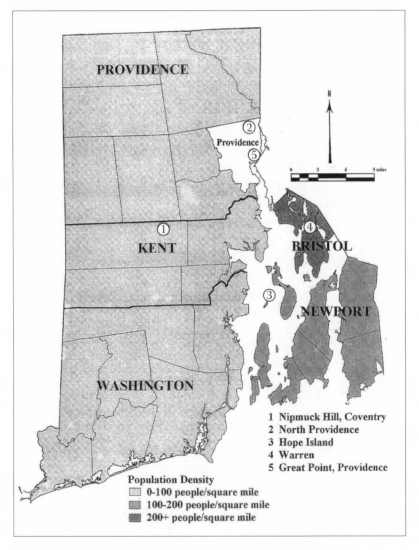

Fig. 4 — *Proposed sites for the first Rhode Island State Prison, 1834. Graphic by Gail Van Dyke. Courtesy of PAL, Pawtucket, Rhode Island.*

BY REFORMING THE DELINQUENT AND DETERRING OTHERS

Prison in Charlestown, across the Mystic River from Boston (Rothman 1971).

After ruling out the sites on the western boundary of the city and in North Providence, the committee settled on Nathaniel Potter's proposal for Great Point "as possessing the most advantages & subject to least disadvantages" (*RCDUASSP*, 5). Potter, knowing that a low bid was an important, if not a determinant, consideration, had presented a shrewd proposal. He had read Haviland's initial plans closely and found a way to cut corners: "There can be a good Prison built on either of the above locations for a much less sum," he wrote, "by dispensing with several parts which in my opinion would not injure the Prison, among which are the leading the particions [*sic*] and the plastering of the Keepers house" (General Treasurer's Records C 0490, 70:B, Folder 2, RISA). With this declaration, the barebones nature of the operation becomes apparent. Not plastering the keeper's house would give it the appearance of a large barn, with exposed timberframing—highly desirable in modern "restorations" of eighteenth-century houses, but a practice that had fallen out of vogue in Rhode Island nearly a century earlier (Stachiw 2001, 23).

In fairness to the other competitors, the committee then asked all six to bid on constructing a prison to Haviland's specifications at Great Point. Only three of the six responded, with Potter underbidding the other two by nearly twenty-five hundred dollars. Thus the committee, in a five-to-two vote, accepted Potter's proposal. The two dissenters, who represented rural districts, objected not to the choice of Potter as builder but rather to the selection of Great Point as the site of the new state prison.

Why Great Point? Why was Great Point—a low-lying, generally useless piece of property subject to periodic flooding—chosen as the site of the state's new prison? Formed at the mouths of the Woonasquatucket and Moshassuck rivers as a glacial outwash plain, Great Point extended into the waters of the Great Salt Cove. The cove effectively divided Providence into three distinct areas: the East Side, settled by Roger Williams in the seventeenth century; the "Weybosset" or West Side, settled by merchants in the late eighteenth and early nineteenth centuries; and the North Side, where Great Point lay, an urban hinterland used for military parade grounds and other sporadic public events (fig. 5).

The aspect with which the committee appears to have been most concerned was the proposed economic viability of the building site, a concern encompassing the cost of the lot, the cost of site preparation, and the site's access to main roads and factories. In terms of real estate acquisition costs,

FIG. 5 — Encampment of the New England Guards, Smith's Hill, Providence, Rhode Island, *by J. H. Bufford and Co., Boston (1844). The Rhode Island State Prison is visible at the foot of the hill, on low-lying Great Point. Lithograph. Courtesy of the Rhode Island Historical Society (RHi X3 2174).*

Great Point, offered by the city of Providence for five hundred dollars, appeared to be a bargain. The city demanded that the state "cause Cove Street to be continued through said lot," thus linking the three parts of the city along the margins of the cove (MSS 144 SS B22 F7, RIHS). The construction of this road and attendant land-filling operations were more than enough to offset any gains won by the relatively low acquisition costs.

Great Point was also a remarkably poor choice from a construction standpoint. Site preparation, encompassing grading and filling the lot and building a wharf at the peninsula's interface with the Great Salt Cove, would ultimately require the displacement of more than eight thousand cubic yards of fill and engender years of bitter litigation on the part of the primary excavation subcontractor. Settling problems due to poor subsurface conditions would become familiar to architects and builders attempting to expand the complex over the next forty years.

Great Point, although technically located within the city limits, was as remote as any site that could be found within the metropolitan area. Travel from the courts required going to the northern end of Benefit Street, crossing a bridge that was occasionally washed out, and navigating along marginal streets in the shadow of Jefferson Plains, a tableland looming over the point. The site offered no clear access to turnpikes or other highways linking Providence with the rest of Rhode Island, or to nascent factory villages north and west of the city.

A review of map and historical evidence helps put the problem of site selection in a different light. In 1797 Great Point is depicted as a series of proprietary privileges granted to John Brown, Thomas Harris's sons, and Benjamin Stelle. No building is shown on any of these lots. Approximately nine hundred feet west of the future prison site is an area described as "English Meadow" with several small houses on it. Nearly three decades later the North Side still appears as a marshy, unattractive spot; Cady's visual interpretation of Providence in 1832 depicts Great Point as open, undeveloped, and isolated, especially in comparison to the burgeoning city south and west of the cove (fig. 6).

Despite this depiction of "blank space," the northwest side of the cove was indeed occupied by the early 1820s: by free African Americans, recent Irish immigrants, and sporadically employed wage laborers. Known derisively as "Snow Town," the area's collection of run-down tenements and "disorderly houses" drew considerable anathema from local civic and community leaders. Joanne Melish (1998, 206) notes that much of this anathema toward Snow Town revolved around the fact that its citizenry was largely African American. One contemporary authority wrote of the district: "Here it is that the scum of the town and the outscorings of creation, nightly assemble to riot and debauch, and in the midst of their bacchanalian revels, the whole neighborhood is kept in a constant state of inquietude and alarm—A viler place never yet existed, and compared with it, St. Giles of London, is a school of morals" (Bartlett 1954, 30–31, quoted in Artemel et al. 1984, IV-B.5). The spatial relationship between Snow Town and Great Point is more evident from later map history. By 1827 English Meadow had been gridded into a series of lanes intersecting Smith Street, and a proposed road (named appropriately Cove Street) had been laid out along the shoreline of the cove. This is the road that the city eventually forced the state to construct as part of its asking price for the land at Great Point.

In addition to cartographic blank space, other documents (city directories and census schedules, for example) deliberately ignored the resi-

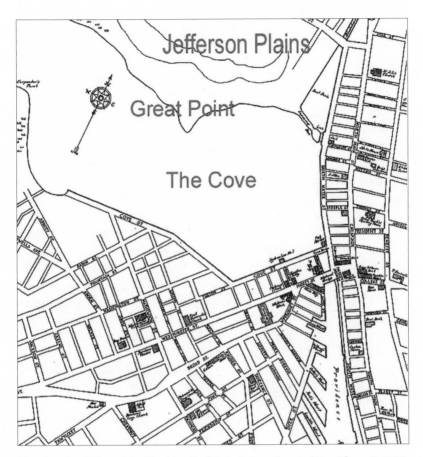

FIG. 6 — *Detail from John Hutchins Cady's depiction of central Providence in 1832. Great Point, future site of the Rhode Island State Prison, is an isolated periphery lying in the shadow of Jefferson Plains.*

dents of this area, as well as their informal title to the temporary houses they constructed on the land of the proprietors. Complaints about Snow Town escalated until 1831, when a race riot erupted in the streets of the settlement. By most accounts the riot began when a group of white steamboat sailors descended on Olney's Lane (Artemel et al. 1984, IV-B.2). A fight between residents and invaders erupted, in which one of the sailors was killed and a second wounded. The white community responded on the second night by cordoning off the street and dismantling six or seven houses. Imposition of martial law led to four additional nights of trouble, including at least one more death and the destruction of a total of eighteen properties (Melish 1998, 207).

Perhaps the decision to situate the new state prison at Great Point, despite its economic drawbacks, was inspired by the recent memory of the Snow Town riots. The siting of the prison can be read as a message on multiple levels. "Respectable" citizens of Providence, who constituted the committee, likely saw the construction of a prison there as a message that society would not endure any more of the riots that had flamed in Snow Town. The inhabitants of these settlements, on the other hand, certainly received the message that many of their tenements would give way to the state's largest public works project to date. This multiplicity of meanings, especially control of potentially rebellious urban masses, may have been an important factor in settling on a final site.

There is a second, equally unsavory possibility for the selection of Great Point. From later correspondence we learn that the prison building committee was trying to purchase additional land for the prison adjacent to the city-owned parcel. This neighboring land was owned by John Brown Francis, the governor of Rhode Island—and, coincidentally, the ex officio head of the 1834 committee. Not surprisingly, the building committee reported that Francis was holding out for a higher price for the formerly worthless land. It is not clear from the land evidence whether Francis eventually won the high price he was asking for the additional property. Suffice it to say that if cronyism and corruption were part of the selection process, it would hardly be the first time in a state with a penchant for political skullduggery.

Evaluating the Planning Process

We have seen that legislators and concerned citizens struggled for more than fifty years to overturn the medieval-based penal code and construct an appropriate state penitentiary in Rhode Island. The documentary record pertaining to this struggle strongly suggests that the effort to change the criminal code in favor of imprisonment was driven by economic considerations, if not notions of potential profit, as much as by the moral discourse of reform and rehabilitation. Thus a close reading of legislative dockets, reports of investigating committees, and newspaper editorials tends to support Foucault's argument linking the creation of the penitentiary to industrial capitalism more than Rothman's (1971) interpretation of society's benevolent interest in securing reform. What larger themes for this study can be discerned from Rhode Island's experience with planning its first state-wide institution?

The first theme is one of financial expediency on the part of the state in planning and executing public building projects, especially reform institutions. The high cost of the proposed prison, compared with the total state budget, was the primary factor inhibiting its acceptance among state legislators. In 1800 the state listed a total of $6,200 in annual expenditures; the disbursement had climbed to $18,300 by 1825, reaching the mark of $92,000 only by 1850. Thus the proposed expenditure of $35,000 to $40,000 in the mid-1830s on a facility for the state's most heinous criminals represented nearly 150 percent of the annual state budget, an amount which proper citizens found appropriately daunting. Although the Pennsylvania-plan prison chosen by legislators would require a higher initial outlay, the state would ultimately make its money back on the relatively low number of guards it would have to hire; better still, no hospitals, chapels, or communal workshops would be required, adding to the long-term savings.

The emphasis on cost leads directly to a second, related theme that will reappear continuously in this book: that of the sacrifice of long-term vision for an immediate gain. The slashing of the number of cells from the 1834 committee's recommendation of fifty to the final number of forty, the selection of Great Point because it was land that could be had cheaply, and above all, the selection of the Pennsylvania plan as the agent of reform all point to strategies for quick success and return on the investment—all of which backfired within the next ten years. In particular the choice of solitary confinement at hard labor as the plan under which the new penitentiary would operate belies the committee's obsession with cost at the expense of the preliminary results at Pennsylvania-system prisons. By the mid-1830s the high incidence of insanity among Auburn's inmates was a well-established fact. Even before a single stone had been set in the ground, worries about costs had outstripped discussion about the proper means of reform.

The final theme is one I will take up directly in the next chapter. It concerns the specific use of material culture—in this case, public architecture—as a means by which the state can transmit a series of direct and indirect messages to different classes in society. The siting of the prison had everything to do with public perception in the wake of the Snow Town riots of 1831. By building the new prison at the northern margin of the city, the state indicated that the informal settlement of Snow Town and other shantytowns, as refuges of the lawless, would no longer be tolerated.

Thus financial insecurity, lack of vision, political corruption, and the perceived need to "send a message" to the taxpayers and the lower classes all played greater or lesser roles in the debate over imprisonment in Rhode Island. In chapter 3, which interprets change in the built environment of the prison, we shall see how some of the challenges and difficulties encountered in the planning process stemmed from the entanglements of the earlier debates. More significantly, we will see the ways in which the darker aspects underlying the process—particularly financial insecurity and the absence of vision—would return again and again to confound those entangled in the business of imprisonment.

CHAPTER 3

"A Monument of Shame and Disgrace to the State"

Building and Rebuilding the Landscape of Confinement

As work crews and subcontractors assembled at Great Point in the spring of 1836, Rhode Island's long-awaited project of constructing a prison began in earnest. For the next four decades the General Assembly of Rhode Island, the board of inspectors, the keepers, architects, builders, and outside contractors would all participate in reshaping John Haviland's original design to suit their own requirements. The speed with which these changes occurred is remarkable; the footprint of the various structures on the prison lot expanded 357 percent over forty years, from approximately 6,912 square feet in 1838 to 24,684 square feet in 1878. Industrial workshops, steam plants, and tier upon tier of new cell blocks all contributed to masking the 1838 complex. By 1878 the observer would have had a difficult time recognizing Haviland's elegant Greek-revival prison hidden within the sprawling institutional-industrial complex that had overtaken the original core.

Certainly a rapidly expanding prison and jail population created the pressures that drove many of the additions and renovations to the Rhode Island State Prison. To view the evolution of the complex simply as a reflexive response to a steadily increasing inmate population, however, is to ignore the larger project of experimentation behind the granite walls of the institution. Few decisions about the prison structure were made without considering the social aspects underlying the state's ideology of reform. Fewer still were made without considering the potential economic benefit of the planned improvement.

The explosion of the prison's built environment and its implications for interpreting changing models of penal reform are the subjects of this chapter. For the first twenty years of the institution's existence, various authorities engaged in a continuous process of manipulating the prison's built environment and the surrounding landscape, and neither reached a "final" configuration satisfactory to the myriad interested parties. Changing architectural tastes, new trends in reform, and above all an economic imperative to produce more goods in the workshops all wrought modifications to the infrastructure. Thus the prison—the ultimate symbol of fixed state authority—may constitute a more flexible and transitory environment than one might initially anticipate. This theorized flexibility has implications for the built environment, labor and power relations.

Central to this discussion of the changing built environment are the power relationships between the general assembly, the board of inspectors, and the keepers of the prison. The general assembly's role in the affairs of the penitentiary is obvious. Its biannual sessions served as the public forum for discussion of the financial, physical, moral, and spiritual welfare of the institution. Its members were especially concerned about the ability of the prison to pay for itself, thus avoiding costly annual disbursements from the state's general fund. The moral imperative of reform was less important to legislators than the economic obligation owed to the farmers, artisans, merchants, and industrialists who had elected them to office.

The keeper's place at the bottom of the hierarchy is also relatively straightforward. At the quarterly meetings of the board of inspectors, which took place in a special room at the prison devoted only to that purpose, he delivered verbal and written reports of the previous month's activities, answered pointed questions about the economic state of the prison, and submitted his accounts for approval. There can be no question about the keeper's lack of control over external affairs. His appointment was annual and required him to post a ten-thousand-dollar bond to the state; he paid vendors out of his own pocket, receiving approval for reimbursement only after a monthly audit; and he was required to explain, often in compelling detail, why the prison labor program was so ineffective. By state law, the keeper's absence from the prison, even for a single night, required prior written permission of two of the inspectors (*An Act in Relation to Officers and Discipline of the State Prison* 1852, Section 5). Given these strictures, it is perhaps not surprising that eight different individuals—generally affluent retired military men who could afford to front the institution's expenses—filled the role of keeper/warden during the prison's forty-year history in Providence.

A MONUMENT OF SHAME AND DISGRACE

Less obvious is the role of the intermediaries in the power relation-ship, the members of the prison's board of inspectors. This committee, formed for the first time during the final days of construction, contained from four to seven members of the Providence elite. Industrialists, jurists, Brown University presidents, and theologians all sat on the board at differ-ent times. Their charge was explicit: "The oversight, management and con-trol of the state prison shall be vested in a board of seven inspectors, to be appointed annually by the general assembly" (*An Act in Relation to Officers and Discipline of the State Prison* 1852, Section 1). Their obligations were to appear at the quarterly meetings and receive reports; to visit the prison-ers and assess their moral and physical well-being; to prepare annual reports to the general assembly summarizing the monthly returns; and to submit formal requests to the legislature for additional funds, especially those relating to construction and repair of the facility.

Although every group in the hierarchy compiled formal, published reports, only the general assembly and the keepers left substantial primary records of their activities. The activities of the board of inspectors are less open to the scrutiny of the historical anthropologist. If we want to be in-formed more about the internal and external tensions in the keeper's world, we can turn to his manuscript daybooks and ledgers, which constitute a firsthand account of the daily business of running a prison. If we are inter-ested in the debates occurring within the chambers of the general assem-bly, we can turn to the published records of those debates and attribute specific ideas, resolutions, and voting patterns to individuals. But the in-spectors, as a volunteer commission with varying agendas, operated in a more shadowy world. Their manuscript *Minutes* (C 490, Box 37, RISA), kept in cursory form, rarely offer any keen insights into the social and eco-nomic processes of running the institution; their logbook, titled *Inspectors' Weekly Visits No. 1* (MS 231.1, Vol. 234, RIHS), is at most cursory in its description of prison life. As members of the local elite, they had almost unrestricted access to jurists, members of the assembly, reformers, mill owners, and others with political and economic clout. Much of the infor-mal decision making, lobbying, and negotiation must have occurred within the parlors of the homes of powerful individuals along the city's East Side and can only be surmised through a careful consideration of rhetoric and performance in the documentary record.

With these considerations of multiple contested relationships of power in the foreground, this chapter begins with an overview of the architectural evolution of the Rhode Island State Prison. In addition to providing a syn-opsis of major construction events, I focus on less prominent but equally

63

important events in the creation of the prison matrix—the enclosure of yard areas, for example, and the creation of formal landscaping in front of the keeper's house. I will return to the relationship between the three primary groups repeatedly, especially in considering the bottom-line financial considerations. Within this discussion I incorporate an archaeological reading of a series of specific institutional actions and the importance of those actions for interpreting changing local and national ideas about punishment and reform.

The chapter concludes with an evaluation of themes for spatial change in the prison. The first of these themes encompasses the structuring of spatiality within the institution. As the built environment evolved, each room, hallway, cell, corridor, and portion of yard acquired a defined purpose. No space was left unregulated; nor was movement, light, or sound. "Discipline," writes Foucault (1979, 139), "is a political anatomy of detail." At the same time, the meaning of that space was subject to interpretation by the different groups negotiating it. Authorities may define and delimit space, but these definitions are subject to contestation by subordinate groups in the institutional matrix.

The second theme, which is primarily concerned with the external aspects of institutional power, addresses the haphazard development of the complex. After all of the plans for a construction or renovation had been set in motion, after the architects had submitted their drawings, a strange inertia pervaded the work of the state. This process, common to institutions, is one in which architectural modification is a product of planning the immediate need to address specific and pressing perceived problems with space.

The third and final spatial theme is the dichotomy between the public and private spheres of the complex. The changing nature of the prison's presentation to the public, especially in the context of the expansion of Providence's urban core, was an important aspect underlying decisions about the prison's infrastructure. Interpretation of the landscape and the built environment suggests a marked disparity between the public impressions of the prison and the invisible areas behind the walls. Similarly, a study of the ways in which the infrastructure was depicted in photographs, plans, and other state documents is helpful for understanding official representations of institutional space.

In addition to the substantial documentary record, this chapter draws on the archaeological record of the complex. Structural information obtained from these investigations can be placed in a discursive relationship to plans, specifications, and other documents calling for revision of the

A MONUMENT OF SHAME AND DISGRACE

complex. This permits the identification of ambiguities and contradictions, as well as an interpretation of the dialectic between what the legislator or the architect conceived and what the contractor actually built. But the importance of the archaeological investigations exceeds the verification or refutation of the documentary record. The unearthing of the complex permitted a unique opportunity to evaluate and experience the spatiality of the institutional environment, and to trace its evolution from a perspective encompassing diachronic and synchronic landscape change (Darvill, Gerrard, and Startin 1993).

The Prison's Evolution

Three primary events stand out over the course of the four-decade expansion of the prison infrastructure: the initial construction of the complex on the model of the Pennsylvania plan (1836–38); the addition of the first communal workshops, to increase economic production and alleviate a marked increase in insanity among the inmates (1845–50); and the total rebuilding of the domestic and economic spheres of the institution, including two cell block wings, a large workshop, and a boiler house (1851–55). No real improvements were made during the final two decades of the institution's history, a phenomenon suggesting two possibilities: either the prison lot was entirely built out, with little room left for architectural innovation, or authorities had resigned themselves to the construction of a new prison only twenty years after the construction of the original facility. Given that the board of inspectors spent most of the 1860s and 1870s repairing the existing buildings and making a series of desperate pleas for a new institution, the latter scenario seems more likely. However, the detectable level of apathy and resignation on the part of authorities is an important aspect of institutional development, and part of the "haphazard development" theme.

Building the Prison (1836–1838)

In contrast to the Eastern State Penitentiary, which had cost the taxpayers of Pennsylvania more than three-quarters of a million dollars, Haviland proposed a much more modest, linear structure for Rhode Island, consisting of a keeper's house, a connecting building, and a cell block running from south to north on the Great Point lot. It is unfortunate that Haviland's elevations have not survived in the mass of documents relating to the construction of the prison. In the absence of visual documentation, we are forced to rely on Haviland's written specifications and the archaeological record to reconstruct his vision for the Rhode Island State Prison.

Four versions of the specifications documents survive. These include a manuscript rough draft, with relatively insignificant strikeouts and substitutions (General Treasurer's Records, Box 70:B, RISA); a clean manuscript copy incorporating the corrections in the earlier draft (*Reports of Committees* 9, 70, RISA); and two printed copies, differing only in the most minor details (General Treasurer's Records, Box 70:B, RISA). In the following discussion I draw on the latest printed copy (cited here as *Specifications* 4), which was the version most likely used by those who bid on constructing the prison.

The printed specifications provide a series of directions to the would-be contractor, including dimensions of structures, materials, construction techniques, and other guidelines to be used in preparing the bid and carrying out the work. The directions begin with the required large-scale modifications to the lot and progress to the enclosure of this improved space with a yard wall. It is only after the prison lot has been defined—when the broadest boundaries of institutional space have been fixed—that the specifications move to the details of the built environment.

Specifications for the yard wall provide insight into Haviland's vision of the Pennsylvania plan. The wall was to be 100 feet (east to west) by 194 feet (south to north); of the front 100 feet, the rear wall of the keeper's house would form the central 46 feet, with projections of 27 feet to either side. It would then run north on either side of the connecting building and the cell block for a length of 194 feet, leaving an area of open space approximately 100 feet by 80 feet between the rear wall of the cell block and the northern line of the yard wall enclosing the complex.

Thus, before a single spade of earth had been turned over on Great Point, we see the first serious spatial constraint to the complex. Short of demolishing the 14-foot-high wall, the only way to expand the prison in the future would be to add buildings with proportions similar to Haviland's structures within this limited space. If we imagine that these future, unforeseen buildings would have the same general width as the rest of the complex (46 feet) and that a minimum clearance between the rear wall of the northernmost building and the yard wall would be 27 feet, then we are left with a building envelope of 46 feet east to west by 53 feet north to south—in other words, a space that would support a building approximately half the size of the cell block. The cell block, as built, contained forty cells on its

A Monument of Shame and Disgrace

two stories; we can assume then that only twenty additional cells (for a total of sixty) could have been added to the prison without destroying the yard wall and extending the boundaries of the property.

The results of these calculations demonstrate a marked lack of foresight in imagining the future extent of incarceration. By 1836 the smallest state prison in use was in Frankfort, Kentucky, which had more than twice the number of cells as Rhode Island. Surely the state, with a steady increase in population and a demonstrated commitment to industrialization and further expansion, would need more than sixty cells to house offenders against the newly rewritten penal code. Yet authorities settled for a building envelope that would accommodate only slightly more than half of the inmates in the smallest state prison in the United States.

Was this failure of vision Haviland's or the state's? It must have been the state's because building committees as far back as 1818 had estimated a need for no more than fifty cells. This is a recurring theme in state building projects: a sum, whether it is a cost estimate, an anticipated number of cells, or the dimensions of a proposed building, is placed on the table (often haphazardly) and thus becomes the standard. Subsequent proposals are measured against this initial sum and derided as "too big" (and thus overkill) or "too small" to accomplish the proposed task. This is especially true in the politically charged world of the state institution, where taxpayer antipathy is always to be expected. Haviland had only provided a prison of the size and approximate cost requested. He could no more specify twice the number of cells than he could demand a much higher quality of building materials. Thus we must question the state's commitment to the project of incarceration.

The contrast in *Specifications* 4 between the building materials comprising the yard wall and those of the fence in front of the keeper's house is striking and symbolic. The yard wall was meant for security, and the details relating to its presumed impermeability are impressive: it would stand fourteen feet tall, with a batter ranging from a twenty-six-inch width at the base to twenty inches at the top; a stone coping would cover the surface of the wall; and the composition of the wall would be of stones "4 feet long and at least seven inches thick" (*Specifications* 4, 1). Twenty-four pilasters at regular intervals along the exterior formed the only ornamentation on the stark, whitewashed structure.

The barrier in front of the keeper's house was to be a much more modest and decorative affair, consisting of a simple wooden pale fence set into granite blocks. Security in the front yard would clearly not be an issue in Haviland's prison; in his mind, the likelihood of an inmate negotiating the two iron doors of his cell, the iron door of the cell block, and the iron door of the connecting building to gain access to the keeper's house was minimal.

More important, the wall and fence specifications establish a dichotomy between the public spaces in the front of the complex, viewed by those passing by on Gaspee Street, and the far more restricted private spaces within the confines of the institution. Haviland's description of the keeper's house, the most prominent portion of the complex, reinforces this dichotomy, which has tangible archaeological components. He describes this structure as a two-story, gable-front house with a barn roof and a full cellar. Several details from the specifications indicate his intent to project austerity and simplicity on the exterior and on the interior: "A plain Doric portico in front as per plan"; "Windows and doors to be cased by plain pilasters"; and "All the Rooms, passages and closets to have a plain astragal skirting of pine 7 inches wide." If we take into account the simple wooden fence enclosing the keeper's yard, the large gable-front house, and the higher, pilastered yard wall, then we begin to see an image of a modest private estate setting, perhaps with an enclosed and invisible garden, rather than an institution for the state's most heinous offenders. This effect would be especially vivid to someone viewing the facade from Gaspee Street. Haviland's architecture has been interpreted as planometric and two-dimensional, and perhaps more concerned with monumentality and classicism than with total structural volume or with the interplay of light and shadow across the projections and recesses of facades. Baigell (1966, 200) has discussed this at length: "[Haviland] rarely, if ever, took into account compositional figure-ground relationships between a structure and the spaces surrounding it. . . . Haviland's buildings are 'removed' from their environment." Certainly the facade of the keeper's house and the impression received from Gaspee Street support this interpretation. The arrangement of structures in a line compressed their collective mass; the gable front, with its broad roof, obscured the connecting building and offered only intermittent glimpses of the cell block from oblique viewing points.

In addition to its planarity, a striking feature of Haviland's design is its internal tension between unity and discord. The keeper's house led directly into the connecting building, which in turn led to the cell block; thus in the plan view of the architect, the prison signals a connected, whole entity. Visually, however, the yard wall separated the house from the remainder of the complex. The prominence of the projection formed by the keeper's house, the separation of the house from the other structural elements, and the picket fence enclosing the public/private interface of the

A MONUMENT OF SHAME AND DISGRACE

front yard all evoke a strong sense of paternalism of the keeper as the physical and symbolic head of his extended "family" of societal offenders.

Linear plans were common in nineteenth-century social reform institutions, particularly asylums (Yanni 2003). The principal difference between the Rhode Island State Prison and contemporary institutions is one of orientation and complexity. American asylums and prisons often had a central administrative building flanked by cell blocks or wards and terminated by pavilions. Subsequent variants on the plan featured additional pavilions "set back *en echelon*, like a row of birds in flight" (Yanni 2003, 31). Under this system the more benign patients could live nearest the keeper's house and the more severe cases could be segregated toward the rear of the complex. Here the effect of the built environment is more simplistic and offers a resounding statement on Rhode Island's conservative ideology of punishment.

The Experience of Incarceration

Initiation into incarceration followed a gradient that began within the realm of the keeper, in whose basement lay the processing rooms for new prisoners, gradually progressing toward the cell block, the realm of the inmate. Haviland's plan included entries on the front (south) and side (west) elevations of the keeper's house. But there is no evidence of access into the basement rooms from the front door. The new arrival to the prison would have been led through the side door of the keeper's house and conducted down a rough-hewn granite stairway underneath the formal entry and into the basement. The front door may have been reserved for the keeper, his family, and important visitors to the complex. On the left side of the front entry was the parlor, the formal domestic domain of the keeper and his family. On the right side was a room furnished for and used exclusively by the board of inspectors at their monthly meetings.

The door beneath the side entry opened into a large hall paved with granite flagstones. Looking forward, the new inmate would have seen three doorways spaced at irregular intervals along the wall opposite the entry. These doors led into a warren of rooms used for storage of clothing and supplies. To the right the inmate would have seen only the stone foundation of the cellar. To the left at the end of the hall an iron door marked the nexus between the keeper's house and the connecting building. According to a *Providence Journal* article written immediately after the abandonment of the complex, a marble lintel over this door bore the inscription "THE WAY OF THE TRANSGRESSOR IS HARD" (*Providence Journal*, January 20, 1879, 2).

After a brief march of twenty feet down the hall, through this iron door, and down four granite steps the inmate stood on the brick floor of the connecting building.

It is difficult to imagine the impressions formed by the connecting building, which was rebuilt at least twice during subsequent modifications. If it was built according to Haviland's specifications, it would have been the lightest and airiest part of the complex. Doors and windows in the connecting building were cased with a single architrave, echoing the stark, clean, Greek-revival sensibility of the entire complex. The twelve-over-twelve windows and the doors into the prison yard would have provided the prisoner with a final glimpse of sunlight before arriving at the iron door of the cell block.

The cell block contained forty cells, ten on each side, twenty on each story, divided by a ten-foot corridor down the center of the building. The overall impression was one of stark, unremitting stone. "The cells are built of unhewn granite blocks, clamped together with iron bars," wrote an anonymous reporter (*Providence Journal*, January 20, 1879, 2). "No white-wash or paint covers them; nothing relieves the cold, rough stone." The inmate would have been led down the silent corridor to an iron door set into pine. The keeper produced a key, and the three-way lock mechanism opened slowly; the door swung out into the corridor, and the inmate found himself in a cell measuring approximately nine by twelve by nine feet. As the cell door closed, pale shafts of light emerged from two window panes set high in the exterior wall. A bunk along one side of the cell was the only furniture in the room. Staring at the stone covering all six surfaces of the cell, the new inmate sat on the bunk and contemplated spending the next year, five years, ten years in total solitary confinement.

Systems within the Prison

But unlike medieval prisons, an Enlightenment-based reform institution could not simply be a dungeon; built in the spirit of reform, it required a living network of systems for heat and sanitation running through the walls, ceilings, and floors. From the ceilings of each cell a five-inch sheet-iron pipe extended into the arch of the corridor. Within the arch the iron pipes connected to wooden pipes, which in turn led to the ridge of the roof, with apertures two inches wide "to conduct the foul air" (*Specifications* 4, 7). Heating pipes ran along the floors of the cells through the cell partitions to the furnace in the connecting building. Individual privy pipes in each cell are discussed at some length: "A circular hole is to be cut through each partition near the floor for the privy pipe 8 inches in diameter" (*Specifications* 4, 6). These individual pipes connected to a central sewer, which ran the length of the building and through the keeper's house, and discharged into the waters of the Great Salt Cove, where tidal action would have dispersed the raw sewage.

These pipes provided more than the passage of the heat, air, and wastewater through the stone walls of the prison. They would come to serve as the prisoners' only means of communicating with one another, through random and codified systems of tapping. "When shut up in the cells," wrote the keeper Thomas Cleaveland, "they exercised under the cravings of the social instinct, which walls and chains cannot repress, every contrivance that ingenuity could suggest, by means of the window, and the pipes passing through the cells, to hold some communication with each other, and they were more frequently successful than would have been supposed possible" (*ARRIGA* October 1845, 26). Thus the fixed, static nervous system of the cell block—the heating and plumbing pipes—took on a new meaning for prisoners and became transformed from the purely functional to the symbolic, serving as a medium of communication in the otherwise silent prison. Space, and its attendant components, is subverted from the moment it is occupied.

Construction Problems

Less than a year into construction, the wisdom of selecting Great Point as the site of the new institution was called into question by contractor problems and construction delays that threatened the entire project. The importance of these setbacks lies in the theme of the haphazard growth of the complex. Such growth took shape, in the milieu of liberal capitalism, as a result of disputes among competing power interests. Its tangible elements encompassed unexpected delays, cost overruns, and substantial disparities between the architect's intent and the built environment.

The state's agreement with the builder James Lewis, dated September 10, 1835, promised $39,771 in return for his completion of the prison by July 7, 1837 (General Treasurer's Records C 0490, Box 70:B, RISA). Lewis failed to report to the job site until late March 1836, thus losing five crucial months from a twenty-two-month project. The work of filling the lot then began, with more than eight thousand cubic yards of dredged material required to bring it to a grade two feet above the level of the Great Salt Cove. Three months into construction, an embarrassed Lewis appeared before the general assembly to request more funds for the project (*Reports of*

Committees 9, 75–76). He had, he submitted, made several erroneous calculations in fixing his estimate for the job, and these mistakes would make it impossible for him to finish the project according to Haviland's specifications (fig. 7).

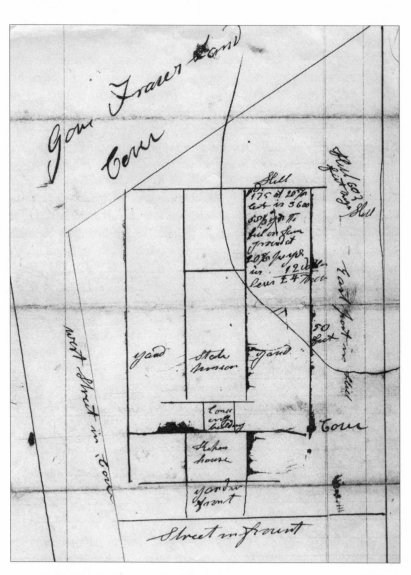

Fɪɢ. 7 — *Sketch presented by James Lewis showing the layout of the prison and the required quantities of additional fill that would be needed to complete the project. Courtesy of the Rhode Island State Archives.*

Surely the general assembly was nonplused by this turn of events. They had driven a hard bargain, sealed it in writing, and initiated the largest public works project in the history of the state. Now the contractor was claiming that his estimates were wrong, and the job was imperiled. After a vindictive debate, in which the representatives of agrarian towns saw their gloomiest predictions about the expense of the prison confirmed, they agreed that more money was probably necessary. However, the general assembly was not about to let Lewis continue without close supervision and surveillance. In addition to reconfirming the appointment of James Warner as state superintendent or clerk of the works, the general assembly appointed a two-person building committee to keep an eye on Lewis, his construction techniques, and his accounts. This committee was authorized to negotiate a settlement with Lewis on completion of the project.

There were at least four interested parties involved in the project now: the general assembly, the general assembly–appointed superintendent, the general assembly–appointed building committee, and James Lewis, who continued to founder. Lewis's inattention to proper preparation of the swampy, low-lying site shocked the building committee; members caught him laying the foundations for the keeper's house not in the clay substratum but rather in the newly deposited fill. Several weeks later they noticed that the partitions between the cell walls were already settling out of plumb, a phenomenon that would require excavating the partitions and reinstalling them. To make matters even worse, the subcontractor supplying Lewis with stone died unexpectedly. Lewis, seeing an avenue to make some of his money back, promptly opened his own quarry to supply the project, transporting load after load of inferior material to the site, where the building committee promptly rejected it as unsuitable (*Reports of Committees* 9, 75).

At this point one might ask why the building committee did not simply fire James Lewis and find another contractor to complete the job. The answer lay in the state's obsession with the financial bottom line, an obsession the committee acknowledged in its report on its problems with Lewis: "Considering the contract for building the Penitentiary as highly favorable to the State if properly executed—they did not feel authorized to proceed to extremities and drive the contractor from the work, nor expedient, to take any course that seemed calculated to produce the same effect" (*Reports of Committees* 9, 75).

Lewis's incompetence finally forced the committee to action. "The work provided a few weeks without any amendment, but rather, from bad to worse." In August 1836 they negotiated a partial rescinding of the contract;

during a respite they called in other contractors to assess Lewis's work. The referees' opinion was that the completed work was completely unsalvageable and that entire sections of walls, partitions, and internal structure would have to be torn up and rebuilt. Lewis was fired from the job, and the building committee completed the oversight of the project, adding an additional year to its total construction time. The final cost of the prison was $51,501.69, nearly $14,000 more than Lewis's original bid.

Nowhere in the literature concerning Jacksonian-era prisons is there a comparable case study reflecting such widespread bungling in the construction of a state penitentiary. Nowhere is there evidence of such a cumulative list of poor decision making. In every one of the key decisions about the prison—opting for the outmoded Pennsylvania plan, selecting a swamp as the site, obtaining a set of generic specifications, choosing the lowest bidder to build the prison—the state had discarded higher notions of reform, as well as any future needs for expansion, in favor of the immediate bottom line. From the initial concept of fifty cells in 1818 to the building committee's unwillingness to fire Lewis—who had, of course, provided a low bid with which the state could happily live—the record is one of sacrificing long-term satisfaction in favor of immediate savings.

We cannot simply explain this away by saying that the state wanted to save money, especially because the 1834 committee was well aware that the Pennsylvania-plan prison would cost nearly one-third more than the Auburn-plan prison. Looking at the events of 1836–38 more closely, a strong sense of legislative ambiguity concerning the whole prison issue becomes apparent. The hesitancy over the project is probably more attributable to a widespread sense of conservatism on the part of legislators from agrarian districts. It is important to remember that Rhode Island in the 1830s had no proportional representation in the general assembly (Moakley and Cornwell 2001, 67). An outlying agricultural town such as Portsmouth, with a population of twenty-five hundred, had as many votes in the assembly as Providence did. Thus, while there was recognition and awareness that incarceration was necessary, the state, torn by internal debate, proceeded with less zeal and considerably more caution than other states. Rather than expediting the project, the intricate system of checks and balances instituted in the oversight of James Lewis's work created tensions over power and authority that ultimately damaged the project. The extent of the damage—the origins of which can be traced back to the 1818 committee—became apparent quickly when the new prison opened.

The Movement to the Auburn Plan (1845–1850)

With the building project completed, Rhode Island's participation in the business of incarceration could finally begin. On November 16, 1838, the first three inmates were marched into their cells in the new prison. Prisoner No. 1 was Elisha Ball, a forty-eight-year-old murderer from Block Island whose death sentence had been commuted to confinement for life; Prisoner No. 2 was Franklin White, convicted of larceny and committed for one year; and Prisoner No. 3 was thirty-five-year-old Lewis Grant of Bristol, serving a two-year sentence for "breaking into a vessel" (Carlson 2002). The three new inmates were under the supervision of Dr. Thomas Cleaveland, the first keeper of the facility (*ARRIGA* October 1840, 51).

Although Cleaveland's initial burden of inmates was small, the state's nascent desire to centralize institutions quickly increased his responsibilities. Before the state prisoners had even moved in, the general assembly acted to abandon the decaying Providence County Jail and to construct a new county jail on the easterly side of the keeper's house (*ARRIGA* January 1839, 34). Little is known about this structure, or the two that succeeded it; a later rebuilding episode, including the construction of the enormous east wing, engulfed the footprint of the previous structures and left no archaeological signature. The specifications for the 1838–39 county jail describe it as a two-story affair having a footprint of sixty feet by twenty-seven feet, with a height of twenty feet (*ARRIGA* January 1839, 34). Thus almost as soon as the yard wall was finished, a portion of it was demolished to make room for a new jail. On the first story were eighteen cells for county jail inmates and those awaiting trial, while the second story held six additional cells and four "apartments" for debtors. It was attached to the back of the keeper's house, the east side of the connecting building, and the southeast corner of the cell block, with access through the basement of the connecting building (fig. 8).

In hindsight, many of the subsequent keepers and members of the board of inspectors admitted that combining the county jail with the state prison—an eminently sensible idea from a financial standpoint—ultimately undermined the reformative agendas of the prison. Unlike state prisoners, sentenced for a minimum of one year, those sentenced to the county jail were incarcerated for a maximum of thirty days. Under these conditions the separation of inmates by offense, age, and gender was nearly impossible. The sheer quantity of prisoners rendered efforts at solitary confinement impossible, as two to three individuals were confined to a single cell. Cleaveland complained bitterly about the impossibility of running a reform

FIG. 8 — State Prison at Gaspee Street, *by Williams S. Hoyt (c. 1845). The hipped-roof county jail addition is visible to the right of the keeper's house. Ink and wash on paper drawing. Courtesy of the Rhode Island Historical Society (RHi X3 1516).*

institution under these conditions and was vehement in his denunciation of sharing the state's only prison with a county lockup: "The lad of seventeen who enters the jail, trembling under the penalty of a one dollar fine . . . remains there until the horrid imprecations, and clanking chains of older villains become sweet music to his ears, and he is discharged a promising, swaggering candidate for the penitentiary or the gallows" (*ARRIGA* October 1840, 52). Judge William R. Staples, Rhode Island's most eminent jurist of the mid-nineteenth century, agreed with this assessment. "In the county jail no means are provided by the State, and no pains taken to reform criminals," he wrote (1853, 20); "[the county jail inmates] are left to brood over their fancied wrongs, and to plan deeper schemes of villainy." To make matters even worse, the portion of the yard wall demolished to make room for the county jail was never rebuilt. The absence of a wall on the county jail side led to further difficulties with the inmates: "The jail being situated in a retired spot, and its walls free of access to any one, the inmates are constantly supplied with *saws, knives, files, keys, lamps, matches,* and the like; and the man who to-day is thoroughly searched, and deprived of

A MONUMENT OF SHAME AND DISGRACE

every thing of the kind, to-morrow finds his cell converted into a well fur-nished machine-shop!" (*ARRIGA* October 1840, 52; emphasis in original). Potential corruption of youth was less a concern for some inspectors. "In the County Jail I found 48 men, women, & boys," one wrote in 1850, adding, "Among the boys are *One in his Seventh year, Two in their ninth year &two others about Twelve years old* = all at labor that can be employed profitably" (MS 231.1, Vol. 234, 98, RIHS; emphasis in original). Others had more visceral concerns about the institution: "Visited the County Jail," noted Inspector Edward S. Williams on August 3, 1847. "The cells have more smell than on previous visits" (MS 231.1, Vol. 234, 54, RIHS).

The expense of dismantling the wall to accommodate the new struc-ture may have forced authorities to reflect on the need to contemplate future expansion more closely. The contradictions inherent in the discipli-nary regimes of the prison and the county jail led to an 1839 assessment that the new infrastructure of both complexes was in serious trouble. The heating system was useless, and despite the best efforts to maintain com-plete silence in the cell block and county jail, inmates were finding ways to subvert those efforts (*Annual Report of the Board of Inspectors* [*ARBI*] October 1839, 26). Thus, Haviland's ideal prison, designed for efficient environmental control, silent self-reflection, and authoritarian regulation, had already outpaced the noble intentions of its creators.

Of perhaps greater significance than the structural and disciplinary problems was the deteriorating mental health of the prisoners in the cell block. In 1839 the inspectors reported a relatively calm atmosphere among those confined: "Their docility and contentment are remarkable, and they readily receive and seem to desire instruction on moral and religious sub-jects: it is hoped that measures can be adopted to encourage and gratify that desire to a greater extent than has been practicable" (*ARBI* October 1839, 27). Noting the severance of wrongdoers from evil influences, their "simple and healthful" prison diet, and the opportunity for the convicts to reflect on their crimes, the inspectors reached the conclusion that "there is good rea-son to anticipate successful results" with what they frankly termed the experiment "to diminish crime and reform criminals," adding that there was also hope that it could be carried off "without pecuniary loss to the state."

Two years later the inspectors and the warden were noting the first cases of insanity among the state prison population. This was by no means unexpected. Marked deterioration of mental health among prisoners at Auburn from 1815 to 1819 had provided the impetus for the development of the congregate plan. Adherents of the Pennsylvania plan had seen a sim-ilar increase in insanity in the Eastern and Western State Penitentiaries but had downplayed it considerably, attributing it to a host of unscientific causes: weak minds, hypochondria, "deviltry," and in some cases "erotic enervation" attributed to excessive masturbation. By 1842 six of the thirty-seven Rhode Island convicts were insane, with others showing "symptoms of derangement" (Anonymous 1877, 27). Cleaveland, who had signed on to be the keeper of a prison, not a lunatic asylum, was so concerned with the problem that he advocated an immediate change in the system of administration to the Auburn plan. The inspectors, having seen the extent of madness firsthand, were compelled to agree with his recommendation. At the January 1843 session of the general assembly, the legislature voted to allow silent, congregate labor within the corridor of the cell block and conceded that the inspectors should study the notion of constructing a communal workshop for the state and county jail inmates.

We should reflect for a moment on the enormity of this decision and ask why the Pennsylvania plan, embraced by the legislative committees of the 1820s and 1830s, was abandoned so quickly once it was actually put into practice. This was more than a simple administrative decision; it was a clear admission that years of legislative planning had failed to address the question of incarceration in a satisfactory manner. More important, the recommended shift to congregate labor would require a total reconception and reconstruction of the five-year-old built environment of the institution, the hiring and education of a new and better-trained staff, and the implementation of an entirely new plan of incarceration.

As with most of the issues surrounding the Rhode Island State Prison, social and economic reasons forced the decision to permit communal labor. The extent of insanity in the institution cannot be dismissed as a peripheral factor. Insanity threatened the entire experiment in incarceration and rendered efforts at reform through moral and educational instruction meaningless. More significantly, insanity compromised the institution's economic viability. The inmates' efforts at labor in solitary confinement had proven so woefully pathetic that the state was losing money on incarceration at a rapidly increasing pace.

Cleaveland, the keeper, discussed these rationales at length in his public justification for changing the plan. The *Annual Report* covering the year 1844 contains what is by far the lengthiest warden's report of any in the history of the prison. This seventy-five-hundred-word document, running a total of twenty-one printed pages, is a resounding denunciation of the Pennsylvania plan, an assessment of its failure in Rhode Island, and a justification for the reconstruction of the complex on the Auburn plan.

78

Cleaveland's contempt for the plan he had administered for six years is striking:

> But the system, thus founded in the most honorable and humane intentions, had the inherent and incurable defect of being in opposition to the laws of the physical nature of its subjects, which no human laws can change. . . . He [the prisoner] is in too many cases carried through "a slow, corroding process" to the derangement, or destruction, both of body and mind. This tendency of the solitary system, it is true, was predicted, upon natural principals, by some eminent opponents, whose benevolent sagacity forewarned, though ineffectually, the friends of Prison reform of the result which they might expect; but experience was necessary to exhibit it, and at an expense which it is painful to contemplate.
>
> (*ARRIGA* October 1844, 13)

To bolster his argument, Cleaveland provided case studies of individual prisoners who had suffered dementia under confinement. Prisoner No. 6, for example, who began to go insane after being confined for a year, "attempted to commit suicide, to avoid being flogged to death, which he was sure would soon be done, though at that time corporal punishment was not allowed in the Prison" (*ARRIGA* October 1844, 20). Prisoner No. 8 "became deranged about the tenth month of his confinement. . . . I have found him in the greatest state of terror and alarm, in consequence of his seeing someone at his window, with a long pike for the purpose of killing him" (*ARRIGA* October 1844, 21). Prisoner No. 40 displayed a similar paranoia; he informed Cleaveland that he had detected a plot

> formed in the Prison yard for taking his life; that he had also seen one of the conspirators at his window, with a gun for the purpose of shooting him, and that he had saved his life by lying on the floor immediately under the window, where the gun could not be brought to bear upon him; afterwards, that they resorted to suffocation, by burning sulphur at his ventilator; and that he barely saved his life by applying his face to the window, where he could breathe the external air.
>
> (*ARRIGA* October 1844, 22)

A MONUMENT OF SHAME AND DISGRACE

Nor was Cleaveland alone in his assessment of the inmates' deteriorating mental health. Thomas M. Burgess, a member of the board of inspectors, visited the prison on June 30, 1841. He found the aforementioned Prisoner No. 6 not working, as well as No. 8 and No. 22; the last "seemed calm but in the opinion of the Warden was not in a state to be trusted with edge tools" (Inspectors' Weekly Visits No. 1, 12). One year later the situation had worsened considerably. Burgess noted that Prisoner No. 6 was now clearly insane and "Nos. 9 and 23 appear to be 'wandering in mind somewhat'" (Inspectors' Weekly Visits No. 1, 19). Fellow inspector George Rice was more blunt in his assessment of November 23, 1842: "I have this day visited all the Prisoners and found four of them Crazy, Say No. 6, 17, 22, and 23 and No. 8, 32, and 35 Fair candidates to become So" (Inspectors' Weekly Visits No. 1, 21).

As far as the financial condition of the prison was concerned, the experiment in silent, solitary labor had proved disastrous. Under the Pennsylvania plan, the institution had lost an average of 25 percent of the potential value of inmate labor to sickness (that is, insanity), a percentage confirmed by a close reading of Cleaveland's account books. Within the period of transition when communal work took place in the corridor, this figure had dropped to a rate of 6 percent loss. Future efforts at communal labor, Cleaveland argued, would continue to improve this situation and reduce the need for appropriations from the general assembly.

Having settled the moral and financial necessities of changing the plan, the board of inspectors began to solicit plans for communal workshops for both the state prison and the county jail. If the institution were going to operate on the Auburn plan, then it was going to have the constituent revenue-generating elements attendant with that plan. Reform had provided the impetus, but financial considerations were the proof needed to transform the built environment of the Rhode Island State Prison.

Construction of New Workshops (1845–1850)

Following the investigations of the board of inspectors, a January 1845 resolution of the general assembly appointed them a committee for the "erection of a work shop with suitable store rooms" (*ARRIGA* January 1845, 65) attached to the northern end of the prison. The potential size of this workshop was severely constrained by the yard wall built in 1837–38. The workshop was to be a one-story, unpartitioned affair with a rough granite foundation; its walls would be solid stone, with light filtering through skylights in the roof. The sum appropriated by the general assembly for the workshop was a paltry $2,000, or $1.13 per square foot. In contrast, the prison had cost more than $15 per square foot. However, the state now had an advantage in letting out building contracts relating to the prison; the resolution following the approval of the workshop authorized the keeper of the county jail "to employ the prisoners in said jail in the erection of such portion of said building" (*ARRIGA* January 1845, 65), achieving some savings in the construction costs. One year later construction began on a second, smaller workshop for the now-unemployed inmates of the jail.

We know relatively little about the interior of the state prison workshop and nothing of the interior of the county jail structure. The only account of the workshop's interior spatiality derives from a journalist's account of an 1845 visit to view Thomas Wilson Dorr's adjustment to prison life. Dorr, the scion of a prominent East Side family, had led a popular rising against the requirement of property ownership for voting in the state. The armed insurrection failed, and Dorr, arrested and convicted of high treason, received a life sentence for his actions. The anonymous journalist reported his visit to the workshop, describing it as "a spacious, airy room, neatly finished, arched and lighted from the ceiling. . . . The room has the appearance of an artist's study" (*The Providence Press*, November 5, 1869, 2). The reporter paid particular attention to arrangements within the room: "The desks are arranged one behind another—and the prisoners sit with their backs to the visitor, and cannot know when they are seen. No loud talking is permitted the visitors—and no questions are permitted to be answered by the keeper" (*The Providence Press*, November 5, 1869, 2).

Members of the board of inspectors confirmed the stunning silence of the workshop. On October 1, 1860, Inspector Francis Wayland reported that he had spoken to only one prisoner during his visit to the prison, an inmate named Jerry O'Brien. "Jerry is the only person who has spoken to me or who seemed aware of the visit of an inspector," Wayland wrote, adding, "The rest as is proper being seated and not turning to look at a stranger did not see me. I consider my visiting so far as protection of the prisoners is concerned to be almost wholly useless. If they do not see the inspector and know that he can be addressed, of what use is his visiting?" (Inspectors' Weekly Visits No. 1, 145).

With the construction of the workshops came numerous additional personnel expenses. Overseers of labor instructed the prisoners in their daily tasks. Additional watchmen were required to supervise the labor process and to monitor the movement of prisoners from their cells to the workshops. Other nonprison personnel appeared more sporadically—a liveryman to deliver raw materials and take away finished goods, representatives of the wholesalers purchasing prison-manufactured commodities. Under the Auburn plan, the formerly forbidding Pennsylvania-plan prison became more permeable, leading to a host of new social and economic relationships within the prison matrix.

The documentary record makes it abundantly clear that with the construction of the workshops, the general assembly of the mid- to late 1840s felt that its role in creating the built environment of the prison had ended. Subsequent requisitions for improving the systems in the workshops and repairing and maintaining the facility met with a general legislative indifference. Here for the first time in the development of the prison complex came real contestation of power between the board of inspectors and the general assembly.

This contestation is most apparent in the increasing time lag between requests made by the board of inspectors in their annual reports and the approval of funds for physical improvements. The *Annual Report* presented to the general assembly in October 1848 provides information about prison-related needs. The inspectors were suffering from the embarrassment of the institution's worst escape. Twelve county jail inmates and Simon Hicks, a state prisoner awaiting execution, had managed to break from the county jail workshop, scramble over a pile of lumber left lying about in the prison yard, and climb over the yard wall to freedom. Simon Hicks was never recaptured. Without citing specific dollar amounts, the inspectors requested funding for a series of improvements pertaining to the security of the complex, including the employment of a night watchman, the construction of a partition wall to segregate yard space, the construction of a lumber and fuel shed to alleviate the problem of lumber in the yard, and the construction of an ironclad emergency door from the county jail workshop into the yard. With the exception of the provision of a night watchman, which was an investment in personnel rather than infrastructure, the assembly funded none of these improvements. One year later the October 1849 *Annual Report* repeated the unfulfilled requests, along with an additional item for repairs to the keeper's house and fence. This request carried a somber warning about the problem in delaying structural repairs: "A small sum will now make good," the inspectors wrote, "what, if neglected, will need very extensive repairs" (*ARRIGA* October 1849, 78). Again the request was rejected and the matter dropped from further debate.

By 1850 the rhetoric of moral reformation and civic virtue had disappeared from the board of inspectors' arguments. Having discerned that the only argument for construction countenanced by the general assembly was

A MONUMENT OF SHAME AND DISGRACE

potential fiscal self-sufficiency, they altered their strategy to argue for new workshop space. Their belief was that the revenues generated by putting more inmates to work could support the smaller projects they envisioned: "The small size of the [county jail] workshop allows but about *one third* of those imprisoned to be employed. . . . We feel that we are warranted in making the assertion, that if our work-shop was extensive enough to give employment to all the prisoners, the close of another year would find a balance in the treasury, after paying the expenses" (*ARRIGA* October 1850, 93; emphasis in original). Later in the same document they repeated this assertion more boldly, raising fears about the ultimate cost of imprisonment to the state: "The State Prison and County Jail are now a heavy tax on the honest industry of our State. The interest of nearly *one hundred thousand dollars* is required each year to carry on their operations. It will always be so, until there is an alteration and enlargement of the present work-shop and cells" (*ARRIGA* October 1850, 93; emphasis in original). The financial argument proved successful, with a second, larger county jail workshop authorized at the same session. For the first time in the history of the institution there was space sufficient for everyone to work—a circumstance that evidently pleased both state auditors and those advocating hard labor as a corrective strategy.

The temporary rapprochement between the inspectors and the assembly led to further goodwill and support for the prison. In June 1851 the assembly approved a total of sixteen thousand dollars for construction of a new cell block on the west wing. This marked the initiation of a five-year building program designed to transform the Rhode Island State Prison into the "smooth-running industrial plant" (McKelvey 1977, 21) that was the hallmark of the ideal Auburn-plan complex. It also marked the beginning of the final legislative effort to create a successful, self-sustaining institution from the complex at Great Point.

The Final Building Program (1851–1855)

The task of designing the new west wing fell to the Rhode Island–born architect Thomas A. Tefft (1826–59). Providence's first college-educated architect, Tefft had completed the design for the Union Depot (the Providence railroad station) while a freshman at Brown University (fig. 9). A devotee of the *Rundbogenstil*, or Romanesque-influenced "round-arch school" popular in Europe, Tefft was a prolific builder of schools, railroad stations, and private houses (Little 1972; Wriston 1940). His plans for the total rebuilding of the prison, on file at Brown University's John Hay Library, reaffirm the state's new commitment to the Auburn plan (Jordy and Monk-house 1982, 169).

In executing these designs, Tefft was careful to observe the structural deficiencies of Haviland's building. Chief among these was the incorpora-

FIG. 9 — Portrait of Thomas Alexander Tefft, *by an unknown photographer (c. 1859). Tefft's numerous commissions included Providence's Union Depot, designed when he was a freshman at Brown University, and the rebuilding program at the Rhode Island State Prison. Courtesy of the Rhode Island Historical Society (Daguerreotype Collection #225).*

84

tion of the outside wall of the cell block as an interior wall of the individual cells. Consequently, as one writer reflected later, "The frost can be scraped from the inside wall of the cell upon any day when the temperature is low, and it is difficult to understand how the inmate, who has succeeded in avoiding suffocation for want of air, can escape being frozen by excess of cold" (Anonymous 1877, 24). The movement of cells to the interior of the building was therefore a marked improvement in managing the internal environment. Tefft also incorporated heating ducts spaced at regular intervals along the outside of the west wing's rear elevation. These ducts conducted hot air from the basement furnace systems, distributing it throughout the three-story interior of the wing. When completed, the new wing was the subject of high praise from the board of inspectors. It contained eighty-eight new cells, built at a cost of approximately two hundred dollars each, and was described as "well-lighted, easily warmed, well ventilated and as secure as any building of this kind that can be constructed" (*ARRIGA* January 1853, 329).

To look at Tefft's sketches for the prison, placing them in a discursive relationship with the archaeological record, is to comprehend fully the slippage between intentions and outcomes in the built environment of the nineteenth-century institution. Among his more striking drawings is a watercolor rendering of the full Gaspee Street facade, in conjunction with

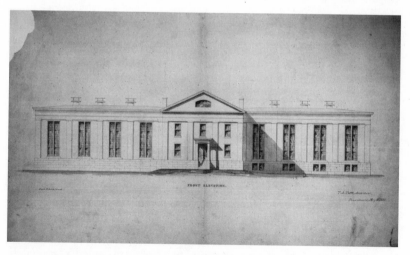

Fig. 10 — State Prison, Front Elevation, Providence, Rhode Island, *by Thomas A. Tefft. Enamored with continental forms, Tefft proposed replacing the outdated Greek-revival facade of the prison with one that evoked Tuscan ideals. Pen-and-ink wash on paper. Courtesy of the Rhode Island Historical Society (RHi X3 7592).*

A MONUMENT OF SHAME AND DISGRACE

a plan view of the keeper's house, connecting building, and cell block. Here Tefft proposes to unify the facade, balancing the west wing with an identical east wing to create a three-story, cruciform structure spanning nearly two hundred feet along Cove Promenade (fig. 10). Equally important, he offered a rebuilding of the cell block in accordance with his vision of the Auburn plan, reducing the size of the cells but moving them in from the exterior walls. Within two years Tefft won the opportunity to complete much of this proposal. The rising rate of convictions demanded still more space to house both state and county jail prisoners. By 1853 the original state prison population of three had grown to forty-nine, while the county jail held eighty-four inmates. The general assembly appropriated funds for a massive building project, including the demolition of the county jail, the construction of the east wing to match the west wing, and the erection of a new workshop and an engine house in the prison yard.

Tefft proposed an ornate Tuscan facade broken at regular intervals by three-story windows. But as Jordy and Monkhouse (1982) have noted, Tefft could hardly resist the opportunity to practice his one-upmanship on Haviland's keeper's house. He covered the wooden clapboard siding with a surface of stone and stucco, obscuring the classical Greek-revival lines of the original structure. A new lunette window appeared in the roof gable, and the entrances on the south and west sides were rendered more stately through the addition of decorative cast-iron *akroteria* masking Haviland's Doric surrounds.

In order to provide a more graceful articulation of the four structural components, Tefft also doubled the width of the connecting building from twenty-six feet to fifty-two feet, recycling portions of the original exterior wall for interior room partitions. The floor, formerly granite flagstones, was now covered with an elegant pattern of bricks laid in a herringbone pattern. In addition to providing much-needed balance to the entire structure, Tefft's reworking of the connecting building affirmed its importance as the nexus of the entire complex. Haviland's building had stressed linear unity, mandating a straightforward progression from the keeper's house to the cell block. Although Tefft's design in no way alludes to the Benthamite panopticon, it stresses the importance of centralization and internal unity in a much more complex structure.

Construction of a massive two-story workshop at the northern end of the site measuring fifty by one hundred feet finally provided a large, well-ventilated space appropriate for a variety of tasks, including cabinetmaking and shoe finishing. Limited views of this structure, combined with archaeological evidence, suggest that it resembled any industrial facility of

A MONUMENT OF SHAME AND DISGRACE

the era (fig. 11). Tall windows along its longer axes provided light into the interior spaces. The industrial order had finally arrived on the Rhode Island prison landscape.

Reinforcing this image of industry was the engine house, the final structure erected on the prison complex. Located in the yard between the east wing and the new workshop, this was a brick-floored furnace building with a chimney on its easterly side. It housed a new system for heating the entire complex; it was also the site of the machine shop, a short-lived experiment in creating semiskilled labor. No elevations of the structure have survived in the documentary record, so its organization and appearance are speculative; however, the chimney was enormous, rising to a height of nearly one hundred feet above the complex and overshadowing that of the Roger Williams Foundry to the east.

Noticeably absent from the rebuilding project was Tefft's proposal to redo Haviland's cell block. The inspectors believed that this was crucial to finishing the reconstruction of the prison, especially because its internal systems were in total disarray. The antiquated cell block—which, on the completion of the rebuilding project, acquired the official term "The Old Wing"—would become the most pressing issue of the 1860s and 1870s, and have an important impact on the abandonment of the complex.

Deterioration, Decay, and Abandonment (1860–1878)

With 176 new cells, the ten-thousand-square-foot new workshop, and a state-of-the-art physical plant, the Rhode Island State Prison should have endured for several more generations. Instead it was effectively obsolete from the moment the building project was finished. Two decades after Tefft had seen his plan realized, the state abandoned it and began planning a new complex of centralized institutions outside metropolitan Providence. We have to ask—as did members of the general assembly at the time—why a twenty-year-old complex that had now cost close to $130,000 (from initial projections of $35,000) was close to obsolescence.

Probably the most important factor underlying these pleas was the decay of Haviland's original cell block. Although it now was reserved for county jail inmates and those held over for trial, the number of convicts falling into this category was staggering, a circumstance that forced authorities to put two and three prisoners in each nine-by-nine-foot cell. Yearly pleas by the warden and the board of inspectors revolved around the insufficiency of the old wing:

While such a building as the old wing of the prison remains, the Inspectors, the Warden and the inferior officers can do but little towards alleviating the discomforts. . . . the General Assembly should initiate some measure of cure for the cure of these crying evils. Procrastination is dangerous. Neglect and indifference are fatal.

(*ARBI* 1867, 14–15)

The Inspectors would again call the attention of the General Assembly to the character of the structure known as the Old Jail. They reiterate their opinion, that it is discreditable to a humane and civilized community and State.

(*ARBI* 1870, 10–11)

The old jail never seemed so unfit for the confinement of human beings as now, and it is hoped that the State and city authorities will give a prompt and serious consideration to the question of building a new penitentiary.

(*ARBI* 1873, 7)

Legislators were not entirely unsympathetic to these pleas. In some ways the inspectors, mindful of the drain on the general treasury, damaged their own credibility by providing wildly unrealistic figures for the reconstruction of the cell block. In January 1863 they noted that most of the estimates received for the work over the years hovered near the twelve-thousand-dollar mark. With seed money of just five thousand dollars, however, the inspectors were convinced that they could complete the project, using revenues from prison industries to make up the balance. Although the assembly actually approved this request (*ARBI* January 1863, 227), the deficit in the institution's accounts rendered the reconstruction impossible.

In the power struggle between the board of inspectors and the general assembly, the inspectors' readiness to promise major renovations for ridiculously small sums damaged their cause (and consequently that of the inmates) considerably. Subsequent appropriations were minor—a rain-water cistern in 1866, a boiler in 1867, a new roof on the connecting building in

FIG. 11 (following page) — Archaeological plan of the new workshop and engine house (c. 1853–55) of the Rhode Island State Prison. Drawing by Dana Richardi. Courtesy of PAL, Pawtucket, Rhode Island.

A MONUMENT OF SHAME AND DISGRACE

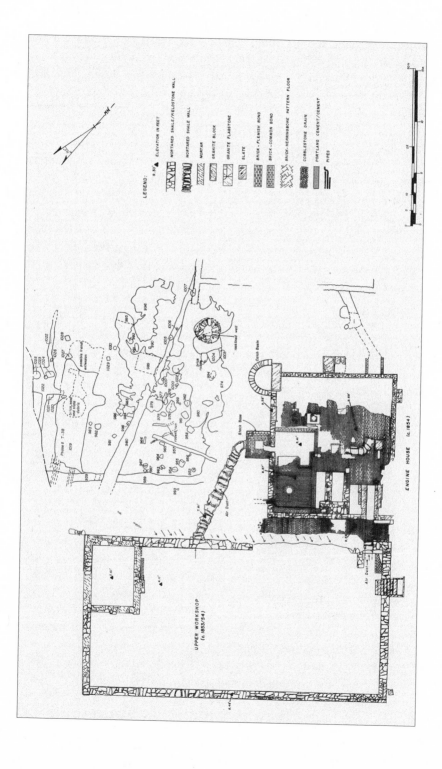

LEGEND:

9.30' ▲ ELEVATION IN FEET

MORTARED SHALE/FIELDSTONE WALL

MORTARED SHALE WALL

MORTAR

GRANITE BLOCK

GRANITE FLAGSTONE

SLATE

BRICK - FLEMISH BOND

BRICK - COMMON BOND

BRICK-HERRINGBONE PATTERN FLOOR

COBBLESTONE DRAIN

PORTLAND CEMENT/CEMENT

PIPES

UPPER WORKSHOP
(c. 1853/54)

ENGINE HOUSE (c. 1854)

1868. These minor appropriations could not stave off decay. In 1867 defiant inspectors wrote that they could not, in good conscience, "adopt any theory or any mode of action which would make the institution profitable at the expense of the equipment and condition of the prison, and the comfort of the prisoners" (*ARBI* 1867, 8). It did not matter that imprisonment was unpopular with taxpayers, the board argued. "The people of the State must not expect to be relieved of the necessary expense of supporting their penitentiaries exclusively by the labor of convicts. There must be expenditures for keeping the prison buildings, the cells, the clothing and bedding in proper condition" (*ARBI* 1867, 8).

Precisely when the inspectors and the assembly arrived at the mutual conclusion that the prison was no longer sufficient is difficult to determine through analysis of the documentary record. By 1869 the general assembly was finally prepared to act on the recommendation for a new prison. After purchasing a farm in Cranston, the legislature constituted the Board of State Charities and Corrections, directing them to start planning "a State workhouse, a house of correction, a State asylum for the insane, and a State almshouse" (*ARBI* 1877, 46). In 1874 the general assembly agreed to build the new prison on the Pontiac road in Cranston, on property already owned by the state. Plans by Stone, Carpenter and Willson, a noted firm of Providence builders, were approved almost immediately, with groundbreaking in the fall of 1874. For all intents and purposes, the Providence experiment was over.

Interpreting Spatiality: Three Themes to Consider

This overview of spatial development at the Rhode Island State Prison raises important themes addressing broader anthropological questions about institutional life. These themes revolve around the essential dichotomy concerning space: that is, the tension between the ways in which humans consciously and unconsciously shape space and the ways in which space, ungoverned and unmaintained, takes on a life of its own within the walls of the institution. In looking at the Rhode Island State Prison, the dichotomy becomes manifest in three distinct ways. The first, which develops over the entire history of the complex, is called here the "gridding" of everyday life, the investiture of every square foot of space with fixed meanings and purposes. However, as I argue below, to view this investiture simply as the increasing regimentation of space is to confuse cause with effect. It is also necessary to look at the ways in which humans moved through that space, and the intersubjective nature of space. How movement is sanctioned (or denied) is as critical as the space itself.

The second visible aspect of the dichotomy is the haphazard development of the institution's infrastructure. After the initial forty-year planning process (1798–1838), legislators and authorities were simply unable to conceive of more than a one-year plan for the prison, an inevitable outcome of reports issued on an annual basis.

The third and final aspect of the dichotomy—and arguably the most important—is the process by which real, empirical space (walls, boundaries, granite property boundaries) is transformed into symbolic representation, both in the landscape and architecture of the prison and in its depiction in two-dimensional mediums (photographs, plans, and sketches). A close look at this process is crucial to untangling the dialogue and dispute over the public and private spheres of the penal institution.

The Gridding of Everyday Life

The process of spatial development within the prison is characterized by the drawing of real and symbolic grid lines over daily routine within the complex. Yet it is not simply a matter of increasing regimentation, as Foucault (1979) would have us believe. Gridding encompasses an essential contradiction at work within the walls of the penitentiary. As the prison population increases and available space decreases, every nook and corner of the prison acquire increasingly specific purposes. For example, when space is not at a premium, the basement of the connecting building can serve a multitude of purposes. As the prison becomes increasingly complex, competing interests attempt to claim that space for particular activities. More important, movement into, across, or beyond a given space can shift meanings to become sanctioned, occasionally sanctioned, or completely unsanctioned depending on a person's position in the institutional hierarchy. In studying this movement we would be misguided to limit our scope to a strict hierarchy of keepers and inmates; to do so would be to ignore the wide range of inspectors, intermediary staff, and visitors both distinguished and ordinary. Imagine, for example, at the end of the day with the prison locked down for the night, a group of loyal underkeepers sprawled on chairs and couches in the keeper's office listening to the keeper's monotonous tales of his service in the Great Rebellion. Now imagine the keeper finding the same individuals in the same positions in the same space but without his personal permission. Thus space has a strong aspect of intersubjectivity, with multiple meanings for multiple individuals. What is sanctioned for some is unsanctioned for others; more important, what is sanctioned for some at specific times is unsanctioned for the same individuals at other times.

How those in charge of the prison's internal space named and defined the internal world of the institution is worth noting. Consider the evidence from the annual inventories compiled by the keepers. The purpose of these inventories was to list all state property on hand in the complex and assign it a value. The first series of compilations, bound in Warden Cleaveland's *Daybook & Journal* (102A, Box 48, RISA), covers the years 1839–45. A later series covers the years 1872–75 (102A, Box 48, RISA). Taken together, they constitute a useful way to trace the increasingly intricate spatiality within the prison.

The 1839–45 inventories are schematic. Categories used to divide space are at the level of large-scale components of the infrastructure: keeper's house, state prison, county jail. The exception is the shoe-making department, a concept encompassing both abstract space (labor) and discontiguous physical space, with equipment located in each prisoner's cell. In looking at this equipment, we can see an emphasis on individuality. Each prisoner has exactly the tools required to perform the task of shoe making: "12 Shoe Benches, 12 Shoe Stamps, 12 Pr. Pinchers, 12 Oil Stones" (Daybook and Journal 1839–45, 25). Books and stationery, stored in the keeper's house, consist of prison and county jail ledgers, the Rhode Island Criminal Code, and (perhaps an ominous foreshadowing) numerous blank ledgers and waste books for purposes yet undefined.

In contrast to these relatively straightforward inventories, which occupy one to three pages, the inventories of the early 1870s, spanning eight to ten pages, demonstrate the extremes to which space has been subdivided within the complex. Although the institution is at this point considerably larger than it was three decades ago, its darkest recesses are more formally gridded. A structure previously described holistically as "the Keeper's House" is now a series of smaller, composite parts, each invested with particular meaning and function.

Using an inventory from the middle of the later inventories (1873), it is possible to trace the physical progress of the warden and his clerk as they compiled the docket. They began upstairs in the keeper's house, where they went through the living quarters of the officers, matrons, and deputies recording beds, lamps, spittoons, and other furniture and utensils. The two then proceeded downstairs, where they listed the furniture in the board of inspectors' room, the dining room, and the kitchen. There is no evidence that the inventory takers went into the warden's private quarters, indicating that there was no state property within the warden's personal domestic sphere.

From the first floor of the keeper's house the two stepped into the connecting building and climbed the three flights of iron stairs to the third floor of the east wing, or county jail. They recorded medical equipment in both the male and female hospitals, and the adjacent sewing room. Heading back down the stairs, they stopped at the second floor (jail—female department) and the first floor (jail—male department) before returning to the connecting building basement—in many ways the nexus of the entire complex—and moving down the old wing, the house of correction. After returning to the basement a third time, they then turned down the west wing and recorded all the property in the state prison and hall. They spent the remainder of the day in the basements of the connecting building and the keeper's house, where they recorded items in the office, cook room, chapel, schoolroom, engine room, and the washing and bath rooms.

The volumes of "Books and Stationery" on hand in the prison also testify to the increasing classification of space. By 1873 this collection has expanded to include maps of Rhode Island, ledgers in duplicate and triplicate for the receipt and release of prisoners, copies of other states' criminal codes, punishment books, and other documents of control. The same increase in complexity is evident in the staff list of the Rhode Island State Prison. As with the built environment and its associated components (including the range of books, documents, and equipment in the warden's office), the staff list becomes increasingly hierarchical, with a greater number of specialists. When Thomas Cleaveland was hired as the first keeper in 1837, he was the sole officer in charge of the three state prison inmates. This situation changed almost immediately; with the addition of the county jail to the complex in 1839–40, the board of inspectors authorized appointment of an institutional underkeeper, whose primary responsibility was the supervision of the new facility. Adoption of the Auburn plan altered this easy paternalism irrevocably. By 1853 the bureaucratization of prison staff had increased significantly. Nine individuals now drew an annual payroll of $3,947: the warden, the deputy/clerk, the underkeeper in the prison, the assistant underkeeper in the prison, two watchmen, the jail overseer, an assistant, and a matron. Twenty-three years later, at the time of the facility's abandonment, the process was complete. The deputy/clerk position had been split into two separate jobs, and there were now four overseers, four watchmen, and the matron, for a total staff of twelve. Nor was there any absence of cronyism in these positions: Frank C. Viall, the

A MONUMENT OF SHAME AND DISGRACE

warden's brother, was an overseer, and Grace E. Viall, the warden's niece, served as the matron.

With the construction of the workshops and the abandonment of the Pennsylvania plan came the need to move inmates through the prison matrix. One of the abstract spatial areas where infractions occur frequently is in the "line"—the shuffling lockstep in which prisoners are taken into the yard, to the workshops, to chapel. Talking in line is not permitted; nor is making eye contact with another inmate; nor is walking too fast, walking too slowly, or stepping out of the line. The successful movement of the line through the complex (in the authorities' eyes) is dependent on the fusing of individuals into a single body, an entity that has as its sole purpose controlled movement through space.

Sound, too, was used as a means of dividing time (and therefore space). The prison bell—seen in other facilities as a drumroll, or today as a public address system—is a means of structuring the daily activities within the prison. But in addition to its functional role as the means of announcing the beginning and ending of tasks, the bell in the belfry over the connecting building serves as a tangible symbol of the power of the state and its ability to divide both time and space into a series of measured, compartmentalized periods.

An even more tangible symbol of the compartmentalization of space is the set of safes, or lockers, recovered during archaeological investigations. These are rectangular lockers measuring eight inches high by eight inches across and sixteen inches deep, having a door with a keyhole. Two examples—one intact and one badly damaged—were recovered from the basement of the connecting building. They are interpreted as lockers for personal possessions removed from individuals entering the prison; the extremely high degree of wear on the lock bolts indicates that the doors were opened and closed repeatedly, suggesting that the lockers contained the possessions of county jail inmates, rather than state prisoners.

It is not difficult to imagine a wall or bank of these lockers lining one side of the connecting building basement. The random artifacts of everyday life—watches, penknives, loose change—are collected, inventoried, and stored in a rectangular grid of identical, officially designated repositories. But here is the most interesting and self-subverting aspect of this regulation: a key fabricated to open the well-preserved locker also fit the badly damaged locker. Thus the capital investment in steel, floor space, and a program of confiscating and returning personal possessions is undercut by the fact that a single key could potentially open all of the lockers.

In addition to serving as a symbol of state regulation, this last example is a prime case study in institutional shortsightedness. The absence of vision is more than a failure to imagine future conditions. It is tied closely to two related spatial phenomena: the uncontrollable and haphazard growth of the institution, in which each decision about space leads to an exponential series of new decisions to make; and the attainment of a level of resignation on the part of frustrated authorities in charge of the prison's spatial matrix.

Haphazard Growth and Development

The building program of the early 1850s marked the watershed of the Rhode Island State Prison's growth and development in any systematic fashion. As we have seen, the power struggle between the board of inspectors and the general assembly resulted in the disbursement of small change for ad hoc repairs to the complex. A second result was the inspectors' increasing militancy for a new complex of state institutions in the suburbs of Providence. Central to this struggle were the pleas for rebuilding Haviland's cell block. It is possible that had the cell block been rebuilt on Tefft's plan, the institution might have survived another decade or two in its Providence location. The refusal of the assembly to countenance throwing more good money away on an inferior structure effectively sealed the decision to abandon the Providence site in favor of a more centralized institutional setting.

Thus we could draw a line between planning and no planning, and put that line at about 1860, after which the only long-term vision for the Rhode Island State Prison was the construction of an entirely new facility. Yet was the physical expansion of the late 1840s and early 1850s or even the initial construction of 1838 truly the result of careful planning? Edward Field, author of the first comprehensive history of the state of Rhode Island, wrote a scathing summary of the poor planning behind the institution: "But the general assembly and the commissioners were misled by the teachings of unpractical theorists of penology . . . and they built a structure of huge, rough blocks of granite, clamped together with iron rods, the only conceivable merit of which was that it seemed so 'impregnable from within' and which soon showed itself in every respect unfitted for its purpose, remaining thereafter for thirty-five years or more a monument of shame and disgrace to the state" (Field 1902, 461). In the most simplistic sense, developments at the prison had to be planned. Authorities knew that the state's population was increasing, crime was rising, and new pressures were incumbent on the institution's cell blocks. They also recognized that institutional viability demanded the construction of larger and better-equipped workshops to keep all inmates at work. And they were surely aware that the eventual expansion of these facilities would tax even the most generous enclosure of yard space and that new land would be required to keep the prison functioning on its current site. But what evidence of long-term planning exists in the documentary and material records of the site? Did anyone—a keeper, a member of the board of inspectors, a legislator—compose a five- or ten-year plan for the prison stating explicitly the need for a total of 150 cells by 1855 and 250 by 1860? The answer to this question is that there is no evidence of long-term planning. The complex evolved only as part of the dialectical relationship between the authorities controlling the financial resources and the authorities responsible for spending those resources in the most efficient manner. Under such a system, with little or no inkling about what the state's financial picture would be in a decade, there could be no question of foresight but only knee-jerk responses to particularly pressing conditions.

The way in which authorities chose to textualize conditions of the prison—by publishing annual reports—was an important factor contributing to institutional stagnation. The reports, issued by the board of inspectors, constituted a performance before the general assembly. By the mid-1840s the format of these rituals was well established; subsequent deviations were rare. The documents always begin with the inspectors' report, a brief overview of conditions in the state prison and county jail. This overview follows a particular order: demographic data, financial condition, moral and physical health of the prison, specific pleas, and a listing of salaries. Next comes the keeper's report, which is always restricted to financial data and a few items of interest that occurred during the year. The reports of the physician and chaplain follow in close order, and the annual report closes with a tabulation of state prisoners, offenses, sentences, and current disposition (whether the prisoner was paroled or died during the previous year).

It is unlikely that many of the members of the general assembly took the time or trouble to read these reports thoroughly. There was no need to do so, for the reports were summarized and submitted to the legislature as a matter of course for their approval. The thirty- to forty-page annual reports were encapsulated in the *Acts and Resolves of the Rhode Island General Assembly* as two-page abstracts. Most significantly, many of the impassioned pleas, such as those cited earlier for reconstruction of the Haviland cell block, rarely made it to the synopses read into the record.

Thus a certain sense of accountability, provided in a ritualized annual report, developed in concert with the institution. To see how this phenomenon played out in the material world, imagine standing along Cove Promenade sometime in 1852, a brief period when the facade of the prison must have presented a truly bizarre architectural spectacle. Reading the building from left to right, one would have first seen Tefft's west wing, with its Tuscan-inspired details, stucco finish, and three-story windows evenly spaced along the front of the building. Adjoining this massive structure was Haviland's elegant Greek-revival keeper's house, its simple porticoes and ornamentation reflective of a different era. Finally, at the right of the complex James Buckland's quaint county jail would have become apparent, its hipped roof and small proportions dominated by both the west wing and the sloping barn roof of the keeper's house—a bizarre amalgam of architectural styles that collectively failed to present a unified ideology.

Institutional growth occurs haphazardly. In the basement of the keeper's house, eyes cast to the floor, we see an excellent example of this truism. The primary north-to-south-oriented hallway is paved with substantial, six-inch-thick granite flagstones. These flagstones once covered the entire basement. But the floors of the four storage rooms on the eastern side of the house present a mishmash of repairs and construction styles. In one room the flagstones have been torn up; in their place are three crude joists of local slate that would have supported a wooden floor. In the second room the flagstones survive in a relatively good state of maintenance. In the third the flagstones have been removed and relaid in a different alignment than those in the hall and the second room; and in the fourth, the flagstones are completely absent, replaced with a series of Portland cement floors that have buckled and been repaired again and again (fig. 12).

Or consider the steam pipe system for heating, located at the interface between the connecting building and the county jail. Because the documentary record contains myriad references to problems with the heating and ventilation systems, we cannot even be certain when these particular pipes were laid, or if they were part of the same episode of repair and renovation. But the pipes cross the stairway into the east wing at an elevation of eighty centimeters above floor grade, effectively blocking the space between the first and second risers of the granite stairs. Thus, to negotiate the stairway, one would have to gingerly step up and over the hot pipe, balance on the second riser, and unlock the door above. To do so carrying something heavy would have been next to impossible (fig. 13).

Cisterns designed for water storage form a third example of the growth of the complex. Throughout the late 1850s the board of inspectors had repeatedly requested new cisterns to improve the condition of the fresh water in the institution. Although the documentary record is not entirely clear on this matter, they seem to have been approved and funded in 1857. In building a cistern and water delivery system, logic dictates that the cistern is built at the highest elevation of the site. Rainwater trapped in the

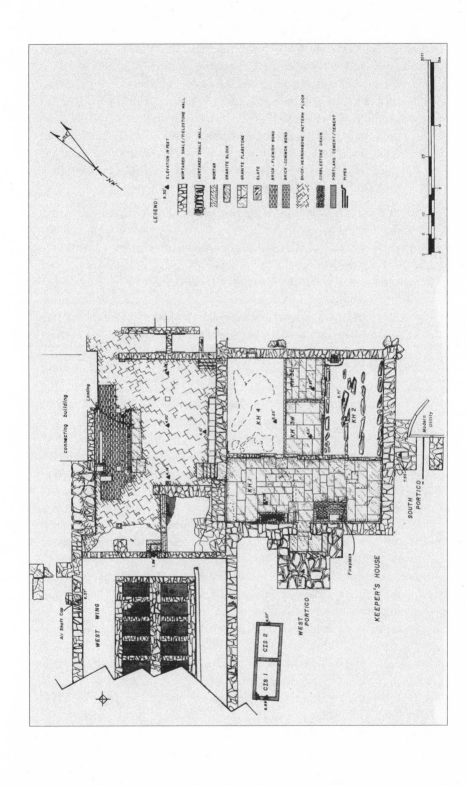

cistern can then be distributed through pipes simply by gravity. The prison cisterns, however, were constructed in front of the west wing—a convenient location, but at the *lowest* grade on the site. The inspectors then requested an additional appropriation for a steam-powered pump system to distribute the water through the complex. Not surprisingly, this request was rejected, probably with a certain degree of amusement on the part of the legislators. The cisterns quickly were converted to trash pits; analysis of the ceramic assemblage indicates that they were abandoned less than six years after they were finished.

To take a fourth and final example, Thomas Tefft designed a clever and intricate system of floor drains beneath the east wing. These drains carried human waste from individual privy pipes in the cells to a cistern in the yard. In dismantling the basement floor of the east wing and mapping the sub-floor drainage system, it quickly became apparent that the drain was laid at an even grade: elevations taken along its course were nearly identical

Fig. 12 (Opposite page) — *Archaeological plan of the keeper's house basement showing the variety of floor surfaces that evolved between 1838 and 1878. Drawing by Dana Richardi. Courtesy of PAL, Pawtucket, Rhode Island.*

Fig. 13 (Above) — *Steam pipes at the interface between the basement of the connecting building and the first floor of the east (county jail) wing. The pipes made negotiating this passageway a dangerous proposition. Photograph by the author.*

A MONUMENT OF SHAME AND DISGRACE

(fig. 14). With no pitch to the drain, waste must have quickly backed up and clogged the entire system, rendering it useless. Confirmation of this derives from the documentary record: the 1873 inventory lists the presence of "80 night-buckets" in the cells of the east wing. Yet the problem persisted; an inspector noted that on August 21, 1877, "Everything appeared in good Condition except the Sewers. In there are large deposits of night soil caused by the backing of water from the Cove" (MS 231.1, Vol. 234, 185, RIHS). As if that were not enough, the night buckets must have been of inferior quality; an archaeological deposit in the yard of the prison yielded a collection of more than thirty enamelware chamber pots, all deposited at about the time the institution closed.

All of these incongruities suggest that a public institution reached a point in its development at which it could no longer be managed with any degree of forethought and planning. Frustrated legislators had seen their generosity subverted by the prison authorities' failure to obtain results. After a certain amount of expenditures, promises to do better, and continued mismanagement, a politically charged institution became supremely unpopular with elected officials. Distancing oneself from the problem was the easiest way of expressing dismay with the state's expenses and gaining the approval of the disenchanted taxpayer.

What of the immediate authorities, the board of inspectors and the keepers? I suspect that they became aware, primarily through fiscal considerations and the indifference of the legislators, that the institution was no longer viable. Their resignation is clearly visible in the decay of the infrastructure. But as always, there is an alternate interpretation, especially for the keepers, who were removed (or chose to remove themselves) from the political process. Remember that the keepers were drawn from the ranks of retired military or police chiefs, and that they were required to pay many of the institution's expenses up front. Under such conditions, financial abuses and misappropriations of labor power were clearly possible. (In chapter 4 I will develop a case study involving Thomas Cleaveland, the most upstanding of keepers, to show that graft or, at minimum, the manipulation of the system was entirely possible.) These lifelong civil servants may have had good reason to avoid stirring up trouble, finding a real interest in maintaining conditions exactly as they were to avoid closer scrutiny. The inspectors, with an avowed absence of such interests—and possibly embarrassed by the physical conditions of the institution—were the ones, rather than the keepers, pressing for changes.

Thus far I have been most concerned with the changing infrastructure and the material world behind the walls of the prison. I now propose to

FIG. 14 — *View of the drainage system beneath the county jail wing, excavated during the archaeological data recovery of the Rhode Island State Prison in 1996. The drain was built with no pitch, causing it to fail quickly. Photograph by the author.*

broaden the focus, turning the discussion toward the larger urban landscape of downtown Providence in an effort to see the dialogue between the evolution of the prison complex and its engulfment by the forces of urbanism.

Public Space versus Private Space

Can we speak of public and private space in the context of the institution? In the sense that the public "owned" the Rhode Island State Prison and could view portions of it clearly from different points in Providence, I believe we can. The danger, of course, lies in ignoring the separate public/private dichotomy within the institution. In this discussion I assume that all portions of the complex visible from a "normal" perspective constitute the broad public sphere. Conversely, all portions *not* generally visible constitute the private sphere. But I will also look at private/public within the complex in order to draw some conclusions about the constitution of social space behind the formidable walls.

In order to address this theme we need to know what members of the public had access to what portions of the prison, and at what times. This is easily resolved through examination of the documentary record, especially maps. A strictly enforced hierarchy of visibility shrouded the gray stone buildings of the prison. Any citizen could view the prison from two primary vantage points: the Cove Promenade, the public park established along the shore of the now-constricted Great Salt Cove; and the open space behind the prison, along the slope of Smith Hill. Of that public, only prison staff members (guards, cooks, liverymen, and contractors' representatives) and state-sanctioned visitors could pass through the gates and into the interior of the prison. It is likely that even this could not be considered totally unfettered access because there were undoubtedly areas within the complex where the presence of outsiders was not sanctioned. Only the board of inspectors and members of the general assembly had knowledge of the full range of institutional space, with all its attendant mysteries and ambiguities.

First, consider the view from the public sphere. I have noted that the prison presented a strong privacy gradient aligned from its northern end, where the most intimate portions of the complex (the cells) lay, toward its southern end, the site of the gates and the keeper's house. The portions owned by the public were the views from the Cove Promenade and Smith Hill. Based on historical maps, I believe that the maximum view shed from the curvilinear sweep of the Cove Promenade encompassed no more than an angle of approximately 45 degrees. High walls and tree plantings tended

Fig. 15 — *The Rhode Island State Prison at full build-out, c. 1870. Note the articulation between the prison and the Cove Promenade, the city's most prominent public park. Silver gelatin photograph by an unknown photographer. Courtesy of the Rhode Island Historical Society (RHi X3 8017).*

to limit this angle of view (fig. 15). The view shed from Smith Hill, with the advantage of elevation, was more substantial and may have encompassed a full 180-degree panorama. Still, the fourteen-foot-high yard wall and the two-story communal workshop blocked the view of the prison yard and must have provided only fleeting and distant glimpses of the inmates moving through the prison matrix.

Architectural and landscaping modifications undertaken in the 1850s and 1860s further defined these views. Archaeological investigation in the front yard, south of the keeper's house, revealed that approximately fifteen to twenty centimeters of high-quality, loamy topsoil had been deposited there during that time. There is also a distinct absence of archaeological

FIG. 16 — *Merchant's bill head (c. 1865) depicting the view south from Smith Hill toward the rear of the prison complex. The newly built prison workshop is at the lower right, as is the stack of the engine house. Steel engraving by Charles Magnus and Co. Courtesy of the Rhode Island Historical Society (RHi X3 1198).*

features in the front yard. By the time the prison had reached its ultimate configuration, the front yard was planted with mature trees and landscaping, and the simple wooden pale fence specified by Haviland had been replaced with a delicate wrought-iron structure. Similarly the construction of the workshop and the engine house in the early 1850s had transformed the view from Smith Hill (fig. 16). From this perspective the prison was indistinguishable from the foundry and machine shop complex to its east. From the south, then, there was a picture of the state as severe but genteel agent of reform; from the north, a more gritty but equally idealistic view of the state as promoter of institutional industry. All surviving historical photographs of the prison were taken from the more subdued view shed of the Cove Promenade. This may be a matter of historical accident and survival; however, it is more likely that anyone who went to the trouble of photographing the prison in the mid-nineteenth century wanted a photograph of a prison, not a factory, and framed the view accordingly.

Looking beyond the Gaspee Street facade, past the Cove Promenade, and to the other side of Providence, we can surmise the extracurricular aspirations underlying Thomas Tefft's rebuilding project (fig. 17). A line drawn from the center of the prison to the opposite side of the cove intersects directly with the center of Tefft's Union Depot, completed in 1849. Considered among his finest works, Union Depot differed from the prison considerably in its remarkable facade of dropped-brick molding and high,

FIG. 17 — View of the Union Passenger Depot and West Side of the Cove *(1858–66)* *by John Gorham. The Rhode Island State Prison, located just past the right edge of the photograph, is screened from the photograph. If Tefft had been allowed to build his city hall in the center of the cove, his work would have dominated the city center. Albumen photograph. Courtesy of the Rhode Island Historical Society (RHi X3 2113).*

crenellated towers. Nonetheless, the siting and massing of these structures and their harmony with one another suggest Tefft's intention to create an evenly balanced weighting of public buildings dominating the two sides of the city's most prominent open space.

Further evidence of Tefft's ambitions for building the center of Providence lies in a third project that was never approved: that is, his project for a new city hall and statehouse on a humanly created island in the center of the cove, directly between Union Depot and the state prison (Bruhn 1988, 270). Submitted and approved in 1850, the plan featured a three-story stone palazzo crowned by a massive dome. Four bridges would connect points on the shore of the cove with the island, an aspect of the design that the local citizenry found particularly absurd. The project indicates Tefft's failure to consider the political climate of the state after the Dorr uprising. The *Providence Journal* was inundated with angry letters "defaming it as 'the State's castle with a moat around it, to be protected by portcullis' or 'a Court House

A MONUMENT OF SHAME AND DISGRACE

with a ditch around it, connected with the jail by a bridge'" (Bruhn 1988, 271). The project was shelved, depriving Tefft of the opportunity to make manifest a sweeping vision for the center of the city.

I do not mean to suggest that this intention was underhanded or devious. It is likely that the elites of Providence found the juxtaposition of the buildings desirable and evocative of what a city center should look like. But it is instructive to see how the process of architecture had changed in the twenty years since Haviland, never having seen the building site, dispatched his specifications to the 1834 building committee. Tefft was not simply responding to the needs of his client, the state; rather, he was actively promulgating his larger vision of a cityscape and the prison's important situation within that cityscape.

In terms of public representation of space, the exception to the overall subtlety of the complex is found in a line engraving on Warden Nelson Viall's official stationery (fig. 18). In this head-on view we see a truly Dickensian interpretation of the institution as factory. Smoke belches from the chimney on the engine house; a deeply cut arc of heavy horizontal striations runs across the sky portion of the image, connoting activity, industry, and other virtues. Large trees obscure most of the east and west wings; the woman and child in the foreground (engaged in an obvious moral lesson) can see only the keeper's house, the chimney, and the mass of the workshop looming behind the walls.

We should not simply dismiss this engraving as fanciful or inaccurate because of its artistic license or its inaccuracy in perspective. Warden Viall selected this image and used it as an unusually large (three-inch height) masthead for his official correspondence. To Viall, this image must have summed up his feelings about what the prison should be: a bustling hive of industrial workers, a genteel and symmetrically planted landscape, a source of moral imagery through which youth could be admonished to act in proper ways.

It may well be too much to ascribe deliberate control of the prison view sheds, whether in real, physical space or in the symbolic milieu of the warden's letterhead, to those in charge of the institution. But certainly there were efforts to control what could be seen and what could not. The privacy gradient that played out in the physical world, especially to those promenading along the shore of the cove, also played out in representational space. Examination of archival sources has failed to identify any photograph, painting, or other rendering of the prison's interior. The single exception is a series of line drawings, possibly made from photographs, published during the demolition of the complex in 1894. But this, of course, is at a time when

A MONUMENT OF SHAME AND DISGRACE

FIG. 18 — *Warden Nelson Viall's letterhead for the Rhode Island State Prison (1867). Here the prison is depicted as the bustling industrial plant that nonetheless conveys an important moral lesson to the boy at the lower left. Courtesy of the Rhode Island State Archives.*

the complex had not been a prison for nearly twenty years. The absence of interior detail holds true for mapping as well. Official plans generated by state authorities show only the black box of the structural walls of the institution. Tefft's 1852 plan for remodeling the entire complex is the only view showing the floor plan and internal room divisions of the keeper's house. Depiction of entrances and exits from the wings, including the Haviland cell block, are noticeably absent from this rendering. Thus in terms of space as represented in official documents available to the public—site plans, photographs, letterhead—the interior of the prison, including the yard space, remained a mystery.

What do we really know about this internal space? I have shown that within the buildings there was steady decay punctuated only periodically by episodes of ad hoc repair. In the state prison wing prisoners sat in their stark cells lit only by single gas jets outside the windows. During the cold winter months warm air rose sporadically from the heating vents; in the summer those fortunate enough to have cells near the ducts enjoyed the occasional updraft of cooler air from the basement. Conditions were far worse in Haviland's cell block, where prisoners held over for trial huddled two or three to a cell, trying to ward off the frost adhering to the walls of the cell. Not even the keeper's house offered comfort to its inhabitants, as he submitted to the general assembly in the *Annual Report* of 1867:

A MONUMENT OF SHAME AND DISGRACE

The centre of the house is a public thoroughfare, always, of necessity, open to the chilling air and inclement storms of winter, and the sweeping clouds of dust in the summer. I will not particularize further, except to say that the two rooms occupied by the whole number of male officers are as unpleasant and as badly constructed as they possibly could be; they contain no windows which can be looked out without mounting a chair, and then it would take a very tall man to accomplish the feat.

(*ARBI* 1867, 22)

The spatial contradiction here is amusing, to say the least; those ostensibly in charge of important, power-laden tasks—surveillance, monitoring, control—were forced to drag chairs to the windows of their quarters and stand on tiptoes to accomplish this task. Furthermore, the increasing complexity in staff led to crowding in the keeper's house. In 1860, for example, Samuel L. Blaisdell, the thirty-four-year-old warden, shared the downstairs rooms with his wife Harriet and their two small daughters, Jane and Grace. Mary Jane Frazier, a domestic servant, assisted the household. Upstairs were the prison staff: John B. Currier, the deputy warden (age twenty-six); the matron; four overseers; and two watchmen. The situation in 1875 was similar: Warden Nelson Viall, his wife, and their two daughters; the deputy warden; and a staff of nine prison officers and the matron all were listed as boarders. Thus thirteen to fourteen people sharing a living space of thirty-two hundred square feet—a situation little better than that of the institution's inmates.

So far we have been concerned with the buildings and walls. What about the space enclosed by the walls? As far as the prison yard is concerned, we know that it was a filthy, muddy area marked by large trash pits of noisome material. Archaeological exposure of subsoil revealed more than two hundred features in the east and west yards, including trash pits, filled wells and cisterns, and postholes. Elongated, difficult-to-define features running north to south through the yards in roughly parallel lines represent rivulets cut through the sandy matrix, areas where the natural hydrology of the overlying hillside scoured through the altered topography, leaving behind mushy, trash-filled depressions in the yards. It is not difficult to imagine these rivulets, fed by melting snow, wending through the yards, an accumulation of organic material, old newspapers, and random bits of trash settling in their wake and staining the subsoil black.

Other equally unpleasant features, primarily related to workshop activity, littered the yard areas. In the southeast corner of the complex, built into

A MONUMENT OF SHAME AND DISGRACE

FIG. 19 — View north of Context 810, a slate-lined trash pit filled with the bone by-products of button production. Note the crude drain in the center of the structure. Photograph by the author.

the yard wall, was a rectangular, slate-lined feature (Context 810) measuring approximately three meters (m) north to south by 1.5 meters east to west (fig. 19). More than ten thousand pieces of animal bone were recovered from this pit, which is interpreted as waste from the manufacture of bone buttons and other implements. The pit became so foul that it required construction of a slate-lined sluice to drain liquid waste from the bones. But those in charge of building the pit demonstrated at least some level of foresight by constructing the feature in the southeast corner of the prison; strongly prevailing winds from the southwest would carry the odor next door, where it would mingle with the acrid smoke from the foundry and, one hopes, dissipate in the air above Providence.

Surrounding the boiler house were piles of ash, slag, and vitrified residue shoveled out from the interior of the furnace. No effort was made to dispose of these materials off-site, perhaps in the misguided belief that they would somehow stabilize the muddy yard areas. It is more likely that they created a wildly uneven topography throughout the prison yard, one through which individuals would have to pick their way carefully to avoid sinking in the wet low spots.

None of this internal disarray was clearly visible to the public. Even the families of prisoners, who were allowed visits by the late 1840s, met with their confined relatives in the sanctity of the office, located in the keeper's house basement. Although they had gone as far as one could progress along the gradient, they were still unable to view the inner workings of the institution. We must ask, then, whether the authorities deliberately mystified the interior world of the prison by not permitting visitors, photographers, draftsmen, or sketch artists beyond the connecting building. By keeping the internal world unexplored and obfuscated, they created an environment shrouded in mystery, intimidation, and fear.

Recall that by the mid-nineteenth century in England the public hanging had lost its ability to cast fear into the common citizenry. Authorities responded by moving executions inside the walls of the prison and creating a standardized set of symbols to announce the completion of an execution: a fixed hour of the day for the death (eight o'clock in the morning), a bell tolling from the prison belfry, a black standard run up the prison flagpole. Angel and 'Liza-Lu, in the final scene of Thomas Hardy's *Tess of the d'Urbervilles* (1979 [1891]), experience this psychological impact firsthand: "Against these far stretches of country rose, in front of the other city edifices, a large red-brick building, with level gray roofs, rows of short barred windows bespeaking captivity, the whole contrasting greatly by its formalism with the quaint irregularities of the Gothic erections. . . . Upon the cornice of the tower a tall staff was fixed. Their eyes were riveted upon it. A few minutes after the hour had struck something moved slowly up the staff, and extended itself on the breeze. It was a black flag" (Hardy 1979 [1891], 329). We should not be surprised that incarceration, as the most severe punishment on the books in Rhode Island after 1852, underwent a similar mystification. Only those who had transgressed against the accepted laws of the state (and those responsible for their safekeeping) could experience the mysteries of prison life.

Thus the overriding contradiction in the spatial matrix of the prison lies in the contrast between appearance and reality: to the exterior world (taxpayers, potential criminals, authorities with no interest in actually seeing the prison), presentations of order, symmetry, industry, virtue, genteel discipline; to the interior world (inmates, staff, official visitors), obsolete systems, buildings requiring extensive and frequent repairs, a yard surface so muddy and filthy that it required boardwalks to negotiate.

The Intransigent Nature of Institutional Space

From the moment the product of state planning was unleashed on the world in material form, those confined within its empirical boundaries (including the wardens and their staffs) subverted that space through an endless range of planned and unplanned actions. Systems used for plumbing, lighting, and heating became conduits of forbidden communication between inmates. The warden's house was transformed from an elegant representation of its occupants' role as paterfamilias into a bustling administrative center for intake and discharge of prisoners. Cisterns designed for the storage and distribution of water supplies became convenient garbage dumps when the pumps designed to move the water into the prison complex became obsolete and failed.

These material examples evoke the essential contradictions concerning the social construction of space, and the relevance of Lefebvre's (1991, 26) truism that *"(Social) space is a (social) product."* Lefebvre is quite specific about the tendency of space to outrun its masters: "The social and political (state) forces which engendered this space now seek, but fail, to master it completely," he writes; "the very agency that has forced spatial reality towards a sort of uncontrollable autonomy now strives to run it into the ground, then shackle and enslave it" (Lefebvre 1991, 26). Within the cultural landscape of industrial capitalism—factories, mills, highways, areas of primary extraction, and retail establishments—space, which is both the means of production and in itself a material product, can only exist insofar as it seeks to re-create itself in more dynamic or profitable ways. Sharon Zukin (1991, 267–75) discusses the phenomenon at length in *Landscapes of Power*. Drawing on the work of Anthony Giddens (1984, 1990), David Harvey (1985), and Edward Soja (1989), Zukin notes, "Space makes material form for the differentiation of a market economy" (Zukin 1991, 268). Lefebvre (1991, 129) takes this notion a step further: "Space itself, at once a product of the capitalist mode of production and an economico-political instrument of the bourgeoisie, will now be seen to embody its own contradictions. . . . The contradictions of space . . . leave history behind and transport those old contradictions, in a worldwide simultaneity, onto a higher level; there some of them are blunted, others exacerbated, as this contradictory whole takes on a new meaning and comes to designate 'something else.'" Yet here we find the essential conundrum of institutional space, which is never intended to "take on a whole new meaning" (or meanings, for that matter); it is meant to be exactly what it is, an interlocking system of gates, walls, cell blocks, and bars designed for the fixed purpose of

A MONUMENT OF SHAME AND DISGRACE

removing deviants from society. When economic, cultural, and social processes undermine that system, the institution becomes obsolete. At the Rhode Island State Prison these processes were evident almost from the day Thomas Cleaveland and his first three inmates stepped through the doors of the keeper's house and began the experiment of imprisonment.

Within a social-reform institution much of human activity is directed at finding ways to subvert the boundaries of space. Inmates invest a great deal of time and attention to escape, the inmate's ultimate subversion of state power. In October 1872, for example, Elisha Peck and Charles Williams escaped from the old cell block. Both apparently had made a long-term commitment to finding a way out: "He [Williams] was continually making keys out of bits of wood and tin," noted the *Providence Journal* (January 20, 1879, 2); "As soon as one was taken away, he would make another, no matter how closely he was watched." After the escape Peck was recaptured in Utica, New York, but Williams disappeared permanently. Peck took part in at least two subsequent escape attempts from the Rhode Island State Prison. In the first he was able to pass a series of five notes to associates outside the prison. This attempt was quashed when one of the associates turned a coded note over to the authorities (319B:1, RISA). Attached to the note are the key and a translation, compiled by an unknown prison staff member. The translation reads:

Jack

I got the note all rite if I don't a new trial im goin to skip from here you work our plan you come for det [?] and bring tools I can see you in the yard and get them keep mum burn this up.

yours, spike

Peck's second attempt to subvert the conditions of confinement had met with failure.

Still, the extraordinary effort of finding a sheet of paper (which was a carefully regulated substance in the prison), developing the code, composing the note, and getting it to the accomplice underscores his zeal to escape the conditions of confinement. A third effort, made with Patrick F. Dennehy, was more desperate and less sophisticated: the two simply overpowered a guard in the chapel and ran for the wall, where they were captured. Thus escapes, illicit meetings between prisoners of different sexes, the stashing of contraband beneath cell floors, and even the forbidden decoration of cell walls are all examples of less forceful efforts to wrest some new and desir-

112

able meanings from the space of confinement. This active subversion was wrought not just by the "powerless" (inmates) but by everyone who operated inside the institutional matrix. Warden Cleaveland, for example, tired of the stark and unremitting gray aspect of his front yard, put inmates to work hauling loam, planting trees, and otherwise gentrifying the formerly austere and forbidding starkness of Haviland's design. The architect Thomas Tefft wrought a similar havoc on Haviland's infrastructure, providing the newly unified complex with the appearance of a humming factory, rather than a relatively small and discrete institution. Outside contractors tore out workshop walls, retrofitted the buildings with more productive systems, and otherwise altered the precarious balance between institutional solemnity and productivity in their drive to wrest more profits from the labor of inmates.

Such actions have an attenuating effect on space and force the contradictions underlying the landscape of confinement to the surface. When space no longer serves the function for which it was designed, it has a steady demoralizing effect on its owners. At the Rhode Island State Prison this was especially true of the wardens, who complained endlessly about the use of their house for administrative purposes. One is also struck by the regularity of complaints from the board of inspectors, the good-natured, prosperous burghers (often with no experience in reform other than occasional philanthropy) charged with maintaining order and rules at the prison. Lacking the financial resources to reconstruct space to serve the purpose of reform and rehabilitation, they simply gave up on the complex and began agitating, fourteen years into the prison's existence, for a new and superior facility. These results strongly support Soja's (1997) argument concerning the importance of "spatial trialectics" underlying the epistemological nature of space. For Soja (1997, 74), spatiality is composed of space as conceived, space as perceived, and space as lived. The basement of the connecting building—which, I have argued, must be seen as the heart of the Rhode Island State Prison—is a premier example of this trialectic. Conceived as a transitional zone between the keeper's house and the cell block, this area became perceived (after the additions of the east and west wings) as a central hallway, an area from which all three wings could be monitored. As actually *lived*, however, the connecting building basement became an area of cluttered debris, a place to pile unused junk, an experimental chapel, bathhouse, and schoolroom. None of the lofty symbolic goals of Haviland's original design seem to have survived long once the daily practice of confinement evolved from the theoretical matrix that had spurred construction of the prison in the first place.

In his discussion of Foucault's work, Soja finds a resonance between his own concept of "Thirdspace" and Foucault's "trialectic of power, knowledge, *and space*" (Soja 1997, 148; emphasis in original). Central to this idea is the Enlightenment-based concept of the *site*, a localized point on a larger grid of streets and streetscapes, cities and cityscapes, all networked together. Foucault's conception of the "heterotopia"—the place of "Othering," whether it be a cemetery, an institution, or a place of illicit sex—is the epitome of the "counter-site":

> There are also, probably in every culture, in every civilization, real places—places that do exist and that are formed in the very founding of the society—which are something like *counter-sites*, a kind of effectively enacted utopia in which the real sites, all the other real sites that can be found in the culture, are simultaneously represented, contested, and inverted. Places of this kind are outside of all places, even though it may be possible to indicate their location in reality.
>
> (1986, 24; cited in Soja 1997, 157)

Heterotopias in modern society are heterotopias of deviation—the focus, as Soja (1979, 159) notes, of all of Foucault's important work. They are malleable, presenting different spaces within one empirical space (within the prison, for example, the counterposing of the Haviland cell block with the more elaborate keeper's house). It is in the last aspects of Soja's analysis of heterotopias that we find the most germane aspects of the prison's spatial environment:

> *Fifth*: heterotopias always presuppose a system of opening and closing that simultaneously makes them both isolated and penetrable, different from what is usually conceived of as more public space. . . . Through such forms of spatial regulation, the heterotopia takes on the qualities of human territoriality, with its conscious and subconscious surveillance of presence and absence, entry and exit; its demarcation of behaviors and boundaries; its protective yet selectively enabling definition of what is the inside and the outside and who may partake of the inherent pleasures.

The concept of countersite is especially pertinent to the social reform institution of the nineteenth century. It has a real, physical sense portrayed on maps, deeds, and photographs, but it remains aloof from broader society, divorced from large sectors of the citizenry by its very nature as a place of punishment or reformation. Institutions are public buildings intended for only a small segment of the public. In choosing to examine the relationship between spatiality and everyday life, I have so far spent little time considering the most important component of everyday life in the prison: that is, the requirement of mandatory hard labor for all state and most county jail prisoners. In chapter 4, I turn to the issues of production and labor in the prison; the discussion begins at the large-scale level of institutional landscape and moves to the struggles over work that scarred that landscape for more than forty years.

CHAPTER 4

"The Privilege of Working"

The Labor Program at the Rhode Island State Prison

"The prisoners perform the labor assigned them with industry and alacrity," wrote the board of inspectors of the Rhode Island State Prison in 1839. "They are under good subordination, showing no disposition to be intractable; should such a spirit be exhibited, it is thought it would soon be quelled by suspending the offender from the privilege of working" (*ARRIGA* October 1839, 27). With this bold declaration, state authorities entered into a four-decade-long experiment in coaxing productive labor from a recalcitrant and generally unwilling inmate population. Unlike the debate over the planning and construction of the prison, in which Rhode Island diverged from the trajectory followed by neighboring states, the state's development and implementation of an inmate labor program were typical of those experienced in other regions of the United States. The first phase was one of initial experimentation, met with unbridled optimism and unrealistic expectations; the second phase was marked by economic and social uncertainty, with production shifting to a variety of formats in an often-desperate effort to accrue revenue and stave off financial ruin; and the third and final phase was one of utter institutional apathy, in which state-supervised labor programs were abandoned in favor of the leasing or sale of convict labor to outside contractors (Conley 1980, 1981,1982; Oshinsky 1996).

In considering this economic and historical trajectory, an interesting parallel is immediately evident between the evolution of the prison infrastructure and the evolution of its labor program. By the mid-1850s, less than two decades after the completion of the prison, all of the major construction and renovation episodes were over. No additional significant investment was made in the buildings or grounds, and the institution was left to decay until construction of a new facility could begin in earnest. The labor program underwent a similar process of decay: idealistic efforts to train prisoners in a variety of tasks eventually led to the abandonment of a state-run program and the sale of inmate labor to outside contractors. These trajectories are no mere coincidence; an important relationship existed between the level of economic investment in the infrastructure and the level of economic investment in the labor program. The two aspects of institutional life were interdependent, and one cannot look at one without considering the implications for the other.

This chapter is especially concerned with three labor-related themes: first, the goals of the labor program, encompassing the range of ambitions and intentions informing work; second, the specific forms of production, including the different strategies used by both state authorities and outside contractors to generate revenue; and third (reverberating through both of the previous themes), the hierarchical relationships between those engaged in production, including inmates, labor superintendents, prison officials, and outside contractors.

The goals of the labor program require thoughtful consideration. In private-sector capitalism the intent is to produce goods that will sell at a price greater than the cost of labor, materials, and transportation—in other words, profit. In the case of the penitentiary, labor is free; in New York and some southern states this led to numerous contemporary complaints by unions over the unfair practice of state-supported production. Thus from the moment the state of Rhode Island announced its intent to produce, it had a distinct edge over the private sector. But this advantage was balanced by the disadvantage of having an untrained, unwilling, and often antagonistic workforce. Those in charge of the labor program were well aware of the shortcomings of their workers and strove to meet their ambitions by matching production with the purported skill level of the workforce. The underlying agenda of other institutional goals—reform, rehabilitation, and vocational training—also reduced the advantage of captive labor.

The range of competing agendas underlying daily work in the nineteenth-century institution is intriguing. Did state authorities genuinely expect that inmate labor could generate a profit for the state? Or did they merely hope that the institution could become self-sufficient, which is a far less ambitious goal than profitability? And what were the other goals beyond revenue generation? There was, for example, an ostensible vocational aspect of labor in which the inmate was "taught a trade" that he or she could carry on after release. The instillation of daily routine, and the development of work as an alternative to crime, also constituted an aspect of labor ideology in the nineteenth-century penitentiary.

Understanding the principles guiding the labor program and the extent to which the program met the goals of its instigators leads directly to the second question: what was the range of production and commodities manufactured in the prison workshops? Interpreting production encompasses more than a simple enumeration of what was made and when. To trace the decisions made by the board of inspectors and the keepers concerning production and labor, we need to look closely at what was made, where it was produced in the prison complex, and most important, what markets (if any) those commodities found. The relationship between prison goods and local, regional, and national trends in consumption was of primary importance in determining the course of the labor program at the Rhode Island State Prison.

Underlying both the purpose of the labor program and its practical development is the question of the relationship between the parties engaged in institutional production and their varying abilities to wrest control of portions of the labor process. It would be simplistic—and ultimately misguided—to cast both "prisoners" and "authorities" as monolithic entities locked in perpetual opposition to one another over the requirement of work. The shifting range of competing interests among the groups involved in production is significant. Inmates, the primary producers in the dark and poorly ventilated workshops, had different agendas at different times. They may have worked to avoid punishment or because labor, no matter how repetitive, was an alternative preferable to sitting in a cell twenty-four hours a day. In times of intra-institutional tension, some may have worked at slow or indifferent paces to express their resentment with the conditions of their confinement. Yet during these same times, others may have actually worked harder than normal to distance themselves from the troublemakers among their number. Thus there can be no single and uniform means of interpreting inmate labor. Production is dependent on numerous variables: attitude of the individual worker, the degree of difficulty of a particular task, and the threats or incentives embedded in the completion of the task.

Now consider the other stakeholders in the process of production: labor overseers, hired to supervise consistent production of commodities; prison authorities, encompassing an increasingly complex staff of specialists over time; contractors, whose livelihood and potential profit depended on the labor of prisoners; and of course the board of inspectors, often critiqued and rarely praised, whose reputations as upstanding community leaders depended on the success of the labor program. In examining these groups it becomes apparent quickly that the range of competing interests must necessarily lead to points of conflict, especially in the context of a penal institution. (In chapter 5, I will look closely at those flashpoints, laying out the possibilities of conflict and their emergence in everyday life.)

The Goals of the Labor Program

What were the goals, explicit and implicit, of the labor program at the Rhode Island State Prison? What historical, social, and economic factors motivated prison authorities to institute mandatory labor? And how did those motivations change over time? I will be careful here about ascribing intentionality to individuals and groups, which is problematic when experiencing human activity through surviving documents and artifacts (cf. Barrett 1987). Nevertheless, the material record, encompassing documents and archaeological remains, is far from subtle on the subject of prison labor. The discussion begins at the level of contemporary nineteenth-century discourse—that of the instillation of routine, vocational training, and institutional self-sufficiency as catalysts of moral reform—and moves toward the more cynical but nonetheless critical notion of profit generation in the penal institution.

Jacksonian Perspectives on Prison Labor

Jacksonian reformers saw labor as essential to the corrective regime. Although the reasons given for daily work varied widely from pragmatic to idealistic, no reformer, no matter how liberal, ever suggested that inmates should not work during confinement. Idealists looked not to the products of prison labor but rather, as Petchesky (1993, 596; emphasis in original) has noted, to the *"doing of work,"* or the instillation of daily routine as a technique for reordering dysfunctional lives. Others saw institutional labor as vocational: teach a criminal a trade, and there would be no need for him or her to return to a previous life of crime. On the pragmatic end of the spectrum was a range of different rationales. In Rhode Island conservative representatives of agrarian districts argued that in a world where corporal punishment was becoming less important, imprisonment should be as retributive as possible (Greene 1963, 20). Those less zealous in their desire to punish but still concerned with institutional costs thought that the labor of prisoners would at least pay for the costs of imprisonment and avoid a drain on the taxpayer-supported general fund.

The debate over the Pennsylvania and Auburn plans of correction was one over labor practice, rather than punishment: should institutional labor be solitary or congregate? Although the debate spilled over into the rhetoric of architecture and moral reform, the empirical issue that separated the two plans was the method of production. In light of the spread of industrialization throughout New England in the 1830s and 1840s, the Auburn plan was arguably more prescient in its recognition of the factory as the organizing force in American life. To advocates of the Auburn plan, the Pennsylvania plan must have seemed much like the antiquated "putting-out" system prevalent in rural districts, in which individuals would produce shoes, palm-leaf hats, and other goods from small shops attached to their houses (Prude 1985). Auburn, in contrast, embodied the concept of the prison as the ideal modern factory: workshops with benches arrayed systematically across the floor space; a silent, docile workforce; and supervision of that workforce through guards stationed at strategic points across the building.

Foucault (1979) considered the development of the Auburn plan an important component of the overall effort to discipline criminals and produce citizen-workers who could be reinjected into the "urban proletariat." I shall return to his thoughts on industrial-capitalist discipline later. But first I will explore the three primary rationales provided by the Jacksonians to support the ideology of institutional labor: the instillation of routine and the development of steady habits, the instruction of inmates in a useable trade, and the need to make reform institutions self-sufficient and less dependent on the morally sound taxpayer.

Instillation of Routine

Routine is a concept central to institutional life. The day is divided and subdivided into countless tasks marked, in the case of the Rhode Island State Prison, by the steady tolling of the bell housed over the connecting building. From the *Rules and Regulations* of 1844 we get a sense of the primacy of daily organization by the positioning of the ritual of everyday life as the prison's first rule:

> 1st. The convicts shall be awakened at sunrise, throughout the year, and such as are able shall commence labor within fifteen

minutes after that time, and shall continue labor, except during the time allowed for meals and reading, which shall be one hour and a half, until half an hour before sunset, between March 20th and September 20th; and until 8 P.M. between September 20th and March 20th. All lights shall be removed from the cells by 9 P.M., and no light shall be allowed in the cells except during that part of the year when labor is performed after sunset, or in case of sickness.

(*ARBI* 1844, 6)

Note the fusion of the natural day, marked by sunrise and sunset, with the ritualized day, marked by specific hours of the clock and artificial lighting. The rule identifies four state-approved activities in the prison: sleeping, working, eating, and reading. Implicit, but not included, in this list is religious worship, a mandatory component of Sunday mornings. As the most active of the five sanctioned activities—and the one at which inmates spent the majority of their institutional lives—constant work necessarily became the focus of inmates' daily routine. Inmates worked ten-hour days, which were unofficially extended during periods of peak production. The work was monotonous, providing little opportunity for innovation or creativity.

One of the most compelling arguments for the interpretation of work as instilling routine is the attempt by prison authorities to regulate work through daily quotas. The *Convict Labor Ledger* (319B:1, RISA) compiled during the shoe-making period, for example, indicates that the keeper Thomas Cleaveland expected each inmate to make one pair of shoes per day. Thus at daybreak, on waking from sleep, the inmate knew that he must produce a pair of shoes by the end of the day. To the warden, this steady and unwavering pace must have become like the rising and falling of the tides, an imposed rhythm of predictability soothing previously chaotic lives.

The development of routine surely had a remarkable psychological effect on inmates. The state prison had an extremely low rate of recidivism of approximately 4 percent over its forty-year history (*ARBI* 1876, 40). In the county jail the rate was much higher; although an exact determination is not possible due to the scarcity of primary documents, its rate of recidivism was closer to 20 percent. A variety of factors contributed to this discrepancy, especially the petty nature of offenses for which individuals were remanded to the county jail. Nonetheless, it is likely that the strict policies of isolation and steady work—rarely in effect in the county jail—combined to make the state prison so unpleasant that few wished to experience its healing forces a second time.

Vocational Training

Vocational training was a second purported rationale for prison labor in the nineteenth-century penitentiary. Just as the moral discourse of religious attendance, state-approved reading material, and education was expected to improve the character of the hardened criminal, so too would the teaching of a trade render him or her metaphysically unable to fall back on deviant ways after release. A frank appraisal of the "trades" taught to inmates belies the notion of vocational training. Labor in the first ten years of the prison's operation (1838–48) consisted of oakum production, manufacture of crude furniture, shoe making, and the painting of decorative fans. None of these activities could have prepared an inmate for a successful career in the outside world. Oakum production, for example, consisted of the tedious peeling of strands from piles of worn-out rope. The strands could then be packaged in bundles for use in caulking ships. The retrofitting of ships' hulls with copper sheathing, which was well in place by the 1830s, suggests that there would have been little industrial demand for oakum pickers by the 1840s.

Shoe production was undergoing a similar transformation. By the 1840s the manufacture of shoes was already mechanized throughout much of New England (Siracusa 1979, 117). Although a role still existed for the small-town local cobbler, hundreds of thousands of pairs of shoes were churned out by the factories of Beverly, Lynn, and Newburyport, Massachusetts. "Vocational training" in the assembly of individual shoes from raw materials would have had little to offer a newly released inmate in a world bent on industrialization. The experiment in decorative-fan production terminated abruptly when the market for such items crashed in 1847. Inmates trained in fan production would have reentered society with a trade for which there was absolutely no demand.

Of all the production activities practiced in the prison prior to the advent of contract labor, the manufacture of stained and grained furniture was probably the most helpful to inmates desiring to learn a trade. Most of the furniture was crude—trestle tables, for example, or simple bookshelves. But all of the furniture production took place in the county jail, where sentences rarely exceeded sixty days. It seems likely that the state was taking advantage of those who were semiskilled, rather than those who required complete education in vocational arts. Thus only capable, male county jail inmates, of all the inmates in the prison matrix, may have had a nominal chance to learn or improve their carpentry skills. In contrast, a state prisoner facing a sentence of five years, for example, had little to do but prepare

123

a single set of shoes during each ten-hour workday for the duration of his sentence. The production of 1,560 pairs of handmade brogans (which is what an inmate serving a five-year sentence would make over the course of his career) hardly seems to have been an inducement to taking on a career as a cobbler at the completion of a sentence. That the inspectors considered carpentry at least potentially vocational is evidenced by a plan, never fully realized, to move furniture production from the county jail to the state prison. "And the convicts could perfect themselves in a trade, that might be the means of gaining an honest living when liberated" (*ARBI* 1850, 3).

If the keepers and the inspectors truly wanted to provide vocational training for the inmates of the Rhode Island State Prison, they would have constructed a textile mill or iron foundry (the staples of the Providence industrial economy) on the penal complex. With skills in weaving cloth or casting metal machine parts, an inmate would have stood a reasonable chance of finding employment on release. The rhetoric of vocational training was just that: rhetoric, promulgated by prison authorities, perhaps to stave off potential complaints from nascent unions about the advantages inherent in state-subsidized labor. The absence of recorded complaints from Rhode Island unions over unfair competition from state industries suggests that unlike the situation in New York, organized labor in Rhode Island felt no threat from the captive labor force at the state prison and county jail. Undoubtedly the completely unskilled nature of the work done at the prison and its lack of application to the outside world had much to do with the silence of the unions on the subject of inmate labor.

Institutional Self-Sufficiency

From the outset of Rhode Island's experimentation with imprisonment, two related concepts dominated the intellectual discourse over institutional labor: profit, with revenues directed into state coffers; and self-sufficiency, with revenues paying for the cost of buildings and improvements to the penal complex. Although both of these concepts require larger revenues than expenditures, self-sufficiency is not at all the same thing as turning a profit. For the moment, I shall examine the issue of institutional sustainability, reserving the question of profit for later in this chapter.

The legislative obsession with the potential costs of a state prison underlying the debate over its construction has already been noted. The 1818 committee to consider the question of building a state prison was especially concerned with possible revenues from the sale of prison goods. This committee took written testimony from Gamaliel Bradford, the warden of the Massachusetts State Prison (MSP), and Sabin Delano, the superintendent of the Vermont State Prison. Bradford was particularly thorough in his evaluation of labor at the MSP and provided printed abstracts showing inmate numbers, offenses, days worked, days absent from work, and other data. Bradford was a realist about the expectations from prison labor: "[The printed abstracts] will taken together form data upon which to ground your calculations. You will see that this mode of disposing ~~with~~ [*sic*] of culprits . . . is an expensive mode of punishment and as such has disappointed the hopes and calculations of many good men who were advocates" (Gamaliel Bradford to Thomas Buffum, September 21, 1818, filed in *Reports of Committees* 8, 21; strikeout in original). Sabin Delano was more positive about Vermont's experience, noting that the institution had begun to turn a profit of nearly two thousand dollars per annum from the woven goods and shoes produced in the prison. But as Rothman (1971, 104) points out, "profit" was a slippery notion in the world of the nineteenth-century institution. Estimates of profit from wardens and boards of inspectors often focused only on the relationship between the cost of materials and the revenues from sale of goods. The ways to juggle the books were myriad; officers' salaries could be left out of the reckoning, for example, or the lingering debt on construction and renovation conveniently overlooked.

Given the poor survival rate of handwritten, original copies of the keeper's reports, an analysis of the Rhode Island State Prison's ability to sustain itself must rely on published reports of financial statistics. The most comprehensive of these is a summary table printed in the *Annual Report of the Board of Inspectors* covering the years 1838 through 1876. The Rhode Island State Prison ran at an average deficit of four thousand dollars per annum for the first twenty-three years of its existence. The first period of surplus was during the period 1860 through 1865, the years of the Civil War. The prison's ability to generate revenue during wartime may well reflect the extent to which New England's manufacturers profited from four years of bloodshed. At the time of the war, the state's inmate labor contract was with the East New York Boot, Shoe and Leather Company—which, in turn, supplied the Union army with brogans manufactured in prison workshops from across New England. As expected, the return of Union army troops to their previous jobs put a dent in the prison's financial status, leading to deficits between 1865 and 1870.

We should look closely at the assertion, stated repeatedly, that the state prison would have had a better chance at self-sufficiency had its accounts not been combined with those of the county jail. Figures from 1849, when the accounts of the two institutions were separated, through 1876 suggest that the assertion had some merit. From 1849 through 1854 the state prison ran at an average annual deficit of $2,201. But from 1855 through 1876 the state prison accrued a modest but noticeable average annual surplus of $1,741. In contrast, the county jail showed surplus only for the war years of 1862 through 1864, and an indifferent surplus at best—$143 in 1862, $13 in 1863, and $80 in 1864. In 1876 it showed a fourth and final year of surplus with a munificent $148. For the period of separate accounting (1849–76), the county jail ran an average annual deficit of $2,250, contributing an average of 74 percent to the overall institutional deficit.

Why was the county jail such a money loser? Revenues from the county jail matched or exceeded those from the prison, belying the notion that its labor was unproductive. The county jail's costs, measured against those of the state prison, were extraordinarily high. The answer may lie in the simple fact that the greater number of inmates in the county jail increased associated costs of clothing, feeding, and housing, costs that could not be offset because of the inability of jailers to put all inmates to work.

As a combined state and county complex, the Rhode Island State Prison and Providence County Jail had little ability to pay its own operating costs. From 1838 through 1858 the institution drew down an average of $5,098 from the general treasury, a twenty-year loss of $101,960. From 1859 through 1863 the prison required no support from the general treasury, and from 1863 through 1876 it ran at a slight loss. More important is the relationship of monies received to monies returned to the state. Over the forty-year history of the prison, the board of inspectors drew a total of $113,950 for institutional expenses, returning only $7,564.30 to the general treasury. Note that the draw-downs are exclusive of construction costs, which totaled $139,981. Thus the gross draw on the general treasury was a staggering $253,931, or $6,511 per annum.

That self-sufficiency was a goal toward which prison authorities strived is unquestionable. Yet no matter how authorities attempted to present data, there is no way to argue that the Rhode Island State Prison ever approached the ability to meet its operating expenses. Still, we should note its importance to the authorities responsible for the maintaining of the labor program.

The Enforcement of Power Relations

In contrast to the rationale of the Jacksonians, Foucault (1979, 231–56) has argued that we should see the concept of prison labor as a veil masking a single, terrible ideology: that is, the state's total control over the body of the criminal, its absolute power over the powerless, its relentless routine of discipline. Labor, according to Foucault (1979, 244), is a necessary component of the process that transforms malefactors into "machine-men, but also . . . proletarians" who will leave prison to take their places in the mills and factories of industrial capitalists. "What, then, is the use of penal labour? Not profit; nor even the formation of a useful skill; but the constitution of a power relation, an empty economic form, a schema of individual submission and of adjustment to an economic apparatus." The interpretation of prison labor as "an empty economic form" is intellectually appealing, especially given the examples Foucault cites. In the Eastern State Penitentiary, for example, prisoners in their cells turned capstans equipped with numerical counters. The capstans were not connected to any mechanism and served only to instill habitual activity in offenders (Markus 1994, 15). Similarly, the English treadmill or tread wheel was a horrific device that forced the inmate to continually climb a series of rotating stairs for prescribed periods of "exercise" or, more explicitly, punishment.

I am not convinced that these examples—limited as they are—provide convincing evidence of labor as purely symbolic and devoid of economic rationale. The treadmill and the disconnected capstan are by far the exceptions in American prison discipline, rather than the rule. Furthermore, such devices were not truly agents of labor; they were agents of the instillation of routine, which is something altogether different. A close reading of the *Annual Reports of the Board of Inspectors* makes it all too clear that authorities were looking for real, empirical methods of production that would produce revenue for the institution. The strategy of the treadmill played no role in a small and rather ordinary facility like the Rhode Island State Prison and is likely more a reflection of eccentric Benthamite reform schemes than of economic intent (Bozovic 1995, 5).

A second and more serious critique lies in Foucault's inattention to the agency of the inmates forced to labor in the prison workshops. From this perspective, inmates cannot be constituted as real, autochthonous subjects, but only as passive dupes participating in their own oppression. Enmeshed in the architectural and social strategies of control, they trudge through their daily lives completely surveyed by those who are manipulating the machine from behind the curtain. Fine-grained historical and archaeological data refute this theorized passivity and point toward a high degree of resistance to the requirement of daily work as well as to the larger issue of confinement by the state.

Unquestionably many aspects of prison life encompassed the visible manifestation of power relations. The shuffling lockstep, in which the individual is subsumed by the mass of fellow prisoners herded across the prison yard, all under the watchful eye of guards, is one of the most striking examples of power display. To state that labor was entirely devoid of value is to ignore both contemporary rhetoric and the very real financial statements and projections produced by prison authorities. Those statements and projections, which caused worry and tension at the higher levels of the prison matrix, are worthy of closer consideration, especially in their pertinence to developing schemes of production.

The Siren Song of Profit

Rosalind Petchesky (1993, 595) has laid out the strongest argument for the "highly productive and highly profitable" nature of prison labor in the nineteenth century. Combining the rationales of the Jacksonians with elements of Foucault's analysis, she argues that the development of a work ethic among social deviants was part of capitalism's all-consuming effort to adapt society to industrialization: "The only acknowledged purposes of prison labor that bore any relation to objective reality were the *production of a disciplined work force* and *the realization of profits*." She goes on to note, "The common aim of all Jacksonian institutions was to reduce idleness and propagate a strict work ethic in the society at large (a society whose dominant conception of deviance was idleness)." Petchesky (1993, 600) correctly points out that the potential profit of the labor process in the Auburn plan led to its adoption by every state except Pennsylvania, which clung to its original experiment despite increasing criticism by the mid-nineteenth century. Auburn prisons provided more than a captive labor force; in the case of the Rhode Island State Prison, which is typical of other institutions, authorities provided outside contractors with the entire infrastructure necessary for industrial production: the workshops, power supplies, storage areas, and security personnel to oversee the work. Auburn provided a plan of management for private capital seeking accumulation. Thus confinement in state institutions and industrialization have a symbiotic relationship, and the accumulation of private profit through the use of public bodies and spaces constitutes a transitional form of industrialization, serving as the archetype for the factory system throughout much of the nation.

These arguments about economic formation, while perhaps overlooking the assertions of the Jacksonians, are difficult to dispute. My contention with the larger argument lies in Petchesky's (1993, 595–96) emphasis on the amount of revenue realized from state sale of inmate labor and the importance of that revenue to state budgets: "The early nineteenth-century institutions of confinement were crucial sources of revenue for the state, and they indicated the state's dependence on private capital at least as much as the capitalists' dependence on the state's coercive power and legitimating authority."

Prison labor in Rhode Island cannot be interpreted as remotely profitable to the state; indeed, the revenue from sale of goods and later the sale of labor barely funded the institution's operating expenses. Still, Petchesky's argument about the *potential* profit in labor is worth considering. Although no one in Rhode Island formally stated that prison labor would serve as a source of general revenue, they may well have hoped that this would be the case and planned production accordingly.

Institutional Motivations

I have presented three interpretations of the goals of prison labor in the nineteenth-century penitentiary. How can these interpretations be balanced and evaluated against one another to determine the underlying goal of labor at the Rhode Island State Prison? I have already pointed out some objections to Foucault's argument about power relations, an argument that is attractive but ignores both empirical data and the testimony of middle- to high-level nineteenth-century bureaucrats. Similarly, Petchesky's point about disciplining social deviants into respectable citizen-workers is well taken, but her emphasis on the profitability of prison is not supported by analysis of fiscal data in Rhode Island. Furthermore no evidence exists, except in the earliest planning stages of the prison, that anyone seriously thought that prison labor would be profitable to the state.

In the absence of evidence to the contrary, we are forced to look more closely at the statements of the nineteenth-century authorities and reformers. Discarding vocational strategy as a somewhat lame justification, we are left with the instillation of routine and the development of a self-sufficient institution as the most likely goals of the labor program. Based on the rhetoric of the institutional reports, I believe that these were, theoretically, reasonable goals that authorities believed could be met with a certain degree of effort. Their own rhetoric returns again and again to this issue. For example, consider the board of inspectors' report for 1849: "And from the ready sale of the articles manufactured, the undersigned have no hesitancy in saying that if the accommodations of the workshop could be enlarged, so that all the prisoners could be put to labor, it would not be many years

THE PRIVILEGE OF WORKING

before this department would nearly, if not quite, pay for its own expenses" (*ARBI* 1849, 23).

This trend of thought continued throughout the middle decades of the century, with authorities ever optimistic despite financial data to the contrary. Some were realists. The board wrote in 1854, "Similar institutions on this (Auburn) System in other states have been made a source of revenue. But it is not probable that our state prison will ever become so" (*ARBI* 1854, 15). A small number of inmates, short terms of imprisonment, the ratio of officers to inmates, and the convicts' need of instruction were all offered as explanations for this failure. Yet some remained optimists, clinging to the idea that the prison could eventually pay its own way. In 1857 the inspectors wrote that they saw "no reason for altering the opinion which they have heretofore expressed, that under ordinary circumstances, with the present management, the State will soon be relieved from any expense for the maintenance of the State Prison and County Jail" (*ARBI* 1857, 5). If we accept the premise that the primary goal of the labor program was to produce a sufficient supply of commodities, the sale of which would support the institution, then the question naturally becomes one of methodology, rather than philosophy: how did authorities attempt to meet the ambitious goals they had defined for the institution?

Production in the Prison Workshops

In addition to its role as a moral necessity, prison labor was conceived of as at least potentially able to sustain institutional operating costs. That it never achieved this goal in Rhode Island is a testament to at least four phenomena: first, poor decision making in selecting the forms of production; second, a total lack of understanding of market forces by the keepers, in their role as business agents; third, collective and individual action by those involved in the labor process; and fourth, the attainment of a certain level of institutional apathy. Graft or corruption is a fifth possibility, although it is nearly impossible to track. In following the trajectory I have developed, the various changes in production over time (which concern the first two phenomena) become increasingly important. Decisions about what goods would be produced in the prison workshops had important reverberations for the philosophical direction of the entire labor system. The following brief history of production at the Rhode Island State Prison pays particular attention to the always-shifting range of commodities produced in the prison and county jail workshops.

Initial Enthusiasm for Inmate Labor (1838–1841)

Shoe making was the first task considered by the board of inspectors as appropriate for the state prisoners. Their 1839 report summarizes the issue aptly: "After procuring all the information in their power as to the kind of mechanical labor practicable with solitary confinement, not injurious to health, easily learned and carried on, and likely to be made profitable, or least liable to loss, the inspectors decided upon that of manufacturing shoes and boots" (*ARRIGA* October 1839, 25). Adherents of the Pennsylvania plan found shoe making philosophically attractive. First, it stressed the individual. As we have seen in the keeper-compiled inventories, each inmate was supplied with the exact same set of equipment and materials within his individual cell. Thus work became a great leveler, with everyone starting with the same tools and no one able to claim an unfair advantage. Second, and equally important, was its ability to be measured and quantified. One could set a goal—in the case of the Rhode Island State Prison, the manufacture of one pair of shoes per day by each prisoner— and assess the prisoners' individual and collective ability to meet that goal. The actual level of production would undoubtedly reflect the inmate's embrace of moral reform and serve as a yardstick in calculating the speed and degree to which the individual was actively engaged in the process of self-reform. Those who were slacking were clearly still enmeshed in their previous reprobate ways, which had brought them to prison in the first place. Those who were meeting or exceeding the goals were shaking off deviancy and becoming productive citizen-workers.

Prisoners in solitary confinement, equipped with workbenches and full sets of tools, produced two types of shoes: brogans and pumps. A brogan was a coarse, mid-length boot consisting of an upper sole stitched or pegged to a square-toed sole and a tacked or nailed heel. It was the common person's work shoe and would become standard military issue during the Civil War (Woodhead 1991, 191). A pump was an even simpler, slipper-like item comprised of an outer sole stitched to an inner sole, with no heel.

Marketing of the shoes produced in the Rhode Island State Prison was initially successful. Ledgers suggest that most of the shoes were shipped to New Bedford, Massachusetts, and marketed as "Whaleman's Pumps"— cheap, almost disposable shoes purchased by sailors heading out to sea.

The shoes had two advantages for seamen: they would not scar the wood of lovingly scrubbed decks, and they could be kicked off easily by a man lost overboard and forced to swim. Other markets for the prison's footwear were less benign. In 1841 Rowland Hazard, the founder of Rhode Island's textile industry, purchased two thousand pairs of brogans from the prison. It is possible that these shoes found their way into Hazard's company stores at Peace Dale, Rhode Island, for purchase by his workers. But Hazard also had mercantile connections to the American South through his brother and business agent Thomas at Charleston, South Carolina. It is equally possible that the shoes were shipped to South Carolina and eventually purchased by plantation agents for use by enslaved African Americans. Thus, a neat irony: shoes made by northern prisoners, funneled through one of Rhode Island's wealthiest merchants, to cover the feet of enslaved southerners. Better still, Hazard could view his purchasing a large portion of the prison stock as a good deed contributing to the success of the labor program and the continued employment of prisoners.

Shoe making would never vanish from the landscape of work at the prison. The initial high cost of tools and workbenches resulted in their being carefully stored, even during periods when other forms of production had superseded shoe making. Authorities would repeatedly return to shoe making when other forms of production failed, primarily as a stopgap measure to keep prisoners employed. The first hiatus occurred in 1843, when national trends in consumption altered production almost exclusively from individual efforts to the collective production of decorative fans.

Prosperity and Failure (1843–1847)

Shoe making had been confined within individual cells when the prison operated under the Pennsylvania plan. Inmates made the shoes; an overseer collected and packaged them; and Keeper Cleaveland shipped them, in large quantities, to wholesalers in Providence and New Bedford, Massachusetts. The adoption of the Auburn plan, first by communal labor in the hall of the cell block and then through construction of the first communal workshop in 1845, forced prisoners into a congregate labor plan. The same reasons that made shoe making suitable for work under the Pennsylvania plan rendered it supremely unsuitable for work under the Auburn plan. With production out in the open, individuals gathered communally but working separately could stealthily measure their progress against that of others. Theoretically, the group as a whole could come to a collective pace, one that would frustrate the best efforts of the overseers to maintain control over production. Shoe making entailed too much individuality for a successful communal labor system.

It therefore became necessary to find an outlet for production that used individuals in separate but contributing roles, merging a hierarchy of tasks into a collective process of production. From a twenty-first-century standpoint the production of delicate, decorative fans by hardened criminals seems unusual. Yet fans were uniquely suited to the large-scale, assembly-line production that congregate labor required. Creating a fan involved at least three distinct steps: pressing the paper and japanning it with lacquer, stenciling the design, and painting in the design with a floral or faunal decoration. Two related steps included the turning of wooden handles on small lathes and the attachment of the rigid portions of the fans to their handles. The final steps involved packing the fans in boxes and gluing labels to their exteriors. Thus six different activities formed a three-tiered pyramid of skill. At the bottom of the pyramid were handle preparation, handle fastening, and packing; on the second tier were pressing the paper and stenciling the design; and at the uppermost tier the painters were responsible for completing the design. Under such a plan prisoners could be matched with tasks appropriate to their skill levels, and production could be increased through a streamlining process. More important, individual pace and progress could be monitored, with the deficiencies in the assembly process identified and remedied quickly.

What did these fans look like? The Museum of Art at the Rhode Island School of Design contains a collection of fans painted in the Rhode Island State Prison workshops (MRISD 36.142, Gift of Miss Margarethe L. Dwight). The collection includes two boxes, which may or may not be the original boxes from the prison; a hand-colored box label; and fourteen fans in various stages of production, including ten finished items. The assemblage was produced by Thomas Wilson Dorr, the prison's most notorious inmate and fomenter of the populist uprising against the state of Rhode Island (fig. 20). That Dorr was permitted to leave the prison with the collection of fans after his pardon in 1845 is a testament to his special status among the prisoners, as well as to the significance of fans as souvenirs of important events. "As the Dwight bequest shows," writes Pamela A. Parmal (1990, 4), "the fan's role as a keepsake or commemorative object was important during the nineteenth as well as the eighteenth century." Since Dorr spent only a year in the state prison, the range of skill evidenced in the fans testifies to the surprising ability of inmates to acquire the ability to paint the objects.

Fig. 20 — Rebel, inmate, painter: convicted of treason and sentenced to life imprisonment in the Rhode Island State Prison, Thomas Wilson Dorr spent the year before he was pardoned painting fans in the prison workshop. Engraving from daguerreotype by W. Warner. Courtesy of the Rhode Island Historical Society (RHi X3 2013).

The articulation between the fan leaf and the handle conveniently divides the leaf into two vertical panels. These panels are generally filled with vertically oriented trailing vines and flowers, including clematis and roses. With some exceptions, the motifs on the fans are remarkably similar to those found on the borders of mass-produced ceramic vessels from the 1840s. Similarly, the scalloped edging of the fan leaf finds parallels in picturesque-revival forms of architecture and material culture.

The RISD collection provides important insight into the production techniques of fans. In an example representing the earliest level of production, the fan leaf has been cut, a handle attached, and the design stenciled onto the fan (fig. 21). In at least two other cases a spoiled fan leaf with a deep crease across its midsection has been reused as a practice model for the novice inmate-painter (fig. 22). On the reverse of this leaf a master painter put a floral design onto the fan and then asked the inmate-painter to copy the image of the bellflowers repeatedly (fig. 23).

At least three different models of fans were made in the workshop. From descriptions in the correspondence between Keeper Cleaveland and his wholesalers, we know that the three models—referred to as Nos. 1, 2,

THE PRIVILEGE OF WORKING

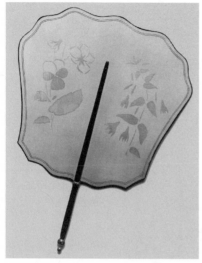

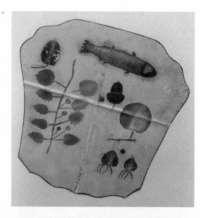

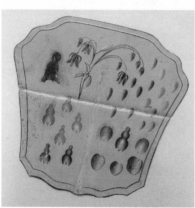

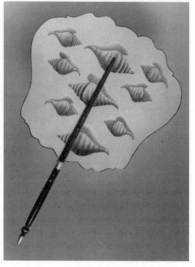

FIG. 21 *(top left) — Paper fan produced in the Rhode Island State Prison showing stenciling for image (c. 1845). Museum of Art, Rhode Island School of Design. Gift of Margarethe L. Dwight.*

FIG. 22 *(top right) — Damaged fan leaf produced in the Rhode Island State Prison and reused as a template for training new inmate-painters (c. 1845). Museum of Art, Rhode Island School of Design. Gift of Margarethe L. Dwight.*

FIG. 23 *(bottom left) — Reverse of the reused fan leaf shown in figure 21, showing the master painter's work at top center and Thomas Dorr's attempts to copy the model below (c. 1845). Museum of Art, Rhode Island School of Design. Gift of Margarethe L. Dwight.*

FIG. 24 *(bottom right) — Completed Rhode Island State Prison fan displaying a design of snail shells (c. 1845). Museum of Art, Rhode Island School of Design. Gift of Margarethe L. Dwight.*

FIG. 25 — Paper box label for fans manufactured in the workshop of the Rhode Island State Prison (c. 1845). Although produced in a penitentiary, the fans were marketed under the name "La Moselle Eventail Elastique." Museum of Art, Rhode Island School of Design. Gift of Margarethe L. Dwight.

and 3—were marketed under the larger trade name "La Moselle Eventail Elastique" (figs. 24 and 25). The means by which murderers, arsonists, and thieves were transformed into producers of French-influenced decorative fans is curious; as a parable for the tensions underlying production in prison workshops, fan production is illustrative of the larger point concerning the relationship of prison-made goods and the outside world, and is worthy of consideration in detail.

The origins of the impetus for decorative-fan production is by no means clear. Based on a partial series of correspondence housed at the Rhode Island State Archives, it seems likely that the New York City firm of Bowen & McManus approached Thomas Cleaveland late in 1842 and inquired about the possibility that inmates could manufacture fans exclusively for sale to that firm (correspondence concerning the fans may be found in Correspondence File 319A:1, RISA; the unsorted file is dispersed over seven different folders). Note that the type of arrangement used here differed significantly from later efforts to sell the labor of inmates to outside contractors. Bowen & McManus wanted an exclusive arrangement to buy fans made in the prison. They were not, however, directly paying for inmate labor, but rather for the finished goods, and even then it was only on approval of the commodities.

Keeper Cleaveland had managed the shoe-making program, with assistance from a labor overseer, in a relatively straightforward fashion. Shoe making required only the purchase of leather stock (widely available in nineteenth-century Providence), supervision of the labor of individuals, and the shipment of finished shoes to local markets. With the prison's entry into the production of decorative fans, his role as business agent expanded dramatically: he was now, in addition to his duties as the moral leader of the prison, responsible for purchasing new forms of stock, generating a product acceptable to a client in a distant market, and maintaining a steady flow of goods for a voracious seasonal demand. Correspondence between Cleaveland and Bowen & McManus lends insight into the tensions of production at the prison (correspondence concerning the fans can be found in Correspondence File 319A:1, RISA; the unsorted file is dispersed over seven different folders). On January 11, 1843, Cleaveland wrote to Bowen & McManus setting terms for the fan contract, including the proposed price of the fans and the freight charges, which he suggested that Bowen & McManus would pay. Their response, dated January 13, 1843, quickly removed any doubts about who held the upper hand in the relationship: "We shall not decide about the fans until we see another sample in the New Style Boxes and we hope, as the boxes will have a *great* influence, that you will be *very particular* and have them got up in the *very best* style. We attach *more importance* to the boxes than we can well make you understand as you are not in the fancy dry goods business" (Bowen & McManus to Thomas Cleaveland, January 13, 1843, 1; all emphases in original). There could be no question, they continued, of Bowen & McManus assuming the shipping charges for the fans. They would pay the charges and deduct them from Cleaveland's bills. Although Bowen & McManus recognized that the cheaply made fans would help them realize an advantage over their competitors, they were all too cognizant of the potential disaster if word got out that their elegant fans, packaged in boxes with French labels, were made by state prisoners:

> One thing more, we wish the whole matter kept to yourself
> as we would not like to have our neighbors, by report from
> Providence or otherwise, hear that we had any thing to do with
> you in the matter, in other words, we do not wish to publish to
> the world that the fans are made in Rhode Island. We do not
> wish you to say how large a quantity you have sold, or to whom

you have sold them, or to what city you sent them. We have no idea or intention of saying the fans were *not* made in RI State prison, but we shall have no objection, if our customers *think* they were made in France.

(Bowen & McManus to Thomas Cleaveland,
January 13, 1843, 3; emphasis in original)

The final lesson Bowen & McManus imparted to Warden Cleaveland was that of petty graft to close the deal: "To *bind* the contract (if it is made) we shall expect a present of *one box*—2 dozen—of the extra, extra, super, super, splendid and magnificent fans to hang up in our windows and exhibit as samples, and to present to some of our friendly editors who will give them a '*puff*'" (Bowen & McManus to Thomas Cleaveland, January 13, 1843, 3).

Cleaveland must have found this engagement much more complex and arduous than the relatively straightforward process of shoe making. No one had demanded samples of the shoes or that they be packaged in decorative boxes. Simple and utilitarian as they were, they had generally sold themselves to local wholesalers. In Providence, Cleaveland was a known quantity, a much-respected figure admired for his honesty. By signing on with Bowen & McManus, he had committed himself and the labor of his charges to a much more complicated form of production and an unequal relationship with a client interested not in philanthropy but rather in turning the highest possible profit from the naive Rhode Islanders.

The prison's relationship with Bowen & McManus would, over the next year, prove generally agreeable to both parties. In early March the retailers indicated that the fans were "indeed beautiful" (Bowen & McManus to Thomas Cleaveland, March 6, 1843, 1). Later in the month they reported that sales of the prison fans were strong and that demand was increasing. This demand led to a request to speed up production in the workshop: "If you can '*grind out*' a thousand Dozen within twenty days . . . we will make you a *low bow*" (Bowen & McManus to Thomas Cleaveland, March 25, 1843). As Petchesky (1993, 600) has noted about institutional labor in the mid-nineteenth century, "Prison discipline quickly came to be subordinated to considerations of production." The wholesalers were calling the tune, and Cleaveland, lured by potential revenues, had no choice but to follow along.

The consequence of the demand for more fans was an extension of the prison working day far into the night. Cleaveland, keeping his silence in accordance with the demands of the client, never indicated in any public document that he was expanding the work day. Cognizant of the pressures they were creating on the lives of the keeper and his family, Bowen & McManus did their best to keep him happy and productive: "We know Mrs. Cleveland [*sic*] must be put to much inconvenience on our account in preparing extra food for those prisoners who work nights & we therefore take the liberty of presenting her with the accompanying dress with our compliments" (Bowen & McManus to Thomas Cleaveland, March 25, 1843).

By May 1843 the huge demand for fans—which were, after all, a highly seasonal item—resulted in increasing pressure from Bowen & McManus. Their level of meddling in the affairs of the prison now extended to the inmates' diet, as they inquired whether the inmates were consuming adequate fat, starch, and caffeine for twelve- and thirteen-hour days:

> What will you do? Can you not with your "*extra help*" give them to us faster. We now would like to know as *definitely* as possible what you can do, from week to week.
>
> Please write us by *return boat*. Please send all the Fans you have on hand if only 20 Dozen and push ahead as fast as possible. We hope your "Black Tea & Bread & Butter" is not short, how is it?

> (Bowen & McManus to Thomas Cleaveland, May 2, 1843)

The "extra help" in this letter probably refers to the county jail inmates, who had been transferred from furniture making to fan preparation. So great was the demand that every working body was needed to keep production up to speed. This must have truly hit home by the end of May, when the spring fan season finally ended: "Yours of the 29th is at hand," wrote Bowen & McManus to Cleaveland on May 31. "We shall be willing to receive the fans only on conditions that you will take *back* all unsold." Still, there was always next year: "Will you now think of the coming year & prepare a great variety of samples. Our Mr. Bowen will probably be in Providence the last of June."

Here, Cleaveland found yet another challenge in the production of fans. He had worked the inmates incessantly for three months. But now, with the season over, he had nothing for them to do. No production could begin on the 1844 models until Bowen & McManus approved the new styles. On June 26, 1843, H. C. Bowen reminded Cleaveland that he would be in Providence in a week: "Will you please prepare as many samples as possible of every description that I may decide what styles to order, also prepare samples of the different shades of color you can make, i.e. paint a lot of plain fans of every *tint* of color you can think of—so that we may select the best." Although the tone of the letter is generally friendly, there is an ominous subtext that the low quality of the later lots of fans—undoubtedly stemming from the sheer pace of production—would not be tolerated in 1844, nor would any delay in the matter. "You will see that it is very important that we exercise our best, *very best* taste in the matter," Bowen wrote, "so that there will be no mistake about them going off at 'double quick time.'"

Despite these warnings, and the lack of occupation for the inmates, Cleaveland seems to have been caught in a strange paralysis, perhaps due to overall exhaustion and what in retrospect would prove to be failing health. Bowen was highly displeased not to have found Cleaveland at home on his visit to Providence: "Our Mr. Bowen was very sorry he could not see you, but suppose it was just as well, as nothing definite could be decided upon as you had so few samples." In mid-August they demanded that Cleaveland come see them in New York with samples; furthermore, they went so far as to compromise the prison's mission of security by demanding that Cleaveland bring with him the unnamed inmate responsible for the finish painting: "It would not be a bad idea to have your Painter come on with you. & we would suggest that he do so. Perhaps it would be a good thing & incorage [*sic*] him if he could accompany you."

The samples, finally prepared, were satisfactory to Bowen & McManus. Production during early 1844 was as frenzied as the previous year's: "We hope you will not stop the 'wheels' *one moment*. . . . We have only again to say push! *push* !! push!!! ahead as *fast* as possible" (Bowen & McManus to Thomas Cleaveland, March 22, 1844). The wholesalers further meddled in the dietary management of the prison by sending quantities of starch, fat, and caffeine to the inmates: "We will ship you a small cargo of 'Bread & Butter' to give your men if by so doing you can 'stir them up.' Black Tea & Bread & Butter are cheap so you must not spare it."

The year 1844 proved to be the last of real success for the fan business. By 1845–46 the prison's fans were no longer popular with merchants. This was due less to the quality of the fans and more to a nationwide consumer shift toward folding, ribbed fans painted with motifs redolent of China and Japan. The consequences for Warden Cleaveland were dire; he had invested thousands of the state's dollars in the paper stock and paints for production of rigid fans. Although he identified a series of new markets for the items, including wholesalers in Philadelphia and other points along the Atlantic seaboard, he was forced to reduce his prices in order to clear inventory:

My prices have been for No. 1 $1.25—No. 2 $1.50—No. 3 $1.75 *cash*. Having a large quantity on hand, & finding the market rather *dull* I have concluded to consign them . . . fixing the lowest limits at for No. 1 $1.00—No. 2 $1.25—No. 3 $1.50 per Doz. . . .

Should you decline selling them will you have the goodness to place them in the hands of some one who will do it, and oblige—

(Thomas Cleaveland to Howland & Taft, December 7, 1846)

So great were the losses from fan production that the general assembly was forced to step in and assess the situation. In an unprecedented step, the assembly passed a bill at its January 1847 session forbidding the production of any additional fans at the Rhode Island State Prison (*ARRIGA* January 1847, 24). Cleaveland, in terminating the industry, was forced to humble himself even further to his wholesalers in an effort to dispose of the stock:

In consequence of recent enactments of our Legislature My present year will close on the 30th of April next instead of on Sept. 30th as formerly.

At that time I shall have to render an account of my proceedings for the six months previous to the Legislature.

Therefore I propose, instead of my present arrangements with you . . . to offer you 25 per cent discount from my present prices (viz. $1. $1.25 $1.50) for all the fans you will cash by the 20th of April next.

I offer the above for the purpose (as you merchants say) of "closing the concern" at that time.

(Thomas Cleaveland to person unknown, February 1847)

The fallout from the debacle continued for some months. In June 1847 Inspectors Thurber and Kimball were dispatched to New York to collect unpaid debts. They spent four days prowling through the wholesalers along Pearl and Williams streets demanding payment for the fans. They paid the cost of their passage and their expenses for four days in New York (a bargain at $14) out of their collections and returned to Providence with $584.41 for their efforts. Fan production at the Rhode Island State Prison had ended once and for all.

I have looked at the documents underlying fan production in great detail because the experience offers three important lessons in liberal capitalism by which those who inherited Cleaveland's disastrous labor program profited. First, state institutions dealing with the private sector had to be careful about pacing the speed of production to match the speed of commodity demand. From 1843 forward, when Cleaveland began dealing with Bowen & McManus, he was caught in a vicious cycle. The fan season was short, ranging from early March through the end of May. By continuing production into June, July, and August, he left the state liable for thousands of fans in the previous year's style, most of which were unsalable due to changing fashions. Thus *all* of the ramifications of production needed to be determined prior to investment in stock and labor training. Second, state institutions driving bargains with the private sector had to be aware that by uniting with private capital, they were undermining the state's mission of punishment and discipline. The supplies of unapproved food shipped to the prison and the "painter's" unexpected and pleasant jaunt to New York City both testify to the erosion of state power under pressure from private capital. Third, and most important, was the lesson that the person invested with the duty of reforming the state's most heinous offenders could not reasonably be expected to serve as the business agent for the institution as well. Cleaveland was a former missionary with some inclination toward the medical arts. He was in no way trained as a factory overseer, let alone a merchant. Thurber and Kimball's trip to New York City, resulting in the wresting of hundreds of dollars in unpaid bills, is evidence of Cleaveland's thorough inadequacy as a financial agent.

The consequence of overproduction and commitment to a single commodity led directly to Cleaveland's desperate search for new and distant markets for goods made in the prison workshop. Markets for fans included most of the major seaports on the Atlantic coast: Boston, New Haven, New York City, Philadelphia, Baltimore, Charleston, and Augusta (fig. 26). Yet a closer look at the data indicates that for all markets except New York City and Philadelphia, shipments consisted of one to two consignments worth less than one thousand dollars. Thus the broad spread of the economic network of fan production is somewhat deceiving. Most fans went to New York and Philadelphia, easily accessible from Providence by steamboat, and the remainder were shipped to points south out of sheer desperation on the part of Cleaveland.

Furniture production, in contrast to the fans, was directed exclusively toward local markets: Providence, Pawtucket, and Warwick, Rhode Island. Two factors may have inhibited shipment of furniture to more distant markets: first, the high cost of transporting large, bulky items; second, and

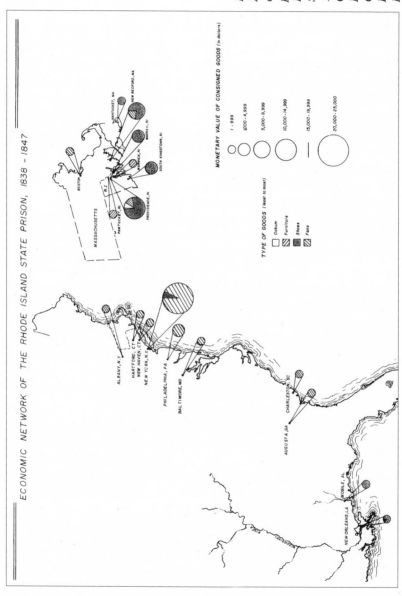

Fig. 26 — Markets for commodities produced in the Rhode Island State Prison, 1838–47. Graphic by Dana Richardi. Courtesy of PAL, Pawtucket, Rhode Island.

ECONOMIC NETWORK OF THE RHODE ISLAND STATE PRISON, 1838–1847

MONETARY VALUE OF CONSIGNED GOODS (in dollars)

1 – 999
600 – 4,999
5,000 – 9,999
10,000 – 14,999
15,000 – 19,999
20,000 – 25,000

TYPE OF GOODS (least to most)

Oakum
Furniture
Shoes
Fans

BOSTON
MASSACHUSETTS
NANTUCKET, MA
NEW BEDFORD, MA
WARREN, RI
R.I.
PAWTUCKET, RI
WARWICK, RI
SOUTH KINGSTOWN, RI
PROVIDENCE, RI

ALBANY, N.Y.
HARTFORD, CT
NEW HAVEN, CT
NEW YORK, N.Y.
PHILADELPHIA, PA
BALTIMORE, MD
CHARLESTON, SC
AUGUSTA, GA

MOBILE, AL
NEW ORLEANS, LA
MISSISSIPPI

more significantly, the New England furniture market was already cornered, not by private firms but by other state prisons. Even in Rhode Island much of the better class of furniture came from other state prisons: "Upon investigation and enquiry it has been ascertained that almost the entire supply of costly Furniture for the whole state is furnished by the States of New York and Massachusetts, a very large proportion of which is manufactured in their State Prisons" (*ARBI* 1850, 8). With a few exceptions, shoes also were shipped to nearby ports: New Bedford, Nantucket, and Warren. The ultimate disposition of the shoes is unknown. Some were certainly sold locally; however, they more likely were loaded onto ships originating from these port cities and traded to distant ports.

Thus, in interpreting the role of market forces on prison production, we should not assume that all markets were local. The prison, as an industrial plant in a fast-growing economy, was inextricably linked with distant markets across the Atlantic world. That the system of internally managed production gave way to external management and control was perhaps inevitable in light of the spread of industrial economies throughout New England.

Resignation and Apathy (1850–1876)

By 1847, at the climax of the debacle over fan production, the board of inspectors was at a loss over how to deal with the complexities of prison labor. Cleaveland must surely have been shaken by the circumstances that had left him with thousands of unsold and unsalable fans: "He was a physician by profession, and had undertaken the duties of a prison official, with the sincere desire to carry out the system adopted at the first. But he soon became convinced that it was not conducive either to the good health or the good morals of the prisoners, and while he endeavored to do the best possible in the circumstances, he felt that success was of very difficult attainment. His physical strength gave way, and on May 1, 1847, he resigned the office of warden" (*ARBI* 1876, 30). Four months later, on September 29, 1847, Cleaveland died at the age of forty-five. It seems likely that his decision to resign was not entirely voluntary. At the May 1847 session of the general assembly, the legislature voted to relinquish its own prequisite of appointing the board of inspectors, investing that ability with the governor. The newly elected governor Elisha Harris, a textile manufacturer from Coventry, was not slow about using his new power. On May 14, one week after the assembly had made its decision, Harris requested and received the resignations of the entire board of inspectors.

The new board, composed almost exclusively of industrialists, held few illusions about the vocational or reformative aspects of labor. They recognized that the infrastructure of the prison would soon require both renovation and new construction, and they were politically savvy enough to know that unless the institution showed better returns on its labor, efforts to lobby the general assembly for the necessary funds would undoubtedly be doomed in committee. Initially they fell back on shoe and furniture making, especially because the means to carry out such tasks were already in place. Within four years, however, they had identified the problems inherent in the state-sponsored labor program: "the Convicts in the prison were employed in shoemaking and the prisoners in the jail at Cabinet making. The State purchased the Stock and disposed of the products . . . the State was liable to loss from the fluctuations of the prices of the articles made, and from the disadvantages under which it came into the market for the sale of its goods" (*ARBI* 1851, 6). Given the disastrous experience with the fans, few could argue with this trenchant analysis. The inspectors' solution was simple: "The inspectors became convinced that a great gain could be made by abandoning the purchase of stock, and confining themselves to the mere sale of labor" (*ARBI* 1851, 6). No longer would the warden have to fill the dual roles of moral leader and business agent. Responsibility for negotiating terms with outside contractors rested solely with the board of inspectors. Furthermore, the pressures on the warden's staff—already on the rise with an increasing prison and county jail population—would be eased by the substitution of state-funded labor overseers with the contractors' own representatives.

The sale of inmate labor to outside contractors eased some of the hierarchical tensions while creating new ones. The state's advantages were clear: they could negotiate a fixed price with a contractor, and anticipation of fees receivable would greatly assist any planning efforts. The return on the sale of inmate labor was minimal but generally steady. For the labor of each state prisoner, Rhode Island received 40¢ a day; for a county jail inmate's labor, 23.5¢ a day. Removal of the burden of oversight allowed the board of inspectors to replace the labor overseers with much-needed new positions, including a matron for the female prisoners and night watchmen.

At the same time, the opening of the gates to outside contractors created the first real break in the membrane of security surrounding the institution. Production of fans had been *externally driven*, with Mr. Bowen's one unsuccessful visit to Cleaveland the only occasion when wholesalers actually attempted to enter the prison. Now the situation was completely reversed: the door was open to those bidding on inmate labor who wanted to inspect the facilities; to the agents of successful bidders (described in the documents as "contractors' representatives"), who oversaw production; and to a wide range of deliverymen and teamsters transporting raw material to the prison and finished goods back to the wholesalers' warehouses. One of these contractors even built and maintained a third workshop just outside the perimeter wall. By 1877 the prison held contracts with a shoemaker, the Providence Cotton Tie Company, a shoddy manufacturer, and a wire-goods manufacturer; they had also been in the unique position of writing themselves a contract for prison laborers to build the furnishings for the new house of correction in Cranston.

What Is the Meaning of Labor in the Nineteenth-century Prison?

In B. Traven's 1934 novel *The Death Ship* we see the patterns of bureaucratic bungling and inmate work evasion illuminated in fiction. Traven's protagonist, Gerard Gales, is confined in a French prison for failing to have proper identification papers. He is then informed that he will have to work while confined:

> Third day: In the morning I was asked by about fifteen different officers if I had ever in my life sewn strings on aprons, I said that I had not, and that I had not the slightest idea as to how it was done. Afternoon: I am called for by eight or nine prison officials who inform me that I have been assigned to the sewing department to sew on apron-strings.
>
> (Traven 1962 [1934], 45)

Gerard develops foot-dragging strategies that, in combination with bureaucratic negligence, result in his sewing exactly one apron string in the course of his ten days in the French jail:

> Fourth day: I have to appear in the store, where I receive a pair of scissors, one needle, about five yards of thread, and a thimble. The thimble did not fit any of my fingers. I complained but I was told to be quiet; they had no other thimble to satisfy my peculiarities. . . .

Sixth day: In the morning I am taken to the shop in which I have to work. Afternoon: I am given a place to sit and to work. Sixth day gone.

(Traven 1962 [1934], 45–46)

In the workshop of a second French jail, Gerard is told to count off "a pile of very peculiar-looking nameless things stamped out of bright tinned sheet iron" (Traven 1962 [1934], 65). He then has to count the same pile again and again and again to ensure that the count is accurate and, more important, to ensure that no bureaucratic retribution falls on his overseer.

Traven's account of life in prison workshops, although fictional, is relevant for understanding the subject position of the inmate-worker as well as that of the state-paid or state-subsidized overseer. In the nineteenth-century prison, work was meaningless to the inmates. To the contractors, contractors' representatives, and members of the prison hierarchy, it was a profit-making scheme. To members of the prison hierarchy and legislators, it was at once a noble idea and a pragmatic means of institutional self-sufficiency.

By the late 1850s Rhode Island's formerly austere, silent Pennsylvania-plan prison had been utterly transformed, not only by the switch to congregate labor but also by the decision to contract that labor out. Inmates who had heard—and to some extent accepted—the rhetoric that labor was a necessary component of their rehabilitation now found themselves in the position of slaves in an industrialized economy, with their labor now strictly a commodity to be bought and sold. We should not find it too surprising that issues of intra-institutional punishment, once rare, became a matter of course in the Rhode Island State Prison during the era of contract labor.

CHAPTER 5

"A Small Amount Has Been Accomplished"

Confrontations and Clashes in the Prison Workshops

We have seen the potential for conflict between inmates, authorities, and outside contractors operating within the matrix of the Rhode Island State Prison. Given that inmates spent up to 66 percent of their entire sentence in the workshops, the domain of labor was the arena in which these groups were most likely to clash. So far the discussion has addressed extra-institutional issues: that is, the decisions concerning the types of commodities produced in the prison, the means of producing those commodities, and the disposition of products to local, regional, and national markets. We have yet to explore the internal world of institutional labor and the oscillation of external tensions into the mechanics of day-to-day production.

Examining patterns of resistance in the nineteenth-century institution requires consideration of both the overt and the covert. Each correlates in the archival and archaeological records of the penal complex. Evidence for overt resistance has a high degree of visibility in the written materials stored in various state repositories. It is manifest in punishment ledgers, statistical compilations, and anecdotes gleaned from the *Annual Reports of the Board of Inspectors*. It may have some tangible and material manifestations in the archaeological record. Covert resistance is obviously more difficult to detect; by definition, successful acts of resistance go unnoticed, unpunished, and therefore unremarked on in the official record. The correlates of covert resistance are exclusively archaeological and therefore less immediately accessible.

Resistance in the Prison: Interpreting the Overt

My survey of the documentary record pertaining to the prison when it was run in accordance with the Pennsylvania plan identified relatively few examples of what I would call overt resistance. This may be because the architectural and social control measures implemented during the state of solitary confinement were somewhat successful in preventing communication, without which there could be no attempts at collective action against the state. The condition of total isolation caused prisoners to turn inward in an effort to wrest some measure of control over their environments. In 1839 the board of inspectors wrote, "The cells are commodious, well-ventilated and cleanly. Many of them are kept by inmates with a neatness and even attempts at decoration which manifest an ambition to deserve approbation" (*ARRIGA* October 1839, 27). This same report describes the authorities' earnest belief that work, even in solitary confinement, could balance out any deleterious effects stemming from the lack of human contact. They noted that before the shoe-making program had been initiated, inmates had simply been locked up with nothing to do. We should not be surprised to find, as the inspectors did, that the delay in starting the labor program "greatly aggravated their discontent and wretchedness" (*ARRIGA* October 1839, 27).

With the expansion of the prison population, the success of the labor program fell off markedly. As early as 1845 the board of inspectors was back-pedaling from its previous predictions concerning the success of prison labor: "The labor of prisoners for the first six months is of little value, the materials wasted in instructing them being taken into consideration" (*ARRIGA* October 1845, 42–43). Efforts to lead the prisoners through a variety of different unskilled tasks, including the manufacture of shoddy (a cheap fabric made from recycled wool), furniture finishing, and fan painting, deteriorated as the new workshop space was compromised by the rising rate of new prisoners and their individual and collective intransigence. After the transformation of the institution to an Auburn-plan facility, increasing examples of punishment appear in the documentary record for offenses relating to demeanor in the workshops. The punishment ledger of 1873 is an especially instructive document; it indicates that inmates were held without food and water for attempts to communicate with one another, for stealing materials, and most seriously, for damaging tools and finished products.

Consider the case of Elisha Peck, a murderer serving a life sentence in 1873. At different points throughout the year Peck was charged with "refusing to work," "destroying tools," and "spoiling prison property," along with a host of more traditional infractions. For the usual misdemeanors ("singing in his cell") he was held without food and water for twenty-four hours. But for the infractions dealing with his misbehavior in the workshop, he was sent to the Dark Cell with a ball and chain for up to a week at a time.

The Peck case raises interesting questions, especially following Scott's (1985) thoughtful discussion of how to identify resistance. Peck's singing in his cell is an action that might have been considered resistance, especially in a prison that practiced the rule of silence; alternatively, it might well be considered a nonresistant attempt to express his own agency and identity. What is important about the incident is that those in charge of the prison could not necessarily anticipate, predict, explain, or tolerate the action, so it therefore became something to record in the ledgers as an act of resistance against the daily backdrop of imprisonment.

Other prisoners demonstrated resistance to the prison system by shirking work and even sabotage. The reports of the keepers and wardens are rife with complaints about the prisoners' inability to learn the simplest of trades. Although it is certainly true that many of the inmates entered the prison from lifelong backgrounds of crime, it seems unlikely that the majority were unable to complete basic tasks such as cutting leather, picking oakum, and making rags. A more likely interpretation is that they were simply foot-dragging and feigning incompetence, an interpretation in line with contemporary resistance theory (Scott 1985).

There are also intriguing hints in the documentary record of collective action on the part of the prisoners. On September 1, 1847, twelve inmates fled the county jail workshop. The timing of the event was well planned; as the inspectors commented dryly, "The escape was made at the time the few officers left at the premises were at dinner" (*ARRIGA* October 1847). The prisoners, left unsupervised, managed to get out of the workshop and across the prison yard, where they used a pile of lumber to scramble over first a coal shed and then the perimeter wall. Eleven of the twelve were eventually recaptured; Simon J. Hicks, a state prisoner under sentence of death, eluded captivity. The board of inspectors refused to blame the officers of the institution, commenting instead that "it is . . . believed that he could have been returned to the jail before this time, had a considerable larger reward been offered for his apprehension" (*ARRIGA* October 1847, 72). Whether this escape was premeditated or not, the prisoners involved took collective action by working together to effect the escape. Once over the prison wall Hicks, the subject of an intensive and well-organized manhunt, may have found refuge among associates in the

A Small Amount Has Been Accomplished

Providence underworld before disappearing permanently from the historical record.

There is another dimension to the story of the Hicks escape: that is, the possible collusion of individual guards acting in tacit solidarity with inmates. Someone, after all, had to leave the lumber piled conveniently against the perimeter fence. Both guards and inmates had reasons to despise the system, particularly in the modern context of the correctional institution (Carroll 1988). Could the sympathies of guards toward their charges result in untraceable acts of "systematic soldiering"?

This example reaffirms the need to interpret actions of resistance on the multiple scales identified earlier. It would be simplistic to set up a two-way relationship of prisoners versus everyone else. In reality, virtually everyone within the institutional hierarchy has some degree of agency in combating the conditions at an institution, including prison staff and wardens. In his ethnography of the contemporary Adult Correctional Institution (ACI) in Rhode Island, Leo Carroll (1988) found that twentieth-century correctional officers (COs) often feel that they are as confined as their subjects. Contributing to this sense of confinement are the COs' fear of attack and their inability to respond with violence; job conditions, including a well-established seniority system and requirements of weekend and overtime work; and an overriding sense that prisoners, with access to state-subsidized educations and medical care, enjoy more privileges than law-abiding citizens. During the early 1970s responses of the COs to these conditions included labor organization, organized sick-outs, and verbal expressions of racism toward African American prisoners. Might not similar issues be visible in the documentary and archaeological records of the first Rhode Island State Prison, in which keepers and underkeepers were locked down with the inmates?

Moving farther up the ladder, the keepers almost certainly experienced frustration with the system they were charged with maintaining. The documentary record is rife with their pleas for various improvements to the prison infrastructure and to the penal system. The same could also be said of the members of the board of inspectors, eminent citizens charged with mediating the relationship between the keeper and the general assembly. The keepers must have had to walk a fine line between militating for funding for improvements and painting a portrait of conditions in the prison that was too desperate. Their forms of resistance are likely to have been more covert than overt.

A Small Amount Has Been Accomplished

Resistance in the Prison: Interpreting the Covert

The massive documentary record is of primary importance in studying contests over power within the institution, as is the record of material remains left behind at the site. However, it is important to note that the discussion so far has focused on *overt* resistance: that is, on strategies that were recognized and defined by authorities as representing inappropriate and evil activities. Yet there surely must have been a culture of *covert* resistance within the institution, constituted of acts that evaded detection at the time; these would have been invisible to the underkeepers, the keepers, and especially the board of inspectors and the general assembly.

In interpreting struggles over power, I will explore acts of covert resistance to higher authority. What might these nineteenth-century acts look like to the twenty-first-century anthropologist? What deeds could have gone undetected, or at least unrecognized as inappropriate activities, by prison staff and authorities? One idea revolves around smuggling and the presence of undetected contraband within cell areas, including liquor bottles, tobacco pipes, or other forbidden goods (Schmidt and Mrozowski 1988). Because the members of the prison staff were under many of the same regulations as the prisoners, caching of contraband might also be an aspect of the underkeepers' activities. There are other possibilities regarding covert resistance. Those in charge of the prison could have been deeply involved in graft and corruption: altering accounts, paying bribes to contractors, or practicing staff favoritism on a daily basis. All of these acts could be interpreted as ultimately concerning power, and none would necessarily leave behind traces in the archaeological or documentary record.

Such deeds could only be possible in a system where power is contested at every level. Solidarity between staff and authorities or authorities and the general assembly might have squelched resistance at any of the lower levels. Fragmentation and dispersal of power, an inherent quality of multilayered surveillance, may have enabled and engendered the various struggles. There is, of course, another possibility: that some acts of covert resistance were recognized and overlooked by those at the next highest level. Some acts of prisoner resistance, discussed above, may require tolerance on the part of the underkeepers. Alteration of records and accounts provides evidence of collaboration or at least connivance between authorities and the board of inspectors.

Resistance, expressed as both collective and individual action, *should* permeate every aspect of institutional life: the imposition of new and humbling behaviors, confinement in cells, and mandatory attendance at religious

153

services. The entire emphasis of the Jacksonian prison program, whether in the Pennsylvania plan or the Auburn plan, was on the erasure of former lifeways and the instillation of new ones. In such a matrix of animosity, how can we even begin to interpret the contestation of power over both time and space?

I suggest that the way to approach the problem is through a strategy that engages the archaeological and historical records as equal partners in the interpretive process. Neither can be privileged over the other since they together constitute the material record of the Rhode Island State Prison. Thus in discussing contests of power in the institution, I first consider the prison workforce. The myriad state-sanctioned documents of control, which reflect the official record of inmate noncompliance with the directives of control, are examined next. The focus then shifts to a geography of resistance across the internal institutional landscape. This is followed by a close reading of the archaeological record and its implications for understanding individual and collective efforts to reshape the balance of power over time and space.

The Prison Workforce

Inmates, as the primary producers in the institutional matrix, constitute the most direct link to the activities in the prison workshops. They spent ten- to sixteen-hour days—the bulk of their time in confinement—laboring at the various tasks. But who were these state and county prisoners? From what economic and social classes were they drawn? And what preparation, if any, did they have for a sentence of hard labor?

Case Studies in Confinement

Some level of demographic analysis of the inmate population is possible through a close reading of committal books, census schedules, and other state documents. Before proceeding to this analysis, I propose to consider three case studies drawn from the file of petitions for pardon that survives in the Rhode Island State Archives. The narrative histories of John O'Brien, Joseph McAdam, and James O'Neill are intriguing because they provide richly detailed descriptions of the circumstance of the crimes, the comportment of the accused at their trials, and subsequent appraisals of the inmates' pre- and postsentencing work habits. Eventually, O'Neill proved to be unambiguously innocent of the crime for which he was convicted. O'Brien's case was somewhat doubtful, and authorities never did fully investigate that of McAdam. Taken together, the case studies demonstrate several aspects of punishment in nineteenth-century Rhode Island: first, the state's determination that no crime should go unpunished, even if an innocent person might suffer; second, the importance of steady work habits, both before the individual was enmeshed in the criminal justice system and after confinement, in assessing reform; third, and most important, how curiously the path could lead from citizen-worker to inmate in the state prison.

"No intent to kill": The case of John O'Brien. Early on the morning of July 4, 1860, a tall, powerfully built man named Daniel Bennet and a friend of his known only as "Johnson" boarded a train at Stonington, Connecticut, and purchased tickets for Providence. The two planned to spend the holiday with a third friend in "the Hollow," one of the less savory neighborhoods in the burgeoning city. Arriving at Union Depot, designed by the late Thomas Tefft, the two met their friend and went to Lincoln's House, a bar in Canal Street, at about 10:00 a.m. The three left quite an impression on the staff of the public house. Between their arrival and their hasty departure at around 11:30 a.m., Bennet, Johnson, and the third man consumed an extraordinary amount of cheap whiskey. One year later John Foster, the bartender, could still remember Bennet: "[D]uring the time he was there, he called for liquor, and drank it, as many as a dozen times I think. I am sure and am ready to say positively that he drank as many as ten times or more" (Affidavit of John Foster, 1–2; the petitions for pardon are all contained in General Treasurer's Records C 1184, 47C:1, RISA; excerpts cited in the pages that follow are from individual documents within the case files).

What happened next is not entirely clear (nor could it possibly have been to Bennet or anyone directly involved in the affair). While standing on the sidewalk in front of Lincoln's House, Bennet saw a machinist named John O'Brien walk by; he and his friends satisfied themselves by screaming some obscenities at him before going back into the bar (Joseph M. Blake to Governor James F. Smith, no date given, 2). O'Brien ignored the insults but did not forget them. Several minutes later he was pushing his way toward Bennet through the throngs at Lincoln's House, accompanied by Timothy Calahan, Dennis Calahan, James Moran, John McGarvey, Stephen Barry, John Curran, and two other men who were never identified.

In many ways John O'Brien was representative of the new immigrants who were finding work in Providence's industrial economy. O'Brien was born in Ireland in 1839, and his parents, Dennis and Catherine, had immigrated to Rhode Island between 1839 and 1847. By 1858 O'Brien was employed at Thurston and Gardner's mills. Three days before the murder, William Nichols had hired O'Brien as a boilermaker at the sprawling Corliss Steam Engine Company. O'Brien was to start work on the Monday after July 4.

O'Brien would never enjoy the opportunity to start his new position. He and his friends set on Bennet and Johnson and proceeded to beat the two thoroughly with their fists and feet; O'Brien, standing on top of the bar, let fly with a kick to the back of Bennet's head. Bennet's local friend fled, never to be identified or questioned. Bruised and bleeding, Bennet and Johnson stumbled out into Canal Street. An officer of the watch noticed that despite being outnumbered, Bennet had given as good as he had gotten and had "a severe bruise on the knuckles of his right hand." Sometime between 3:00 and 4:00 p.m., Bennet and Johnson were conveyed to the watch house to sleep off the effects of the alcohol and the fight. The next day at 9:00 a.m., a Dr. Ely recorded "no alarming symptom" for Bennet; lying on his back, he projected the image of one recovering from "a severe debauch." Six hours later a Dr. Collins visited Bennet and called for him to be removed to the Dexter Asylum for medical treatment. By 5:00 p.m. on July 5, when the two doctors arrived at the asylum, Bennet was dead.

John O'Brien and his identified accomplices were arrested and remanded to the Providence County Jail to await the results of a grand jury investigation. In September the jury returned a true bill against them, finding that they "being of evil minds and dispositions unlawfully and wickedly in and upon one Daniel G. Bennett [*sic*] . . . did beat, strike, and kick upon the head, face, neck, breast, belly, sides, back, and other parts of the body," with Bennet's death resulting. All were charged with murder; all pleaded not guilty.

At the trial the defense, led by the attorney Joseph Blake, revolved around whether it could be said with certainty that the beating in Lincoln's House had led directly to Bennet's death. A perfunctory postmortem by the two doctors had noted the cause of death as "intoxication and violence." Dr. Ely testified that he could not attribute the death to one cause or the other; Dr. Collins, however, testified "that there were appearances which he could not account for upon any other supposition than that of death from violence" (Joseph M. Blake to Governor James F. Smith, no date given, 4). Inexplicably, of the six defendants, O'Brien was the only one found guilty. Blake brought forward a motion for a new trial; a cart man had seen Bennet involved in a fight earlier in the day, which resulted in a wound to his head.

The bartender, John Foster, came forward and reported that he had served Bennet and his friend ten glasses of whiskey in the two hours they had sat in Lincoln Street, a circumstance overlooked during the trial. The request was denied. On February 7, 1863, John O'Brien was sentenced to life imprisonment at hard labor in the state prison.

Six years after Bennet's murder, Blake began the laborious process of assembling a petition for his client's pardon. "I thought when O'Brien was sentenced, that if his conduct in prison should be such as to confirm my favorable opinion of his character, I would in a year or two petition for his pardon," Blake wrote in a letter to Governor James F. Smith (Joseph M. Blake to Governor James F. Smith, no date given, 2). After reviewing the evidence in the case, he noted his recent discovery of a third time that day when Bennet had suffered a blow to the head: "Information given me by Hon. Walter S. Burgess [indicates] that after said quarrel in Canal Street, when said Bennet and his Connecticut friend were being taken to the Watch-House in College Street, he resisted the Police Officers and was 'clubbed in the head' by them" (Joseph M. Blake to Governor James F. Smith, no date given, 5). This information too had never surfaced at the original trial.

Amazingly even O'Brien's former prosecutor, now in private practice, expressed sympathy and support for a pardon. "I certainly have no objection to the exercise of executive clemency in this case," wrote the same Walter Burgess who had provided Blake with the key information about the earlier fight, "and should feel I must confess considerable personal satisfaction should he be restored to his liberty" (Walter S. Burgess to Joseph M. Blake, March 20, 1866, 1). Burgess, who had hoped for a conviction of manslaughter at best, had been stunned when the law and order-minded jury had returned a conviction for murder in the case: "I was always satisfied that John had no *intent* to kill the man who insulted him," Burgess declared, adding that he was pleased indeed that Blake was going to all the trouble to prepare the petition (Walter S. Burgess to Joseph M. Blake, March 20, 1866, 1; emphasis in original).

One of the key documents in the petition for pardon was an appraisal of the inmate's behavior and his conduct at work in the state prison. On March 14, 1866, Warden Richard Blaisdell provided an affidavit concerning O'Brien's tenure in the prison. After reviewing the case and significant dates, Blaisdell wrote, "As to [O'Brien's] conduct, I also certify that ever since I have been connected with said prison as Warden & Deputy Warden it has been good, and such as to indicate a good disposition and kind feeling to others" (Petition of John O'Brien, Certificate of R. W. Blaisdell).

No record exists of John O'Brien's receiving a full pardon from the governor. He was, however, released from the Rhode Island State Prison on June 2, 1866, for "expiration of his sentence." This suggests that as a compromise between keeping him in prison and pardoning him, the authorities may have consented to alter his conviction to manslaughter, with an appropriately shorter sentence than the life imprisonment he had received for Bennet's murder. Whatever the reason, reprieve came too late. On November 19, 1866—less than six months after he was released—the Providence city clerk recorded John O'Brien's death from "chronic pleurisy" at his mother's home. Wrongful conviction, hard labor, and the relentlessly severe conditions at the state prison had all taken their toll on the unfortunate John O'Brien.

Joseph McAdam steals a watch. The case of Joseph McAdam, convicted and sentenced to two and a half years in 1865 for stealing a watch, illustrates at least the potential importance of preconviction work habits for would-be recipients of pardons. Born in Massachusetts in 1845, McAdam had moved south to Rhode Island with his parents in the late 1850s. In 1864 he enlisted in the Second Rhode Island Infantry Regiment and was stationed at Fort Adams in Newport. Private McAdam was a member of Company G, newly formed to offset significant regimental losses at Spotsylvania and the Wilderness region in Virginia. While Company G awaited its orders to join the regiment in Virginia, its members amused themselves by wreaking havoc on the local citizenry. Thomas Tilley, city marshal for Newport, later described to Governor Burnside the events of September 23, 1864, that led to Private McAdam's arrest. The night started in a Thames Street saloon, where the barkeeper told Tilley that at "about 12Oclock six Soldiers amongst whom the two convicted came to his saloon and purchased a bottle of liquor each and then blew out the light and ran away without paying for it, he knew them well as they had been at his place often" (Thomas Tilley to Governor Ambrose Burnside, June 1, 1867, 1–2). The besotted soldiers continued to wend their way back to the fort. Along the way they stopped at the house of a man named Rutherford, who "heard some noise in the yard & opened the window up stairs and asked what they wanted, they said Water, he came to the door with a pail of ice water in one hand and a lamp in the Other, he found six soldiers and noticed one had very sore eyes and told him he would give him a receipt that would cure them" (Thomas Tilley to Governor Ambrose Burnside, June 1, 1867, 1). Rutherford's reward for this act of kindness was a vicious assault in which the soldiers threw him to the ground before beating him thoroughly. One of the soldiers used a slingshot to bring down a bystander named Duffy, who tried to break up the melee. The next day Rutherford and Duffy appeared at the fort and identified McAdam as the one who had led the assault. Tried and convicted of larceny on a person in September 1865, McAdam was sentenced to two years and six months at hard labor commencing on November 23, 1865 (*Newport Daily News*, November 24, 1865, 2).

During his trial McAdam did little to help his cause. Tilley recalled that "his conduct when sentence was pronounced was extremely ugly," adding that a key witness had later reported that McAdam "threatened him severely I think he said he would be the death of him when he got out" (Thomas Tilley to [?] Stevens, March 13, 1867, 1). A year and a half later, with a year remaining on Joseph's sentence, McAdam's brother and father (both named Peter) initiated a petition for a pardon, representing that Joseph "was never before charged with any crime and up to that time had always maintained a good character with his employers" (Peter McAdam and Peter McAdam Jr. to Governor Ambrose Burnside, January 22, 1867, 1).

Some ambiguities did exist in the case. The prosecution's case rested on Rutherford's complaint that McAdam had stolen his watch during the assault. Tilley noted that when Rutherford and Duffy went to the fort, the commanding officers turned up several watches from the knapsacks of Company G, none of which was Rutherford's (Thomas Tilley to Governor Ambrose Burnside, June 1, 1867, 2). McAdam did indeed have a watch that was not his own, but it belonged to a man named Daniel Weaver, who had been recently attacked by a group of soldiers (McAdam claimed to have bought the watch from a fellow soldier at a remarkably low price). Furthermore, McAdam had had no opportunity to call witnesses who would support his alibi. Arrested as Company G marched from Fort Adams down to the ship on which they would sail for the South, he must have watched in dismay as the ship carrying his potential witnesses weighed anchor, got under way, and disappeared into the broad Atlantic Ocean.

McAdam *pere et fils* solicited supporting letters from their brother's former employers as testaments to his good character. Willard B. Scott testified, "McAdams [*sic*] was in my employ about eighteen month [*sic*] before the war. . . . The boy was a very good, honest, industrious lad, and not a person that would be apt to commit such a crime, as that with which he is charged" (Willard B. Scott to Governor Ambrose Burnside, January 22, 1867, 1). William Haskell, Scott's former partner in the jewelry manufacturing business, echoed Scott's defense of their employee: "He was an industrious, honest, well behaved boy giving entire satisfaction to myself and my partner. I do not believe him guilty of the crime for which he was convicted, and should be glad to see him released from prison" (William Haskell to Governor Ambrose Burnside, no date).

Thus the habits and industry of the citizen-worker prior to imprisonment were crucial standards for the appraisal of character in the ritual of the petition for pardon. Of even greater interest is the emphasis on the honesty and character of the petitioners in the process—in this case, Peter McAdam and his son, who included letters from their own employers as part of the petition package. "Peter McAdam, the father of Joseph McAdam . . . has been in our employ seventeen years," wrote Messrs. Congdon and Carpenter, "and we value him for his honesty, sobriety, and faithfulness, and we have confidence that any statement he may make can be relied upon" (Congdon and Carpenter to Governor Ambrose Burnside, January 22, 1867, 1). S. G. Arnold, the employer of Peter McAdam Jr., offered a ringing endorsement of his charge: "Peter Jr. has been with me for the past five years & is still in my employ. He is truthful, honest in every respect and I place full reliance on his statements" (S. G. Arnold to Governor Ambrose Burnside, January 23, 1867).

Despite the endorsements of all three members of the McAdam family as positive examples of sober workers, the petition for pardon apparently failed. Perhaps the references all sounded too similar; perhaps Joseph McAdam was simply too close to the end of his sentence. He was granted a token two days' sentence reduction and was released from the Rhode Island State Prison on May 22, 1868. His activities after his release cannot be traced.

The strange case of James O'Neill. The case of James O'Neill was considerably more convoluted. On October 15, 1862, the *Newport Daily News* reported on "a disturbance . . . of a most disgraceful nature . . . indicative of the grossest insubordination" at the Providence camp of the Twelfth and Thirteenth Regiments. Members of the Thirteenth Regiment had been playing "foot-ball" on the Dexter Training Ground when a dispute erupted. Several officers trying to break up the quarrel were injured severely, especially one Lieutenant Taber of the Twelfth, who suffered a broken cheekbone in the fray.

Lieutenant Taber was a popular officer in his regiment. The *Daily News* reported that a group of soldiers from the Twelfth Regiment, Company D, formed with the sole purpose of punishing the attackers from the Thirteenth. Laying siege to their targets, they chased them across the training ground and into a nearby blacksmith shop. Precisely what happened inside

A SMALL AMOUNT HAS BEEN ACCOMPLISHED

the blacksmith shop could not be determined, but James Simmons, the drummer for Company D, received "the fatal stab in the abdomen with a dirk knife" (*Newport Daily News*, October 15, 1862, 2). Simmons's attacker fled the camp. The *Daily News* noted mournfully that "James Simmons is reported more comfortable, although but little hopes are entertained of his recovery." The paper's worst fears were confirmed two days later: "James Simmons is dead. . . . Gone! Not on the field of battle with the flag of his country waving o'er him; Gone, not in the hour of victory, with the shouts of triumph wafting his spirit on his heavenward way, but killed ere he saw the field of carnage—butchered and murdered by the hands of the assassin" (*Newport Daily News*, October 17, 1862, 2). The death of one of Newport's soldiers at the hands of one or more recruits likely from Providence infuriated the *Daily News*: "It makes us almost weep to think such things can happen, and to know how it wrings the blood from out [of] young hearts that love."

Little more was reported on the murder of James Simmons until nearly a year later, when the *Providence Daily Journal* trumpeted the news of "An Important Arrest" (*Providence Daily Journal*, September 2, 1863, 2). One James O'Niel [*sic*], a deserter from the Twelfth Regiment, had been arrested in Pawcatuck, Connecticut, just across the border from Westerly, Rhode Island. He had drifted from Providence to Boston to Westerly, where he had found employment in a local mill. Rumors about his involvement in the murder of Simmons had followed him throughout his wanderings. The *Journal* saw the persistent association of these rumors with O'Neill as convincing evidence of his complicity in the crime: "When O'Niel was in custody, he said 'I know what you've arrested me for; you haven't arrested me as a deserter, but for killing that soldier.'" In the eyes of the *Journal*, O'Neill continued to implicate himself: "And so he continued to talk of the affair on the Training-Ground, about which no other person had said a word. His voluntary information is conclusive as to his guilt" (*Providence Daily Journal*, September 2, 1863, 2). An officer and two enlisted men who had served with O'Neill in the Twelfth Regiment quickly identified him as Simmons's murderer. One month later he pleaded not guilty in Rhode Island Supreme Court (*Providence Daily Journal*, October 12, 1863, 2). On January 7, 1864, O'Neill, convicted of murder, was sentenced to life imprisonment at hard labor in the Rhode Island State Prison.

Everything concerning O'Neill's arrest, conviction, and imprisonment was clean and tidy. There was just one series of details that everyone (except O'Neill) contrived to overlook. O'Neill, a native of Manchester, England, who had immigrated to Philadelphia, had served in the 109th

Pennsylvania Regiment. He had never belonged to the Twelfth Rhode Island Regiment and had never met any of the regiment's witnesses who testified that they had seen him kill Simmons. On the day of the murder he had been confined to a convalescent camp in Bolivar Heights, Virginia, a circumstance he explained patiently to the Reverend Augustus Woodbury in an undated and convoluted letter: "I respect the XIX Deuteronomy 18 and 19 says against false witnesses. I don't want any body punished but I think it hard to be kept in prison and have to work at hard labour just for false witnesses" (James O'Neill to Augustus Woodbury, letter not dated).

To his credit, Woodbury took O'Neill's story seriously and began to look into the matter. Gradually the facts behind the case began to emerge. O'Neill's brother-in-law, Sergeant Thomas Brady of the First New Jersey Cavalry, testified that he had run into James at a convalescent camp in Virginia near the time of the murder. O'Neill had relayed to him a harrowing story about the Battle of Cedar Mountain, Virginia:

> I asked him what he was limping about and he told me he was
> wounded at Cedar Mountain on the 9th day of August 1862, he
> was taken prisoner and lay Twenty seven (27) hours on the field
> until our forces captured the field again, he told me that a rebel
> lieutenant filled his canteen with water, and gave him some
> biscuit, and the rebels carried him under a large tree to keep
> the sun off him, and there left him as our men were coming up,
> and they had to leave, that was all the conversation we had.

(Affidavit of Thomas Brady in the Matter of James O'Neill)

Further confirmation came from Joseph Wilmarth, a former member of the Twelfth Regiment. Authorities conveyed Wilmarth to the Rhode Island State Prison and asked him to identify James O'Neill as the James O'Neill who had served in the regiment. Baffled, Wilmarth signed an affidavit asserting that the man in prison "is a total stranger to me" (Affidavit of Joseph Wilmarth in the Matter of James O'Neill).

Was there a second James O'Neill? And did the two resemble one another closely enough to cause this level of confusion? Woodbury, now head of a formal investigatory committee, had an ambrotype made of O'Neill and dispatched it to Philadelphia with Justice of the Peace Charles A. Collis. Thomas Reed, a loom fixer, deposed that he recognized the man in the ambrotype as James O'Neill, whom he had known for twenty years. For a time O'Neill had lived in his father's house in Manchester. "I last saw him on a Sunday in the middle of November 1862 in Carrol Street, Kensington,"

A SMALL AMOUNT HAS BEEN ACCOMPLISHED

Reed affirmed. "He was wounded—he was just out of the hospital" (Affidavit of Thomas Reed in the Matter of James O'Neill, 1). Michael O'Brien, a weaver, had run into O'Neill at about the same time in November, when O'Neill was still recovering from the leg wound received at Cedar Mountain. O'Neill had told him that he was going back to his regiment. "I have looked at the accompanying ambrotype marked with the letter A and recognize it as the likeness of James O'Neil [sic] of whom I have testified," concluded O'Brien (Affidavit of Michael O'Brien in the Matter of James O'Neill, 1).

The committee wrote to the adjutant general's office for the muster roll of the 109th Pennsylvania and to the former paymaster of the regiment for confirmation from the payroll records. O'Neill's presence on both sets of documents in September and October 1862 finally convinced state authorities that they had the wrong man. On April 19, 1872, O'Neill, who had been kept unaware of the ongoing investigation, was dumbfounded when authorities told him that he was pardoned after serving more than eight years for a murder he had not committed. "Then the good news was broken gently to him and he appeared dazed with happiness. He came out of the prison and said 'How sweet the air smells'" (*Providence Journal*, January 20, 1879, 2). The state awarded O'Neill the munificent sum of two hundred dollars and sent him on his way under the care of his brother-in-law. Perhaps of greater significance, a bill to restore the death penalty (abolished in the state in 1852) "dropped out of sight with great celerity" (*Providence Journal*, January 20, 1879, 2). O'Neill, whose "mind had been seriously injured" during his time in prison, died penniless in Philadelphia some years later.

It is difficult to draw many conclusions from the case studies of O'Brien, McAdam, and O'Neill. They represent only 3 of the approximately 847 individuals who found themselves confined behind the granite walls on Gaspee Street. Their cases do point to some broader conclusions, elaborated below. First, the state punished mob activity, especially that which led to violence against citizens, seriously and with all dispatch. Second, the state's targets of punishment were the powerless and dispossessed. Although many of the inmates in the Rhode Island State Prison no doubt deserved to be there, the wrath of the state fell particularly hard on those without influence or powerful friends. Third, and most important, was the equation of nonnatives with criminals. O'Brien was born in Ireland, O'Neill in England to Irish parents, and McAdam in Massachusetts to Irish-born parents. Taken together, they constituted a class that middle-class Providence viewed with deepening suspicion.

Demographic Analysis

Between 1838 and November 1878 a total of 912 sentences were made to the Rhode Island State Prison, representing a total of 847 individuals. Of these individuals only 32 were women, a remarkable circumstance; viewed in concert with census data, we are left with the unmistakable impression of the "maleness" of the institutions. When Thomas Cleaveland assumed his duties as the first keeper of the state prison, he had 3 inmates, all men. Fifteen years later, of the 193 individuals who had been committed to the state prison since it had opened, only 7 had been women (*ARBI* 1854, 14). The trend continued to the end of the institution's tenure in Providence (table 2). On January 1, 1876, for example, 56 prisoners—all men—filled the cells of the state prison. In the county jail there were 135 inmates, 128 of whom were men. Thus only 7 of the 191 inmates in the entire complex (3.6 percent) were women. At the close of the year the ratio was similar: 86 state prisoners, all men, and of the 161 county jail inmates, 14 women, constituting 5.7 percent of the institutional population.

Age categories are relatively similar for the two institutions; they may not be meaningful, especially considering the duration of sentences. But there is certainly a real difference in the two populations in terms of ethnicity. The majority of state prisoners were southern New Englanders, born and raised in Rhode Island, Connecticut, and Massachusetts. The county jail, however, was a different story. An assessment conducted at the end of 1867 found that in that year a total of 870 individuals had passed through the revolving doors of the county jail. Of these, 406 (47 percent) were natives of Ireland; Rhode Island natives constituted 18.4 percent of the county jail population. This disparity reflects the anti-Irish sentiment prevalent in Providence through much of the mid- and late-nineteenth century. Irish workers tended to be picked up, first by the watchmen and then by the more formal Providence police, for vagrancy, loitering, and a wide range of other questionable offenses. The virulent rhetoric of nativism was occasionally appalling. An 1894 letter from an anonymous citizen of Providence to the editor of the *Citizen*, a Boston newspaper choked with anti-Catholic sentiments, expressed this prejudice succinctly: "The religious faith of those committed [to Rhode Island state institutions] stands in the proportion of three Roman Catholics to one Protestant. In the face of these figures, is it not about time that the American portion of our people and the better element of our foreign citizens, united against the pauper and criminal element governing our cities?" (*Boston Citizen*, January 6, 1894, 2). The writer went on to exhort residents of Providence to be ever vigilant, and to "see to it that her police and militia are not filled from the dangerous classes."

TABLE 2

Demographic Profile of Rhode Island State Prison
and Providence County Jail Populations

Year	Number		Age[1]		Gender[2]		Nativity[3]		Literacy[4]	
	SP	CJ	SP	CJ	SP	CJ	SP	CJ	SP	CJ
1840			30	24	17:1	23:1	17:1	nd	nd	nd
1860	67	87	31	22	33:1	19:1	33:1	1:2	100%	100%
1865			29	25	11:1	14:1	22:1	1:2	70%	40%
1870			28	21	24:1	18:1	48:1	1:1.5	100%	51%
1876	56	135	33	22	56:1	16:1	56:1	1:2	100%	48%

SOURCES: Manuscript Federal Census Schedules (1840, 1860, 1870); Manuscript Rhode Island Census Schedules (1865); Annual Report of the Board of Inspectors (1876).

[1]Expressed as the median age of the inmate population.

[2]Expressed as the ratio of male to female inmates

[3]Expressed as the ratio of American-born to foreign-born

[4]Expressed as the percentage of prisoners listed as able to read and write

The literacy rate for state prisoners was especially high and compared favorably with the general population. In 1860 the percentage of inmates who could not read or write was zero. Five years later the state prison literacy rate was 70 percent; five prisoners (14 percent) could read but not write, and six (16 percent) could neither read nor write. These returns suggest a surprisingly high ability of prisoners to at least read and write their own names. In 1875, for example, 6 percent of all citizens of the state of Rhode Island could neither read nor write and 2 percent could read but not write (Perry 1887, Table XLII). But we do not know the literacy rate of the inmates prior to entering the prison or what degree of the literacy derived from the educational component of the institution. Wardens from Thomas Cleaveland forward had instituted an aggressive educational program; by 1857 authorities had assembled a prison library of nearly six hundred titles, ranging from the vocational (*Allen's American Farm Book, Cabinet Maker's Guide, Handbook of the Useful Arts*) to the inspirational (*Autobiography of a Blind Minister, Beecher's Letters to Young Men*) to the virulently nativist (*History of Popery, The Papal Conspiracy Exposed, History of the Protestant Refugees*).

Thus the results of demographic analysis are ambiguous. We are left with the interpretation that the "average" state prison inmate was a white male, New England born, who could at least write his name and read. The average county jail inmate was a white male, more likely to be first- or second-generation Irish born, who was less likely to be able to read or write. But what, if anything, do these tendencies suggest about the inmates' abilities to comprehend and comply in the requirement of daily work?

Perhaps a better guide to the demographic composition is seen in the occupations of prisoners before incarceration. For the state prison, the first evidence we have is from the 1860 federal census. No occupation is given for fifty-four of the sixty-six inmates. However, because the remaining twelve were all artisans (blacksmith, stonecutter, painter, silversmith), it is possible that the census taker did not record laborer as an occupation. None was listed as owning property: "The *State prison system* settles accounts quite as effectively as does the executioner of the rich bourgeois State," wrote Bukharin and Preobrazhensky (1969 [1922], 87; emphasis in original). "Its shafts are directed, not against the rich, but against the poor." Five years later the Rhode Island state census was considerably more specific. Here we see a breakdown between laborers (n = 24, or 66 percent) and a variety of artisans, farmers, and mariners. In 1875, the last year for which occupations are available, we see a real cross section of society emphasizing industrial occupations (machinist, engineer, plater).

The analysis of occupations suggests that based on inmates' previous experiences, there was no inherent reason for the labor program to fail. In terms of trades and occupations, at least as recorded by authorities, prisoners had a wide range of abilities that might well have proven useful in an industrial operation. At the very least, they were used to work, with a surprising number classified as skilled or semiskilled artisans. Unfortunately, we have almost no firsthand accounts evaluating the skills of the individuals or assessing their respective work ethics. The analysis leaves us dependent on the paradigm of resistance and all its attendant aspects of human activity.

Documents of Control

I have already noted the increase in the mechanisms of control—seen in the steady accumulation of ledgers, maps, and a telegraph system—in the warden's office of the Rhode Island State Prison. The realization of the need for these items, their maintenance and upkeep, and the sporadic innovations (keeping ledgers in duplicate, for example) are all concepts that spring from twin needs: the need to control (which is the raison d'être of the penal institution) and the need to document, justify, and otherwise shield local authorities from the scrutiny of state overseers.

The earliest surviving document of control is the *Convict Labor Ledger* (319 B:1, RISA), a leather folio purchased from a local stationer, which indicates Thomas Cleaveland's enthusiasm for the new labor program. Written in his sprawling hand is the title: "Amount of Convicts Labor in the R.I. State Prison Commencing Oct. 1. 1840." The ledger's span (October 1840 through March 1843) covers both shoe making and the transition into fan painting. Entries are broken out by week, with the number of the prisoner, the work s/he was engaged in, and the value of the work completed during the week.

From this document we learn much about the mechanics of daily production during the regime of shoe making and gain insight into some of the labor program's structural deficiencies. First, we are able to see the gendering of work in the prison. During the period covered by the ledger, there was but one female inmate in the state prison. Instead of making shoes, she was put to work sewing clothing, linens, and blankets for her fellow inmates. On November 28, 1840, Cleaveland noted that the prisoner, known only as No. 17, had made "Four Shirts and 4 Pillows; No. 17 Previously Made 20 Comforters, 12 Shirts, twenty towels & Sundry Mending." It is not clear whether Cleaveland considered shoe making inappropriate for a woman or whether her sewing skills were more valuable than the production of additional shoes.

The ledger also notes the staggering amount of work lost due to sickness in the Haviland-designed state prison. In his weekly summaries Cleaveland provided two figures at the bottom of the page. The first is the total dollar value of the goods produced during the week. Interestingly, No. 17's sewing contributions are valued at zero, reflecting both the use of the items within the prison and a dismissive attitude toward "women's work." The second figure is the dollar value of work lost on account of inmate sickness. The sickness figures were incorporated into monthly statements as well as occasional notes by Cleaveland. On December 12, 1840, for example, he wrote, "By the above it will be seen that 37 1/2 per cent of the labour during the last five weeks is lost from sickness consequently a small amount has been accomplished." The unanticipated extent of disease in the dungeonlike cells, combined with the increase in insanity, caused the board of inspectors to backpedal from their previous predictions concerning the success of prison labor (*ARRIGA* October 1845, 42–43).

A SMALL AMOUNT HAS BEEN ACCOMPLISHED

But the most important observations from the ledger lie in the occasional marginal notes relating to discipline, especially for offenses concerning labor. These notes are scrawled in the right-hand side of the ledger and, prior to the development of documents reporting exclusively on punishment in the 1870s, represent the only way to track such offenses in the 1840s. They probably do not represent the complete realm of offenses but can be considered a representative sample of infractions in the Pennsylvania-plan prison.

Cleaveland and the board of inspectors always asserted that much of the initial success in the shoe-making program came from the inmates' sheer relief at having something to do other than stare at the gray stone walls of their cells. His marginalia bear this contention out. During the twenty-eight months covered by the ledger, reports of discipline breaches are rare. Not surprisingly, most concern attempts by inmates to communicate with one another or with people passing by on Gaspee Street. On October 31, 1840, for example, Cleaveland noted that "Nos. 14, 15 & 16 violated the rules of the Prison by talking through the windows. It being their first offense no punishment was imposed." On June 12, 1841, a similar offense occurred, with a harder punishment: "Nos. 17 & 20 were cut short of their regular allowance of food one day for talk with each other out the windows."

In some cases we are left ignorant of the punishment. An example is an entry dated September 25, 1841: "No. 8 violated the 7th Rule of regulations by being impertinent to the underkeeper Mr. Greene and was punished accordingly." No offenses were taken more seriously than failure to participate in the requirement of daily work. On July 13, 1841, Cleaveland noted that "No. 25 Refusing to work was put upon no allowance [of rations] and cont'd obstinate four days when he retur'd to his duty." More frequent than the marginal notes are entries on the left-hand side of the ledger, next to the numbers of the prisoners and the particular tasks in which they were engaged. Those inmates failing to produce at least six pairs of brogans or pumps during the work week have the notation "discipline" next to their output, but no specific mention of what that discipline encompassed.

Other than the letters and inventories discussed above, documents concerning fan production are limited. It is possible that the frantic rate of production during the years 1844–46 outpaced the administration's ability to maintain accurate ledgers. Alternatively, perhaps the ledgers disappeared with audits and other accounts pertaining to the fans. At least one inmate was disciplined for slowing the production of fans: "No. 35 having

A SMALL AMOUNT HAS BEEN ACCOMPLISHED

been repeatedly guilty of tearing fans, the warden was authorized to cause moderate corporal punishment to be administered," wrote Inspector Thomas M. Burgess in 1845 (MS 231.1, Vol. 234, 36, RIHS). The sloppiness in paperwork during the fan-production era is countered by a mania for compilations during the regime of contract labor, when we see entirely different, more rigorous forms of controlling time, production, and unruly labor. Instead of assessing inmate compliance by quantifying the individual's production, authorities implemented a system of time books (319A:2, RISA). The time books have categories for inmate name, inmate number, and hours worked, with days ordered horizontally across the ledger. Summary monthly tabulations list the number of hours worked by state prisoners and the number worked by county jail inmates. These are then multiplied by the daily amounts paid by the contractors to arrive at the institution's monthly returns on inmate labor.

The difference in record keeping reflects the underpinnings of the philosophical shift in labor policy. In the more idealistic era of shoe making, what counted most was that inmates were working steadily and developing the habit of daily labor. Now, with the state's gamble on contracts with outside firms, record keeping became essential. Inmate labor lost to sickness or other factors was no longer a matter between authorities and the inmate; it was a matter of lost revenue for the institution's coffers and would be punished accordingly.

Thus we should not be surprised that, when labor is tied directly to revenue, new systems of incentives and punishments are implemented. The great innovation in incentive is "good time," or credit toward reducing the overall sentence. But no innovation is without counter-innovation: at the same time legislators approved the implementation of good time, they instituted *deductions* of credit for intra-institutional offenses. These deductions were compiled and quantified in a series of punishment ledgers covering the years 1872 through 1877 (319C:2, RISA) and constitute a solid basis for examining points of conflict within the prison walls.

It is admittedly difficult to look at some of these offenses, from a late twentieth-century perspective, without a certain sense of amusement at their apparent triviality: "Early Rising," "Humming in Cell," and "Destroying his Pants" are some of the more unusual examples. But as we look more closely at offenses, it becomes clear that the vast majority of inmate actions are directed at slowing down the machinery of the workshops, whether literally (by sabotaging machinery, for example) or figuratively (by avoiding work). With the 1872–77 punishment ledgers, we finally have an emic way of tracking the relative seriousness of offenses in the minds of prison authorities. Rather than abstractions ("punished accordingly") or corporal discipline (noted but rarely quantified), punishments are now provided in empirical, quantifiable terms of "good time" lost by the offending inmate. These are given, next to the names and offenses, by figures denoting the days lost, which almost always range from one to three. Marginalia supply information about extraordinary supplemental punishments ("in chains," "in solitary confinement"). Rather than take the initial assumption that punishment was handed out more frequently for offenses pertaining to work, we should look more closely at the data and see what they indicate about the geography of resistance within the complex.

A Geography of Resistance

I chose to analyze the data by tabulating the locations within the prison complex where a total of 1,306 offenses occurred between the years 1872 and 1877 inclusive. Because the location of the offense is noted in 82 percent of the incidents, we may assume that to prison authorities, *where* an offense occurred was equally as important as the nature of the offense. The geography of offenses encompasses both fixed space (cell, chapel, workshop, schoolroom) and abstract space (in line, unspecified). I next quantified the offenses by location, which yielded striking results. The number of offenses recorded in the workshop (789) is more than 1.5 times the number of offenses recorded throughout all other areas of the prison complex combined (517), including those unspecified and unknown (fig. 27).

This finding leads to an important question: does the extraordinarily high number of offenses in the workshop reflect a higher level of inmate misbehavior in this particular area? Or was work so important that authorities chose to enforce a different standard in the workshop, one with greater strictures than elsewhere in the complex? Realistically, the two are linked inextricably. If inmates spent nearly two-thirds of their sentences at their benches in the workshops, then it stands to reason that there were substantially more opportunities for deviant behavior there than in the chapel, occupied for one hour a week. At the same time, mindful of this opportunity, authorities enforced the rules in an especially strict manner. Collective action with dangerous objects was more possible in the workshop than at any other locus, if for no other reason than the amount of time inmates spent there. That possibility kept the workshop at the nexus of resistance and retaliation.

An analysis of the workshop infractions reinforces authorities' vision of a silent and disciplined workforce. Using the geographical breakdown, I

WORKSHOP (789)

CELL BLOCK
(117)

WASH ROOM (4)

LINE (100)

Fig. 27 — *A geography of resistance: locations and numbers of intra-institutional offenses, 1872–77. Photograph by the author.*

calculated the number of offenses and the days of good time deducted by location (table 3). Dividing the latter by the former yields the average deduction for an offense committed in a particular sector of the prison. The message of "respect work" was imparted seriously in the workshop, where penalties averaged significantly more than elsewhere in the institution.

We now need to look more closely at the problems in the workshop to assess the nature of noncompliance (table 4). The range of offenses can be grouped into three larger categories: attempts to communicate (whether by looking around, talking, whistling, or making eye contact); destruction of tools and materials; and general misconduct, including "persistent bad behavior," fighting, and most intriguing, attempts to evade work through self-mutilation.

We might well stop here and ask what these offenses and their frequency say about both the perpetrators and the punishers. First, the figures should not mislead us into thinking that the workshop was a scene of perpetual chaos and strife. Between the years 1872 and 1877 there were 1,872 days of work. With 1,306 offenses recorded, this works out to an average of

TABLE 3

Locations and Numbers of Intra-institutional Offenses, with Average "Good Time" Deductions, 1872–1877

Location of Offenses	Number Deducted	Total Days Deduction	Average
Shop	789	2316.5	2.94
Schoolroom	5	13.0	2.60
Unspecified/ unknown	233	580.0	2.49
Line	100	246.0	2.46
Chapel	58	131.0	2.26
Cell	117	257.0	2.20
Washroom	4	7.0	1.75
TOTALS	1306	3550.5	2.72

SOURCE: "Punishment/Discipline Books," Rhode Island State Archives (319 C:2), Providence.

A SMALL AMOUNT HAS BEEN ACCOMPLISHED

TABLE 4

Intra-institutional Offenses in the Prison Workshop, 1872–1877

Offense	Years Noted	Total Incidents
Attempts to Communicate		
Talking/making noise	1872–77	346
Looking/gazing around	1872–77	184
Communicating	1872–77	68
Singing	1872–73; 1875	5
Making grimaces	1876	1
Destruction of Tools or Materials		
Wasting cane or stock	1874–76	19
Damaging/destroying work	1872–73; 1876	11
Destroying tools	1872–73; 187	4
General Misconduct		
Disorderly conduct	1872–76	61
Refusing to work	1873–75; 1877	40
Fighting	1874–75	2
Carelessness/neglect/laziness	1872–76	18
Leaving bench	1872; 1876	7
Stealing	1872–75	23
TOTAL		789

SOURCE: "Punishment/Discipline Books," Rhode Island State Archives (319 C:2), Providence.

a recorded offense every 1.4 days. Yet remember, we are only able to measure *recorded* mayhem. We lack the ability to discern the vast range of offenses that went undetected or unpunished. Those actions surely must have shaped the entire atmosphere of the workshop, infusing the industrial operation with a silent but discernible tension throughout its granite walls.

The implications of the recorded actions for interpreting the archaeological record of the site are intriguing. One would expect offenses grouped under the subheading "Destruction of Tools or Materials" to have a much more visible archaeological component than those grouped under the subheadings "Attempts to Communicate" and "General Misconduct." An offense such as "Throwing cane down the privy" would lead the twentieth-century archaeologist to the privy, where, after digging faithfully through layers of waste, she would be rewarded with a bundle of unused and water-logged chair-seating cane. Thus the archaeological record bears out the historical record, and everyone is satisfied that the resistive act did indeed take place. Similarly, if prisoners were destroying tools—and one would expect that the tools would have to be truly destroyed to be discarded from a low-budget industrial operation like the prison's—then our archaeologist could pace the distance of a hearty throw from a door or window of the workshop, excavate neatly, and expect to be rewarded with a pile of rusty, discarded metal objects.

Such a scenario has already been realized in the archaeology of industrial New England. In an important study from western Massachusetts, Michael S. Nassaney and Marjorie R. Abel (1993, 1996, 2000) looked at the archaeological remains of the John Russell Cutlery Company (1870–1936), where they identified a clear example of "systematic soldiering" among the workforce. They first developed a context for technological change in Russell Cutlery, drawing on issues confronting workers: layoffs, wage cuts, deskilling, and general working conditions (Nassaney and Abel 1993, 267–69). In their examination of archaeological deposits of ruined knife blanks, they raise the question: "Do wasters represent fossilized evidence of a proletarian class-consciousness—a hidden transcript—in the work place?" (Nassaney and Abel 1993, 265). Otherwise-skilled craftsmen, imported from Lancashire for their considerable talent in fashioning knives, found ways to slow down the pace of production by ruining nearly finished products and thereby resisting the creeping industrialization of the plant.

But what about the material correlates of the other two categories of malevolent activity, communication and misconduct? Should we simply assume that because these actions become manifest in a word, a gesture, or an emotion they vanish into ether, leaving no trace on the internal landscape of the prison? Quite to the contrary, it is in these very actions that we find the most compelling archaeological evidence of the contestation of power—that is, in the constant reshaping of the prison's built environment to suit the productive and controlling needs of both authorities and outside contractors.

Rebuilding the Landscape of Confinement: Three Examples

January 14, 1874, was a quiet day in the prison workshop. No one was punished for any offenses, and work continued as usual on boots and brooms for the local firm of Gilman & Greene. Within the workshop, guards walked up and down the rows of workbenches, ensuring that silence was maintained and that production continued its steady pace. At the end of the day the small steam engine in the basement was shut down for the night, the inmates were formed into lines, and the contractors' representatives and prison employees made the rounds of the building to ensure that all was in order.

That night a heavy snow fell on the spires and steeples of Providence. The streets were deserted and quiet in the "excessive cold" of the January night. Shortly after 12:00 a.m., a police officer on Cove Street noticed a plume of jet-black smoke against the clear night sky. He sounded the alarm, but too late; despite the best efforts by the full Providence Fire Department to haul hoses over the prison wall and douse the flames, the attic of the workshop was fully engaged. By the time the firefighters managed to control the blaze, the workshop was in ruins. Fully half of the structure had burned away, leaving a thick layer of soot and ash blowing across the trampled and muddy prison yard. For the first time since the inception of labor in the prison, the industrial process had stopped completely.

A subsequent investigation, conducted by the board of inspectors, failed to determine the cause of the fire. The investigation cleared the prison employees, the guards, and the contractor's representatives of any malfeasance; inmates, though not implicated directly, were considered ultimately responsible for igniting the blaze. Within one week plans for punishing the inmates were in place. They would be put to work rebuilding the workshop, laboring for ten-hour days in the coldest depths of a New England winter. Furthermore, prison authorities trumpeted, the new construction—involving the cross-laying of floor members to create a nearly impenetrable flame retardant—would be virtually fireproof and impermeable to further efforts to derail production.

A SMALL AMOUNT HAS BEEN ACCOMPLISHED

We can well imagine what inmates thought as they dragged the new wooden joists across the prison yard and painstakingly hoisted them into place. The simple lesson from the fire was this: burn down the workshop and we will design a workshop that cannot burn. Better still, inmates, under close supervision, would participate fully in their own oppression by constructing their new cage. Such a task would give them, in the eyes of authorities, intimate knowledge of the ultimate futility of similar acts of sabotage against the state.

Now consider movement through the complex. Remember that numerous official complaints concerned the line, where unruly activities such as talking, joking, and walking too fast could accelerate into violence or an attempt to escape. Unsanctioned movement, after all, could lead to disruption and chaos on the march from the cells to the workshop. But how could authorities control this mass of workers, exposed to fresh air only twice a day, and prevent them from spreading out across the yard and taking collective action against the outnumbered prison staff? Again, the answer was relatively straightforward: over a period of years prisoners laid out cobble-lined pathways, two feet wide, connecting the points of egress and ingress. No mention of this path building occurs in any prison records. But surely the painstaking labor involved in systematically laying out cobblestone after cobblestone (estimated at more than ten thousand total) must have imparted authorities' lessons about the need to move in a controlled and orderly fashion.

A third example is more poignant and, though not executed with malice, expresses indirectly the indifference of authorities to the emotional well-being of their charges. In 1857 business for the prison-manufactured furniture was particularly poor. The contractors running the shop, J. H. Field & Co., had expressed disappointment with the unruly and undependable labor of the state prisoners and were obliged to cease operations at the prison until the larger economic situation corrected itself.

One solution to keep the state prisoners busy involved a lot of land west of the prison, between the wall and Park Street. Warden S. L. Blaisdell, noting that the area was useless, contrived to put the land into production by creating a market garden. Thus men who had served five, ten, and fifteen years in solitary confinement suddenly found themselves out in the sun pushing wheelbarrows of fill to create an even grade and a strong southerly exposure. We can only imagine the improvement in morale and overall psychological health of the inmate population. But by the time the land was filled, graded, and ready to plant, the economic circumstances were such that Field & Co. were ready to resume production. Inmates returned to their lathes and drill presses in the grimy workshop, and the care of the garden was turned over to prison employees. The message this time, while perhaps not intentional, underscores a larger point: the prison exists to make obedient, *industrial* workers out of its "citizenry." The market garden would do in the time of unforeseen shortfall, but no reasonable prison authority in the urban Northeast would consider turning his charges into farmers rather than factory workers.

The final example of the reshaping of the built environment in response to problems in the workplace is perhaps the most dramatic. Notations in the 1872–77 ledgers contain "Dark Cell" as a punishment for repeat offenders or those committing especially heinous offenses. In the official reports, only one mention of the Dark Cell is made: "The Dark Cell is used as a means of punishment for the more serious offences," wrote Warden Nelson Viall in 1870, "but never for a more definite period than one night" (*ARBI* 1871, 13). Longer stays were, however, possible for the recalcitrant: "it is left to the convict himself to decide when he shall be released by promising obedience to the rules."

In the final phase of archaeological investigation, this block of eight cells was uncovered in the basement of the west wing. The cells here measure only four by six feet across the interior—barely enough for a man to lie down in. They were in the dankest portion of the complex, closest to the cove basin, and utterly devoid of light. It is not difficult to imagine the notorious Elisha Peck squatting in one of these cells, listening to the water seep in through the slime-covered stone walls. Here is institutional authority's ultimate response to unruly labor: to bury it, often for days at a time, in the deepest, darkest hole imaginable. It is the final expression of the state's frustration and apathy, and represents the ultimate expression of the built environment's capacity to terrify short of the tomb.

The Dialectic between Labor and Landscape

In tracing the history of forced labor at the Rhode Island State Prison, I have noted a sharp and noticeable change in the institutional matrix between the regimes of labor under the Pennsylvania plan (1838–45) and those under the Auburn plan (1845–78). Myriad forces are engaged in the dialectical process: profits, as expressed by the labor program's ability or lack of ability to pay for itself; tensions between prison managements, retailers, and outside contractors; and inmates, as agents of individual or collective action in resisting the requirement of daily work. Ultimately the phenomenon underlying the more immediate alterations in penal labor is the commodification of prison labor, and its transformation from an idealistic agent of reform and rehabilitation to a more crass agent of revenue for the state. Many of the problems that wracked the internal world of the prison stemmed from forces largely outside the control of local authorities. The failure of the decorative fan business is the most important of these for examining the effects of the market on prison discipline: because retailers in New York City no longer had need for fans made in the Rhode Island State Prison, an entire regime of local officials fell at the hands of the state. Inmates who depended on meager incentives in their work—an extra meal of "Bread & Butter" and "Black Tea," for example—found themselves transformed into industrial slaves with only the hope of eventual sentence reduction guiding daily work. At the same time, they also found themselves penalized of that "good time" for the most trivial of offenses, such as looking around the workshop during their ten-hour days.

The importance of the commodification process lies in its transformation of the built environment, from solitary cells of discipline to factory-like workshops marked by cobblestone paths. It is in the foundations of the workshops, the spoil piles outside their doorways, and the wretched confines of the Dark Cells that we see the peak of cynicism reached by prison authorities in the 1870s. With the completion of the commodification process, labor had run its true course, and within the walls of the Rhode Island State Prison inmates found themselves the unwilling subjects of the state's experiment in forced labor for the benefit of the private sector.

CHAPTER 6

"A Sort of Uncontrollable Autonomy"
The Reinvention of the Social Reform Institution

"The work of building the new State Prison has made satisfactory progress during the past summer and autumn," wrote the board of inspectors in 1876, "and the Inspectors look forward to its completion with the hope that it will prove to be amply adequate for many years for the needs of the State" (*ARBI* 1875, 11–12). "The old jail," they added confidently, "will disappear." During the final year of the Rhode Island State Prison's existence in Providence, authorities terminated all labor contracts with outside firms and put inmates to work making tables, desks, and other items to supply the new institution. Nelson Viall's clerks carefully packed the ledgers, correspondence files, telegraph machine, and other items in the warden's office. Inmates, although cognizant of the impending move, were deliberately kept in the dark about the actual date, lest they formulate a plan for a commotion or disturbance during the transportation process. Late on the night of November 27, 1876, Viall's staff, supplemented by members of the Providence Police Department, moved down the cell block hallways, formed the inmates into lines, manacled them to one another, and set out through the cold night for the new penitentiary.

Late-night revelers returning home must have gaped at the spectacle of shackled inmates shuffling through the streets of Providence under heavy guard. The convoy approached the outer limits of metropolitan Providence and then marched nine miles along the country roads. By early morning they had arrived at the forbidding, neo-Gothic entrance of the new penitentiary at Howard, a small village in Cranston (fig. 28). As the *Providence Journal* (January 20, 1879, 2) reported: "Warden Viall kept his own counsel as to the time and manner of the removal, and the prisoners were in their new quarters before people knew that the New Prison was to be occupied at once." Inside the warden's house—as in Providence, located at the front of the complex—they found the gas jets blazing and a receiving clerk, pen in hand, waiting to fill in the pages of a brand new ledger.

Along Gaspee Street the dawn hours of November 28 were strangely quiet. For the first time in nearly forty years, the bell over the connecting building failed to toll its commands to rise, to eat, to work, and to pray; the few machines remaining in the workshops were left idle; and curious citizens of Providence must surely have tested the wrought-iron gates of the prison, pushed them open, and viewed for themselves the decaying buildings representing the material world of state-sanctioned punishment, a world that few of the law-abiding had seen in the history of the institution.

Those of a particularly thoughtful nature among the citizenry might well have pondered an inevitable question: how could the first and most formidable of state institutions—built as the largest public works project in the history of Rhode Island—have become so utterly obsolete as to be abandoned after a mere forty years? From a late twentieth-century perspective, we should take that question a step further and ask what its failure said about the nature of the social reform institution and the nineteenth-century industrialized state's care for the deviant, the disenfranchised, the poor, and the insane. Most important, from the perspective of this study, is the question of future practice: what contributions can anthropology, and specifically historical archaeology, make to the study of social reform institutions?

Here I will try to tie together three major themes—landscape, labor, and the contestation of power—in an effort to draw some broader conclusions about the changing meanings of reform institutions in the fully industrialized state. The discussion begins with a brief consideration of the Smithfield Town Farm and Asylum (hereafter the Town Farm) in Smithfield, Rhode Island. Established in the same year as the Rhode Island State Prison, the Town Farm experienced a more spectacular failure than the prison through an especially lurid scandal concerning the mistreatment of inmates. The goals, sizes, and settings of the two institutions make comparisons between them difficult. Nonetheless, the abandonment of the Town Farm six years before the demise of the prison points to some broader implications underlying the failure of Jacksonian-era institutions and the changing landscape of American reform in the last quarter of the nineteenth century.

Howard, R. I. State Prison and County Jail. Front Entrance.

FIG. 28 — Howard, R.I., State Prison and Jail. *Designed by the firm of Stone Carpenter and Willson and completed in 1878, the facility, now known as the Adult Correctional Institution, is still in use. Post-1907 postcard view. Author's collection.*

The discussion then shifts to explanations for the failure of the Rhode Island State Prison. By "failure" I do not simply mean state and local authorities' acknowledgment that Great Point was no longer feasible as the site of the state's central penal complex. "Failure" in the sense of a social reform institution encompasses a much broader definition; used here, it is more akin to a failure of long-term vision on multiple levels. On a strictly material level, it means that all of the carefully designed systems for housing, feeding, punishing, and reforming prisoners had become outmoded, antiquated, or otherwise unusable. On a symbolic level, it means that the penal institution had lost its ability to perform its function as the material embodiment of the state's moral virtue. Confidence in the institution on the part of legislators, administrators, inmates, and the public had been irrevocably eroded. Finally, on a metaphysical level, it means that all the best intentions of legislators and local authorities, reformers, and crackpots had been bested by forces beyond their proponents' control. In this case, I argue that the unchecked forces of spatiality and the active human subversion of space and its state-designated meaning had defeated the purpose for which the institution was constructed.

181

The chapter concludes with some ideas for further study of social reform institutions. Archaeological investigations of institutional sites are rare (Cotter et al. 1988; De Cunzo 1995). There are reasons why archaeologists may not have found the opportunity to examine asylums, orphanages, and poor farms. Some of these revolve around logistics: excavating the Rhode Island State Prison encompassed the removal of twenty-five hundred cubic yards of fill; extensive coordination with clients, contractors, and unions; and the creation and implementation of an extensive site-safety and health plan to ensure that no one was injured on what was, after all, a relatively dangerous site. Thus institutional sites, especially those in urban areas, are much more likely places for compliance-funded cultural resource management studies than for summer field schools. But there is surely more to the problem than logistics. I suspect that the large scale of boarding schools, monasteries, asylums, and convents and the difficulties of associating artifacts with individuals or even groups have been seen as daunting problems, resulting in a lack of attention to them as archaeological sites. That this is so is unfortunate, for their primary contribution is the provision of insight into the organization, redefinition, and subversion of space—all important phenomena underlying the contradictory aspects of space within the context of industrial capitalism.

How Capitalism Takes Care of Its Own

At different moments in time the debate over the Rhode Island State Prison both reflected and deviated from the Jacksonian-era national debate over penal reform and prison industry. Centralization of state institutions at Howard, a process that began in the late 1860s, reflects the most important trend in mid- to late nineteenth-century reform: that is, the abandonment of the experimental notion of Jacksonian-era institutions and the collection, segregation, and isolation of "deviants" in state-sponsored locales near the metropolitan cores.

These trends are especially evident in the treatment of the poor and the insane. In Rhode Island, as in most New England states, care of these less fortunate citizens was delegated to the town level for most of the nineteenth century. The case of the Smithfield Town Farm and Asylum offers an important counterpoint to the Rhode Island State Prison. Conceived in the same spirit of reform as the prison, the Town Farm became the site of perpetual neglect and abuse, deviating markedly from the prison in the absence

A SORT OF UNCONTROLLABLE AUTONOMY

of an underlying agenda of reform. Its failure to deliver on its promises provides an important case study with insight into the late nineteenth-century rationale of transferring the burden of care from towns to the state, and helps explain the centralization of marginalized citizens in large-scale state institutions.

Caring for the Poor and the Insane: The Smithfield Town Farm and Asylum

Prior to the establishment of town institutions for the poor, many Rhode Island communities boarded indigent families at town expense. A practice common in the eighteenth century was the "auctioning of the poor," by which more prosperous residents would vie to become low bidder on a pauper (Rothman 1971; Katz 1996, 14). In return for the low bid, paid for out of the town's general fund, the winner would have the right to put the individual and his or her family to work, a circumstance that naturally led to unspeakable abuses.

Town overseers of the poor were authorized to assist less severe cases of poverty on an individual basis. This form of "outdoor relief" had its medieval origins in the Elizabethan poor laws. In Smithfield, a small agricultural town ten miles north of Providence, records of town council meetings indicate that overseers of the poor billed the town for caring for the sick, providing firewood, and burying the dead. With steadily increasing numbers of individuals and families requiring relief, however, the trend was one of streamlining and efficiency as towns across New England sought to bring the poor together in local institutional settings: "Just as the penitentiary would reform the criminal and the insane asylum would cure the mentally ill, so the almshouse would rehabilitate the poor" (Rothman 1971, 179).

The decades between 1820 and 1840 witnessed the construction of sixty new almshouses in Massachusetts towns. Other states, including Rhode Island, were part of this trend; by 1850, when Thomas R. Hazard made his survey of the state's town farms, he was able to point to fifteen different institutions with a total of five hundred inmates (Hazard 1851). The town farms shared three philosophical strategies with prisons: the removal of "deviants" from society, the development of work regimes, and the instillation of unvarying daily routines in the lives of the inmates.

Euro-Americans had settled Smithfield toward the end of the seventeenth century. As part of a vast tract termed "the Outlands," the town had

had a steady agricultural base for nearly two centuries when industrialists began to make use of Smithfield's abundant water resources for mills and factory villages. The forces of industrialization engendered large-scale class realignment in the town, with numerous farms consolidated into larger holdings and the release of itinerant displaced farmers and their families (Garman and Russo 1999). Smithfield's decision to purchase a farm for the relief of the poor was reached on October 27, 1834, when a committee was authorized to buy a suitable property (Smithfield Town Meeting Records, October 1834). No record of the construction of the Town Farm survives, nor do any photographs or paintings. Based on the archaeological evidence, it was likely a dormitory-style, multistory structure with gable-end entrances and chimneys along the roof peak. Maps show the Town Farm as a T-shaped structure. The keeper's house constituted the base of the T, serving as an entrance into the institution. As with the Rhode Island State Prison, built at the same time, the underlying idea was to project a patriarchal ideology, with the keeper as head of the needy family.

By 1839 the Town Farm was already in a state of financial mismanagement. At the March 29, 1839, town meeting, Arnold Aldrich II and John Foster were appointed to review the accounts of the Town Farm "from the time the Town bought the farm up to the present time . . . so as to show the inhabitants of said town the expense they have been at in supporting the poor of said Town." The results of the inquiry were never printed. Indeed, the relative absence of the Town Farm from the town meeting reports may indicate that it was generally ignored in the 1840s and 1850s.

The state inspector Thomas Hazard, who visited the Smithfield Town Farm in 1850, found conditions generally acceptable but objected to the lack of segregation of inmates according to class (the poor, the insane, the debilitated). However, this situation was not unique to Smithfield. It was only in the larger, urban institutions of Newport and Providence that Hazard found the appropriate conditions of segregation (Nicolosi 1989, 3). In response to this criticism, the town authorized construction of a new, separate asylum building. The specifications given in this order are the only evidence of the construction plan:

> Voted that a suitable Building for the accommodation of the
> Insane Paupers of the town of Smithfield be erected on the
> Asylum Farm in said Smithfield with a suitable yard connected
> therewith . . . and that Spencer Mowry Esq. be a committee to
> examine buildings for similar purposes in other places; to draw
> a plan of said building & cause the same to be built either of

wood, brick, or stone . . . to be so located as not to join the present Asylum house apparently erected a second, separate building on the property exclusively for the insane.

(Smithfield Town Meeting Records, August 19, 1854)

As McBride, Soulsby, and Clouette (1991, 8) point out, this is an important document because it indicates a great deal of foresight on the town's part in terms of segregation and the special nature of the asylum. At the same meeting, Smithfield indicated its willingness to bring back its "Insane Paupers" from Butler Hospital, "when suitable accommodations shall be made for them at said Asylum." The building is the result of Spencer Mowry's careful analysis of the town's needs for its mentally ill population.

On October 24, 1870, a scandal erupted over Smithfield's treatment of the poor. Assuming the pen name "Humanity," an anonymous writer to the *Providence Journal* leveled charges concerning the abuse of the poor and insane under Smithfield's care. These accusations encompassed everything from staff theft of the inmates' property to physical brutality to de facto, town-approved murder. The identity of "Humanity" cannot be determined. The author's references to "our town" and "our community" suggest residence in Smithfield. As there are repeated references to medical terms and the physical condition of some of the inmates, it is tempting to speculate that the author was one of the local doctors who sometimes attended the inmates. The author's charges, and the authorities' staged response to those charges, wrought important changes to the system of poor relief.

The council's response to Humanity's charges was swift, with a special town meeting held on October 25, 1870, to address the situation. The town council, after having Humanity's letter read into the record, appointed a five-person committee "to investigate the whole matter." The committee was also charged with publishing its findings, perhaps an indication of the town's confidence in the system's vindication. In the original record the words "Providence Journal" are scratched out as the venue of publication and replaced with "pamphlet form for distribution & the result of the investigation to be published in the Providence Journal." Evidently, the town wanted a more permanent record than that afforded by a war of letters to the editor.

The investigative committee met twice in rapid succession. Their meetings must be seen as a ritual performance in which both tradition and drama were integral to the committee's actions (De Cunzo 1995, 3). On October 29, 1870, they convened at the Town Farm "for the purpose of ascertaining in

185

the first place, the general provision made by the town for the support of such of her poor as were provided for at the asylum" (*Report of the Committee of Investigation* [*RCI*] 1870, 1). There they found what they recorded as generally decent conditions. Their description of the living arrangements indicates that the two buildings on the property, the Town Farm and the asylum, had deviated from their original purpose of separating the insane from the indigent. Separation now was by gender (although who lived in which house is uncertain). The 1870 census shows four female and nine male inmates, so it seems more likely that the women were occupying the asylum building and the men the Town Farm. Regardless of who lived where, the separation by gender, rather than classification, evokes Victorian sensibilities of propriety rather than Jacksonian ideas of reform and inmate classification by offense.

Having found the overall conditions at the Town Farm satisfactory, the committee then turned to the specific accusations leveled by Humanity (1870, 1). The first charge was that the keepers, the assistants, and by implication the overseers of the poor had all practiced physical violence on the inmates. Humanity's proof was the testimony of a former inmate, derided by the committee as "of weak mind" (*RCI* 1870, 2). The committee heard testimony from two individuals, Asa Burdick and Simon Smith, both of whom were former keepers of the Smithfield Town Farm and Asylum. After hearing the testimony of these two, the committee concluded that the keepers "have endeavored to do their duty faithfully and without undue severity" (*RCI* 1870, 2). There is no record of the inmates testifying regarding this accusation or at any time during the proceedings.

The second charge was that the town had contributed to the death of James E. Angell, an insane pauper whom Humanity claimed had been locked in the basement until his condition became fatal (1870, 1). Testimony from Obed Paine, overseer of the poor, revealed that a range of circumstances contributed to Angell's death. First, there was some question of whether Angell was a legal resident of Smithfield or whether he belonged (and was therefore chargeable) to another town. Second, Paine was waiting for the state farm in Cranston, then under construction, to be ready for the reception of the insane. Third, Paine claimed that he had tried and failed to obtain a place for Angell at the Butler and Dexter asylums. Paine finally did find a place for Angell at the Worcester State Hospital, but Angell died en route. The investigative committee failed to find serious wrongdoing on Paine's part. They found that he may have been too conservative in his

A Sort of Uncontrollable Autonomy

actions, but they respected his watchfulness on the part of the town's financial interests.

The third accusation was the most poignant. The Mowry family, consisting of a mother, son, daughter, and infant—all unnamed except for thirteen-year-old Nancy—was being supported at town expense on a small farm some distance from the Town Farm. Paine, as overseer of the poor, allowed the family fifty cents a week for subsistence from the town's general fund. Humanity's accusation (1870, 1) was that this pittance was insufficient to prevent starvation in the family: "Poor Nancy over ate herself — on wild grapes — and sickened and died. Dr. Nutting says that this child contracted a disease resembling the *black vomit*; and that nothing but grapes appeared to come from the stomach; and the mother says that the child subsisted on grapes for the last few days of her life, although the mother would hardly be willing to believe that her child died of starvation." In this case, with death and implications of starvation, the town felt compelled to take evidence from Nancy Mowry's mother; from one Mrs. McCoy, who shared the house with the Mowry family; and from Dr. Nutting, the physician. Mrs. Mowry testified humbly that Nancy "had never been well" and that the overseer "gave her all she asked for" (*RCI* 1870, 4). Mrs. McCoy also testified to the solicitous nature of the overseer. Dr. Nutting's testimony is curiously worded in sharp, staccato phrases neither confirming nor denying the accusation: "Vomited a black substance like black vomit. [I] Knew nothing about her food when sick. Mother was a very poor nurse.... Diet would not produce the black vomit; want of food would not produce it. Saw the matter Nancy threw up. Saw no grapes. Did not say that nothing but grapes came out of her stomach. The grape story belongs to other parties. I said nothing about it" (*RCI* 1970, 4).

The final charge was an especially lurid tale concerning "not very bright" seventeen-year-old Susan Tifft (*RCI* 1870, 5), who lived with one William Mowry on a nearby farm. On September 12, 1870, at two o'clock in the morning, the arrival of Mowry and Tifft at the asylum awakened the keeper George R. Weaver. In the wagon lay a dead infant. Weaver admitted Tifft to the asylum on the basis of a standing order she carried with her. The note, signed by Obed Paine, ordered the keeper to take her in when she appeared and to release her at her pleasure. Weaver, horrified by the grisly scene, summoned Dr. Nutting, demanding an inquest. Nutting, according to Humanity (1870, 1), took one look at the scene and after saying "I've seen worse than this," refused the demand for an inquest. The dead infant was buried at the Town Farm burial ground in an unmarked grave. Eight days later Susan Tifft demanded to be released, and she returned to William Mowry's farm.

In his testimony at the committee hearing, Weaver adopted a perspective of "only following orders." Mowry, for his part, said that Obed Paine had told him that Mowry should keep Susan at his farm as long as she could pay, then take her to the asylum. Paine denied this last accusation, saying that when he had learned that Tifft was pregnant in July, he had urged her to go into the asylum but that she had declined, saying that the unnamed father of her child (presumably Mowry) would support her.

Finally Dr. Nutting testified, again in what reads as an equivocal manner: "I said 'I have seen worse things than this,' but did not say nor mean that I had seen worse things 'done here'" (*RCI* 1870, 6). Dr. Nutting's reply to the question of the cause of death must also be seen as self-serving. He reported that the child was not murdered, a finding that greatly relieved him. However, he also noted that the ultimate cause of death was violence: "Did not think an inquest necessary. Did not think there was any violence. Child was still-born. The mother had been dreadfully kicked and pounded, about a month before the child was born, as she said, and she had felt no motion of the child since that time. . . . Decomposition had been going on two weeks or more before the child was born. My remark was made to relieve Mrs. Weaver's mind" (*RCI* 1870, 6–7). In this matter the committee finally found some measure of fault, determining that Paine had acted inappropriately in placing Susan Tifft with William Mowry: "If Susan Tifft was a proper subject for the town's care, the town should have seen to it that in her case there should not have been—as there was—a violation of every idea of decency and a disregard of every sentiment of humanity" (*RCI* 1870, 6).

The committee's report closed with some important recommendations. They had, after all, been charged with investigating "the whole matter." The committee had praise for Obed Paine and the others involved in poor relief, noting that any mistakes that had been made came from the head, not the heart. But they also found that the present system was untenable. The buildings required a significant investment; more important, the farm was saddled with much more land than could effectively be worked by the inmates and the hired help. In many ways these conclusions are reflective of the demographic composition of town authorities. No longer were they the members of the founding families of Smithfield, eager to participate in national debates about poor reform. The new local authorities were either industrial capitalists or their trusted agents. From their perspective, issues of efficiency and economy—a foreshadowing of Taylorism—were much more significant than philosophical experiments. More important was the blight of the Town Farm on the community and its corporate identity. It is important to remember that at the time the Humanity incident occurred, the nation was anticipating its celebration of the centennial (Praetzellis, Praetzellis, and Brown 1988, 198). Town histories were in preparation across New England, and the stigma of a blighted Town Farm inhabited by those marginalized by larger society was an unappealing aspect of model company towns and corporate paternalism. Thus the special committee's recommendations—which included selling the Town Farm and establishing "advisers of the Overseer of the Poor" in every major village of Smithfield—were strikingly modern, and in keeping with the sensibilities of industrial capitalism. The advisers (appointed by the town council, naturally) would administer local poor relief, thus ending the Dickensian experiment of the town farm and asylum. In December 1870 the town council voted to accept the committee's report and authorized a committee to sell the Town Farm. Augustus Aldrich was contracted to draw a map of the property, and the few remaining inmates were moved to Howard and other state institutions. Smithfield's forty-year-old experiment in reforming the poor had officially ended.

The Lessons of the Town Farm

The bitter lessons of the Town Farm testify to the changing notion of care in the third quarter of the nineteenth century. No longer could individual towns afford the expense or the potential liability of an institution. Note that one of the reasons cited for abandoning the Town Farm was the large investment that the buildings would require to make them more habitable. Towns found that the mismanaged, often decrepit facilities did much to undermine civic pride; in fairness, there was also a broad recognition that individual communities were unable to provide the expertise to deal with a steadily increasing population of the dispossessed and the debilitated.

From this recognition grew the notion that care of the poor and the insane was no longer an issue for local communities, but for the power of the state and its attendant bureaucracy. The state, for its part, does not seem to have contested this matter and indeed embraced the concept of centralized institutions. Certainly there were logistical imperatives at work. Under the town farm system, local authorities caring for "strangers" or those who could not establish that they were residents of the town charged the state for those individuals' food and clothing. The state, in turn, would pursue reimbursement of these funds from the communities of the inmates' origins. The sheer volume of correspondence between towns and the state on file at the Rhode Island State Archives testifies to the monumental inefficiency of this system. Had so-and-so, now an inmate of the East Greenwich Town Farm, truly been born in North Providence? Because there was no centralized state record system prior to the 1850s, making such determinations required a series of back-and-forth trips between the towns in question, the taking of affidavits, and the compilation of extensive (and often contradictory) documents in case files.

Under a central, state-operated system these questions would be no longer relevant. With large-scale facilities, all those who had been marginalized at the town level—the poor, the insane, the orphans, the juvenile offenders—could be collected in one location. Conversely, this assumption of responsibility by the state, and the implementation of care by those with at least some level of professional training, could engender a much higher degree of segregation and separation of inmates within the central institutional complex. Orphans with criminal tendencies, for example, could be sent to the industrial school; those with records of better behavior could be placed in a boys' home to await adoption. Just as prison inmates would eventually be "graded" by their behavior under confinement, so too could all of society's outcasts be classified, constituted in groups, and set on a course for reform, rehabilitation, and release.

For each of these classes of human beings the state would provide a designated space: an asylum, an orphanage, an almshouse, an industrial school. Each of the spaces, while under control of different administrators, would come together as an institutional whole. Under centralization, there would be no more random economic disbursements to counties, towns, or even individuals for poor relief; there would be the Rhode Island Board of Corrections and Charities, which would hold sway over the component spaces, meting out state appropriations as necessary. Better still, in terms of economic gain, the power of labor could be more efficiently harnessed. At Smithfield, administrators complained that the thirteen inmates could do little to support the institution in terms of labor or even self-sufficiency. At Howard, however, there would be five hundred paupers to work the state farm, theoretically resulting in far more productive results.

The most important concept underlying the collective institutionalization of the marginalized lies in the material manifestation of state power. As the institutions at Howard began to take material form, no one could fail to notice the commanding presence of the gray, turreted institutional buildings on a prominent hillside west of Providence. The very names of the constituent complexes acquired resonance for generations of Rhode Islanders. With the construction of the new facilities, Rhode Islanders saw the ability of the state to implement detention and surveillance at previously unheard-of levels. Keeping the material embodiment of state power foremost in mind, I will now return to the Rhode Island State Prison, and the ways in which its institutional failure meshed with practices of collectivization, classification, and segregation initiated by the state.

Why the Prison Failed

It is a relatively simple matter to consider the history of the Rhode Island State Prison and identify reasons why it did not survive in Providence. From the initial debate in the early 1800s a range of ambiguous goals and competing interests guided its conception and implementation. For some legislators, the prison represented punishment in the most rigorous and uniform manner possible; for others, it served as an opportunity to realize some level of economic gain from the labor of society's most heinous offenders; for still others, it offered Rhode Island a chance to catch up with the broader, established reform movement in Jacksonian America.

Thus it should come as no surprise that the practice of imprisonment in Rhode Island proved to be as muddled as the debate over the abstract concept. Legislators found the prison a civil necessity that was supremely unpopular with taxpayers; inspectors found their own best efforts to reform the institution thwarted by imperatives of fiscal expediency; and prison administrators, many of whom entered the office with noble expectations concerning their duties, found themselves reduced to glorified bookkeepers charged with inventorying prison stock and justifying requisitions for paint and other trivial supplies.

Absent a clear, unwavering vision of the goals and rationale of imprisonment on the part of authorities, it follows that inmates, on the receiving end of the mixed messages, developed a wide range of responses to the conditions of their confinement. Some went dutifully to the workshops every day, kept their gazes on their work, and served out their time quietly in the hope of pardon or parole. Others attempted to derail the system that exploited them by slowing down the machinery, both symbolically and literally. Still others engaged in remarkable patterns of violent activity serving no other purpose than the expression of rage and frustration at the conditions of confinement; such activity was almost guaranteed to bring retribution from prison authorities. In the search for answers explaining the inability of the Rhode Island State Prison to deliver on its promises,

191

some larger explanatory categories are readily visible. These include the harsh realities of the economic world of the nineteenth-century penitentiary, the misguided siting of the prison at Great Point, and the debilitating effects stemming from the contestation of power at multiple levels of the prison matrix.

Economic Explanations

The economic woes of the Rhode Island State Prison have been discussed here at some length. The prison infrastructure never permitted all inmates of the county jail and the state prison to work at the same time. Inmates who did not work, whether because of sickness, malingering, or inadequate facilities, represented financial liabilities to the system because nothing supported their housing, clothing, and feeding other than disbursements from the General Assembly of Rhode Island.

We cannot, however, simply blame the economic debacle of the prison on the few inmates who did not labor in the workshops. Few of the wardens were fiscally savvy, as Thomas Cleaveland's unfortunate venture into the fan market proved. In retrospect, it seems misguided and almost cruel to have selected dedicated reformers such as Cleaveland and invested them with full financial responsibility for the operation of the state's most prominent institution. Furthermore, the product of the prison industry program was, for a variety of reasons, of limited value. As we have seen, the selection of prison goods was probably aimed more at the instillation of routine habits than at potentially profitable commodities. Finally, money received from the general assembly was often spent unwisely, particularly in the development of the prison's built environment. The examples supporting this argument are myriad, as the steady decay of the institution indicates.

Thus there seem to have been solid economic rationales underlying the decision to abandon the Providence site in favor of a more centralized state institution: the institution could no longer support itself, the workshops were inadequate, and the infrastructure was decayed and, primarily through overcrowding, no longer adequate for the hundreds of inmates double- and triple-bunked in cells meant for individuals. Still, it is difficult to argue that any of these economic problems actually caused the abandonment of the Rhode Island State Prison; they are better seen as symptoms of large-scale, structural problems and are unsatisfying in their ability to address the root causes of institutional failure.

Geographic Explanations

Geographic explanations for the prison's failure revolve around the state's decision to build the prison at the edge of metropolitan Providence, which had engendered some measure of debate in the general assembly. Recall that proponents of other sites for the prison had selected sites near quarries or, in one case, adjacent to water power and neighboring mill villages. Yet Great Point, a site with few advantages from the perspective of potential prison industries, had prevailed, largely because of the political impropriety associated with the ownership of contiguous property by Governor John Brown Francis, who was also a site selection committee member.

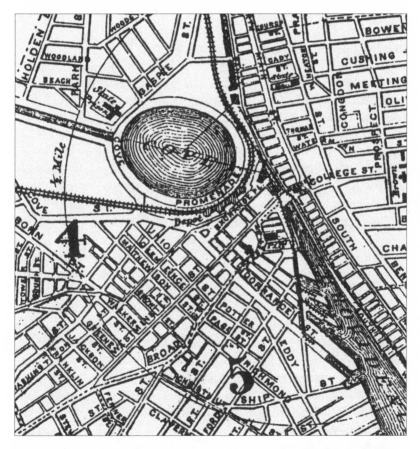

FIG. 29 — *Detail from the 1870 Beers'* Map of Providence, Rhode Island *showing the extent to which the urban core had enveloped the formerly remote Great Point location of the Rhode Island State Prison.*

A second and unintentional aspect of the siting, however, is the city of Providence's rapid growth in the 1850s and 1860s that stretched the limits of the city far beyond what they had been in 1838. Within a matter of twenty years the development of the urban core overwhelmed the prison (fig. 29). We have seen how the site changed rapidly from a remote, sandy peninsula accessible only by the most tortuous city roads to an important landmark on the urban landscape demarcated by Tefft's Union Depot and the Cove Promenade. The integration of the prison into the metropolitan core, while initially promising, ultimately undermined its force as the material embodiment of moral virtue in the fully industrialized city-state of the late nineteenth century.

Power-oriented Explanations

Explanations considering the contestation of power as an impetus for institutional self-destruction are attractive as means of interpreting failure. Arguments concerning the erosion of state authority through collective and individual acts of resistance are increasingly visible in anthropological, archaeological, and historical literature. They are especially compelling because they turn our attention away from the dominant, forcing us to consider closely the actions of those previously considered powerless. John Wood Sweet's (1995) study of race relations in New England provides an especially intriguing argument concerning the end of slavery in Rhode Island. Through close examination of legal evidence, Sweet (1995, 335) notes that the rhetoric of the American Revolution engendered a more explicit demand for freedom on the part of the enslaved. Slave owners found themselves losing control over the enslaved until they were forced to promise freedom for fixed terms, a process that led to the adaptation of the Gradual Emancipation Act in 1784.

Applying this rationale to the Rhode Island State Prison offers some interesting possibilities, especially because the contestation of power at multiple levels is so vivid. It would be tempting to speculate that the steady increase in documented acts of disobedience, in concert with the undocumented actions recovered archaeologically, made the institution no longer tenable. But ultimately all of these explanations cannot account for the fact that Rhode Island legislators did not abolish the prison, as they did the practice of slavery; they simply moved it from its location in Providence to the newly developed centralized facility at Howard, where it survives today. Nor does this move indicate that inmates or administrators had "won" any contestation of power. Quite to the contrary, the construction of the sprawling edifice and its association with the state farm, the Sockanosset Home for Juvenile Offenders, and other institutions reinforced the visible manifestation of state power over both its weakest citizenry and its minions of bureaucrats and administrators.

Yet the contestation of power in the prison matrix leads to the important observation underlying all of the aforementioned explanations: namely, the sense that the formally demarcated space of confinement and punishment had become no longer tenable. The warden's house, cell blocks, and workshops could not serve in any effective manner the purposes for which they were originally designed. Thus the failure of the prison may be a parable about the liability of space to reconstitution and redefinition, and about the illusory nature of spatial control.

Such conceptions of space are admittedly difficult to problematize in the material world. Looking beyond the internal world of the Rhode Island State Prison, we can see two closely related spatial processes at work in the late nineteenth-century city-state. The first is the collection, classification, and isolation of deviants on the geographical margins of cities. The second is the reclamation of formerly abandoned "waste lands" to form more comprehensive and formally designed urban cores.

Last Stop: Howard

As the example of the Smithfield Town Farm and Asylum demonstrates, the Rhode Island State Prison was not the only Jacksonian-era institution foundering in Rhode Island during the 1870s. Local poorhouses, asylums, orphanages, and other institutions were unable to deliver services to their charges, a circumstance directly attributable to the post–Civil War explosions in population and homelessness. As early as January 1867 the general assembly had appointed a committee to start considering sites for a complex of institutions—a state workhouse, a house of correction, a state asylum, and a state almshouse. In envisioning this complex of institutions, the newly formed Rhode Island Board of Corrections and Charities selected the small village of Howard, a crossroads on a hillside in the rural town of Cranston.

Unlike the situation in the 1830s, the debate over a centralized complex of institutions moved much more quickly. In May 1869 the general assembly approved an appropriation of $22,500 for the purchase of the Howard Farm (Report of the State Charities and Corrections Committee

195

1883). New appropriations followed quickly: $30,000 for a house of correction (1870); $164,000 for a workhouse (1872); $456,000 for the new prison (1874–78); and $124,649.25 for a reform school (1878 and 1879). Subsequent general assemblies would take up a state home and school (1890), a state sanatorium for consumptives (1904), and a state school for "feeble-minded" children (1907).

Rhode Island's implementation of a central institutional complex proved to be as ill-fortuned as the original construction of the state prison. Perhaps the most graphic account of the various institutions is Dr. Henry A. Jones's *The Dark Days of Social Welfare at the State Institutions at Howard, Rhode Island* (Jones n.d.). Having served as the physician for the complex at the turn of the century, Jones was all too familiar with the demoralizing world of Howard, beginning with the arrival at the depot of train cars of the insane, the criminal, and the poor:

> Many of them [the train's passengers] had looked with despairing eye through the car windows to what to me appeared to be a stately castle of grey stone, ovaled-windowed, massive, and turreted, and architecturally attractive; but to these in this car, it was the grim castle of despair, the place of sorrow, of resignation, and of death! It was the State Prison!
>
> I was startled to see the train disgorge itself. Out upon the wet snowy platform, a handcuffed group were hustled, slipping and clanking down the slippery steps of the car. Calls and shouts from sheriffs in blue uniforms straightened up this motley crowd into a semblance of order, save one poor female, who, clanking her shackled wrists as one would a bracelet, screamed out some unintelligible language which showed she was insane.
>
> (Jones n.d., 7–8)

Late nineteenth-century maps of the state institutions, especially after the construction of the new state prison, are the most visually compelling representations of the scale of the Howard institutions, including the train depot cited by Dr. Jones, the temporary sheds where segregation and classification of new inmates occurred, the single road system linking all of the various institutions, the power plants supplying light and electricity to the buildings, and the individual fire stations (thus decreasing dependency on outside forces). Above all, we see the vast tract of blank space around the complexes, reflecting the remoteness and isolation of the site and the physical isolation of the dispossessed from "respectable" citizenry.

A SORT OF UNCONTROLLABLE AUTONOMY

I suspect that there is much more to be gained from closer study of the relationship between the institutions at Howard. Their pointed efforts at self-sufficiency, their monumental architecture, and their geographic isolation are all as intriguing as the Jacksonian institutions that had pre-dated them. It is these qualities especially that make them attractive for further research.

Cycles of Change on the Gaspee Street Lot

It is worth looking closely at the subsequent history of the Gaspee Street lot on which the prison complex stood for forty years in order to see the extent to which the visible manifestation of "prisonness"—the decayed buildings and grounds of the complex—traveled in and out of the city's collective consciousness from its abandonment in 1878 until the present day.

One of the more curious aspects of the site's history is the tenure of its subsequent owner, the city of Providence, which petitioned the state for release of the property. Given the dilapidated state of the buildings and their location near the foul waters of the cove, legislators agreed to this request with little debate. The city, in turn, saw a tremendous opportunity. It had recently established a city yard at Kinsley Avenue, two blocks west of the

FIG. 30 — Rhode Island State Prison, *c. 1880. Signs of the swill men's occupancy of the keeper's house include the wagons, chicken coops, and laundry hanging on the line. Silver gelatin print by an unknown photographer. Courtesy of the Rhode Island Historical Society (RHi X3 8017).*

197

FIG. 31 — Normal School and State House, Providence, R.I. *Completed in 1900, the normal school filled the former prison lot, while McKim, Mead, and White's Rhode Island State House (1895–1904) dominated the former Jefferson Plains. Post-1907 postcard. Author's collection.*

former prison. The prison would make an ideal boardinghouse for immigrant city workers that was convenient to the city yard and the downtown area (fig. 30). Thus, a neat irony: buildings and grounds deemed uninhabitable for the state's worst criminals were deemed acceptable and even desirable for housing Portuguese and Italian city street sweepers and "swill-men."

The boardinghouse occupation continued until 1889, when the buildings finally became too dilapidated for that use. As a central parcel in what was now downtown Providence, other state and municipal interests eyed the lot for more aesthetic purposes. The prevailing group proved to be a state commission, appointed in May 1893 and charged with selecting a site for a state normal school, or teacher-training college (Report of the Commission to Select and Purchase a Site and Erect Thereon a Building for the State Normal School [Normal School Commission] 1899, 1). Spurred by the planned construction of the new Rhode Island State House at the summit of Smith Hill and the ongoing filling of the cove basin, the Normal School Commission envisioned an informal triangular urban core embodying civic virtues (figs. 31 and 32). The key points of this triangle would be government, represented by the new state house; industry, represented by the Union Depot rail station and yards; and education, represented by the new normal school (fig. 33). Construction of the normal school began in

A SORT OF UNCONTROLLABLE AUTONOMY

Providence, R. I. Bird's Eye View, Normal School Gardens.

FIG. 32 — Providence, R.I., Bird's Eye View, Normal School Gardens. *Where the prison buildings had stood, there remained only the new driveway into the normal school and a newly planted formal garden. Post-1907 postcard. Author's collection.*

the summer of 1895; the *Providence Visitor* (June 28, 1895, 1) reported that demolition of the prison was a public spectacle: "Large crowds gather daily to watch the work of razing the old State Prison on Gaspee Street." Undoubtedly some former occupants of the complex stood in the crowd and cheered as the granite walls came down.

When finished, the normal school, joined by the adjacent Henry Barnard School in 1928, served as the state's only teacher-training institution for more than fifty years (Adams and Tait 1994, 15). The hard-fired, yellow-brick walls of the complex formed an important focal point of the Smith Hill area, spurring other civic construction in the vicinity—the Rhode Island Medical Society building (1914) and Veterans Memorial Auditorium (1928), for example. Nonetheless, by the 1980s the two buildings, which now served as the University of Rhode Island's Providence campus and state offices—were deemed no longer necessary in light of the current redevelopment of Providence's metropolitan core. Long-deferred maintenance (which had, after all, plagued the administrators of the Rhode Island State Prison) had taken a severe toll on the infrastructure. The parcel of land, situated in the heart of metropolitan Providence and adjacent to Interstate 95, held a commanding value in the Providence real estate market.

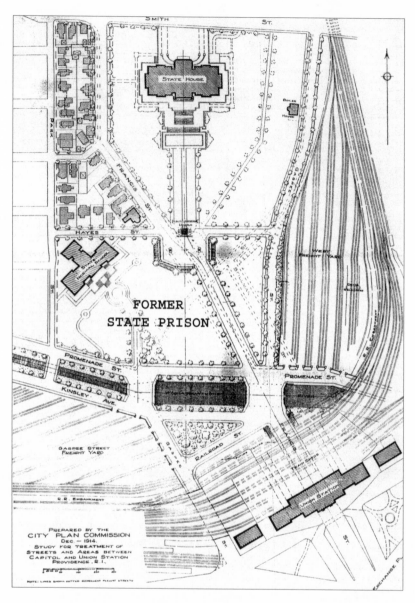

FIG. 33 — Proposed Plan for Development of the "Public Garden" *(1914). Advised by Frederick Law Olmsted, the City Plan Commission envisioned a new urban core overlying the former landscape of deviancy (City Plan Commission 1915, 2).*

FIG. 34 *(Opposite page) — Cycles of change: exposed for the final time, the ruins of the Rhode Island State Prison, framed by McKim, Mead, and White's Rhode Island State House, give way to the Providence Place Mall. Photograph by the author.*

Thus in a cycle lasting slightly more than a century, the Gaspee Street lot was transformed from prison complex to teacher-training college to upscale retail mall, a neat reflection of the progression of American values in the twentieth century. Space once regarded as forbidden, the domain of society's worst offenders and their warders, is now demarcated by Pottery Barn and Banana Republic. No sign of the site's history appears in the new mall; project proponents, although supportive of the archaeological investigations in the context of federal and state compliance, did not feel that the site's gloomy history was an enticement to upscale consumers (Richard Duggan, personal communication 1997).

Although the developers can hardly be faulted for their concerns—a marker commemorating the last execution in Rhode Island would indeed provide strange context to Nordstrom's—one of the supreme ironies of the prison's history lies in its ability, as an archaeological site, to attract crowds. Field personnel were constantly amazed at the crowds observing daily progress on the excavation from the adjacent Francis Street Bridge. At the conclusion of the excavation, the mall developers sponsored a public day, offering free tours of the site. More than fourteen hundred people lined up for the opportunity to take a last look at the prison. Thus for a brief moment

A SORT OF UNCONTROLLABLE AUTONOMY

the prison infrastructure, demolished once, was temporarily part of the city-scape until a second, more thorough demolition eradicated it for the final time (fig. 34).

The Inflexibility of Institutional Space

In the minds of nineteenth-century reformers, disciplining the deviant required regulation of three related aspects of human experience: regulation of *time*, seen through the steady and unwavering tolling of bells to mark the day's activities; regulation of *behavior*, seen through the instillation of work patterns and moral education; and most important for imprisonment, regulation of *space* and movement through space. When any of these aspects became subverted, the project of reform could no longer follow its intended course, and new strategies (such as building new penitentiaries) had to be adopted.

In the requirement of spatial regulation lies the essential contradiction underlying the nineteenth-century reform institution. English and American reformers had conceived penal servitude as a purifying experience for the reprobate, an experience in which the inmate would be isolated from all contact with outside society and reshaped, through labor and moral education, into a productive citizen. Yet these institutions could not be the carefully controlled utopias their advocates imagined; no nineteenth-century American institution could escape the all-encompassing economic context of industrial capitalism. This context shaped decisions about prison industries; more important, it penetrated the heart of the reform project, altering it irrevocably. Although the prison was meant to be separated from the outside world of capital, production, and profit, it could never be so. This experience was shared by other utopian-minded people—the Shakers, the Amish, the New Harmonists—all of whom found their best efforts to escape the world of capital thwarted by economic imperatives.

The failure of the Rhode Island State Prison was ultimately a failure to regulate the spatiality of imprisonment. This flaw has broader implications for state-sponsored projects, especially institutions. By their very nature institutions embody the tensions and contradictions between the goal to reform and the larger goals of capitalism. Thus all those confined within the prison's walls become prisoners of the contradictory ideology of reform. Unable to adapt to unpredictable changes, such as an increase in inmate capacity or the disappearance of markets for prison goods, its inflexible interior space becomes ever more rigid. Indeed, such institutions were doomed to failure from the moment the architect's pen touched the paper. The concept of the ultimate prison is an illusion, yet one that continues to find financial and governmental support in the present day.

A Role for Historical Archaeology?

Within the past twenty-five years, historical archaeology has undergone a major transition in research orientation. A subfield that had its origins in the reconstruction of houses, fortifications, and business establishments of great men has been transformed into one in which the search for the marginalized—Native Americans, African Americans, Creoles, Métis, poor Euro-Americans, and others—is the primary focus of research. Indeed, historical archaeology often markets itself on the argument that archaeological excavation is the only way to recover information concerning the lives of those who only existed as names mentioned peripherally in slave ledgers, census records, and other documents of control.

Yet despite the level of interest in "marginality," broadly constituted studies of institutions are relatively rare. With notable exceptions, archaeologists have generally overlooked prisons and poor farms and asylums. Numerous factors contribute to this gap in the archaeological record. One stumbling block is the immense size of many former institutions, which tend to retain sprawling blocks of standing architecture and landscaped grounds. A second is the association of institutions with aspects of American social history that many find distasteful or unpleasant or depressing. Perhaps the most significant is one of problem orientation in American historical archaeology. Simply put, the artifacts that land in the screen during the excavation of an institution are mundane and above all repetitive (fig. 35). The point of disciplining is not to support ambitions or dreams; it is to create unity among a body of individuals and to stamp out any nonconformity. Ceramic deposits for the prison, for example, consisted of vessel after vessel of white graniteware in a limited number of forms.

The uniformity of assemblages may be the most significant challenge in the development of archaeologies of social reform institutions. Historical archaeology has paid a great deal of obeisance to the artifact recovered from the ground. Ink and human sweat are expended on exacting typologies and chronologies of nails, for example, or on the question of whether pearlware first appeared in the American colonies in 1778 or 1780 (Seidel 1990). The innovative archaeology of spatial boundaries has gone a long way toward countering the tyranny of the individual artifacts. As Patricia Hart Mangan (2000, 205) has stated eloquently, "If space can be understood as the context in which human behavior takes place and therefore helps to shape its form, then its study can illuminate changing economic, political, and ideological relationships." Some recent studies have produced exciting interpretations of the manipulation of space under feudalism, mercantilism, and industrial capitalism. J. Edward Hood's (1996) work in Deerfield, Massachusetts, for example, has demonstrated that English settlers of the Connecticut River Valley went to great lengths to establish town and settlement patterns reflecting the conditions of social and economic inequality that had dominated English society. James A. Delle's (1998) study of Jamaican coffee plantations is a powerful interpretation of the ways in which planters actively manipulated housing, field patterns, and production areas to provide maximum surveillance of the enslaved. Most significantly, studies by Ross W. Jamieson (2000) and Mangan (2000) confront the problem of spatial reckonings head on, providing entirely new ways to conceive the lifeways of their distant subjects.

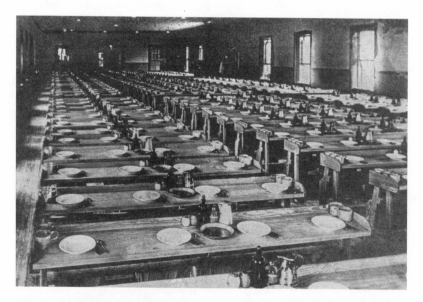

FIG. 35 — *Wisconsin State Prison, Wasau. A typical turn-of-the-century view of a prison dining hall emphasizing the importance of discipline through material culture. Post-1907 postcard. Author's collection.*

All of these studies, and others, seek to understand the peculiarities of liberal capitalism and its effects on the structuring of the material world. What better way to study this phenomenon than by looking at institutions, the state-designated repositories for those who found themselves on the outermost fringes of this world? Thus Howard and other centralized institutions of the late nineteenth century, while perhaps not offering individual artifacts that can be linked in a one-to-one association with individuals, households, or groups, offer a rich potential for exploring the construction of deviant space on the grandest scale possible, and the subversion of that space by the inmates of the institutions.

Examples of such subversion are everywhere. During a recent survey on a boarding-school property, a team of archaeologists under my direction identified numerous illicit campgrounds in the woods and fields surrounding the campus. These campgrounds followed an almost-identical pattern: a fire ring, often with a grill overlying the circle of stones; several chairs, appropriated from school buildings, placed at random intervals around the fire; and a scatter of cigarette butts and liquor bottles. Once again inmates, the generally unwilling occupants of an institutional complex, find ways to subvert the approved demarcation of space, turning the gaps in the space to their own uses. Surely the further study of boardinghouses (Beaudry and Mrozowski 1987a, 1987b, 1989; Mrozowski, Ziesing, and Beaudry 1996), homes for "fallen women" (De Cunzo 1995), orphanages, and other heterotopias will offer both similar and divergent insights.

But perhaps the most compelling reason to look more closely at institutions in the course of further research lies in their ability to capture the stories of individuals whose lives were caught in the torrent of social, cultural, and economic phenomena deriving from the Industrial Revolution. Microhistories of these individuals, while tremendously difficult to pursue, are rewarding in their ability to reconstruct the overwhelming atmosphere of societal upheaval in mid-nineteenth-century America. The case files of the petitions for pardons are often tremendously detailed; in those that were taken seriously, one sees the friends and neighbors of both criminals and victims coming forward, the statements of witnesses and employers, and the opinions of learned jurists—all articulating and reconstituting the world of the underclass in a truly historical-anthropological manner.

Consider Patrick F. Dennehy, who with the notorious Elisha Peck planned the crude escape described in chapter 3. Paroled from the Rhode Island State Prison in 1893 after serving twenty-one years, Dennehy promptly published *The Convict's Story, and Other Poems Descriptive of*

Prison Life (1894), a collection of earnest yet execrable verse about prison life. Consider this excerpt from "'Tis a Folly to Fret":

> No one will envy my present position
> Imprisoned for life is no happy condition
> The process of taking my life may be slow,
> Yet I'll be happy in spite of my foe. . . .
>
> Ten thousand dollars, I'm told they would give
> To keep me in prison as long as I live.
> For eighteen long years they have made it a go,
> Yet I may conquer in spite of my foe.

(Dennehy 1894, 43)

In the preface to the volume Dennehy noted that his intention had been to "write up my case and show the public the injustice of the sentence I received twenty-one years ago, giving my experience during the long term of imprisonment" (Dennehy 1894, preface). "I have not been able to carry out this plan," he added, "but I shall endeavor to do so at a later date." Dennehy never carried through on his plans, a circumstance in which literary critics must surely rejoice at the expense of historians.

Or consider Ed McKearney, an inmate of the county jail. Given the gaps in the documentary record, we know nothing about McKearney or his crime or even the duration of his sentence in the jail. We do know that while he was locked down in the cells, jammed in with the debtors, petty criminals, and vagrants, he managed to secure a piece of roofing slate. On the slate McKearney carved his name for posterity, accompanied by a crude image of a horse. Was the horse simply a material reminder of long-ago life on a farm? Or did it symbolize a longing for freedom and unfettered movement? McKearney's artwork was discovered and taken away; it was later reused to line the animal bone trash pit of Context 810.

Thomas Casey, the writer of the letter that opens this volume, never received his pardon from the state of Rhode Island. He continued to be in and out of trouble, receiving as much as four days in solitary confinement (presumably in the Dark Cells) for his aggressive and occasionally violent behavior. He was finally released in 1868, on expiration of his sentence. During the winter of 1871 he caught a particularly virulent cold, which developed into pneumonia; on March 23, 1871, he died, having spent thirteen of his thirty-four years in state institutions. He was buried in a dismal patch of ground at the corner of the North Burial Ground in Providence, not far from the graves of inhabitants of the Providence institutions.

A SORT OF UNCONTROLLABLE AUTONOMY

To stand in the place where Thomas Casey and hundreds of his fellow inmates, including the insane, the poor, and other castoffs of industrial society, are buried is to experience a small measure of the isolation they experienced during their lives of confinement. The triangular plot is neatly bounded on its three sides by a busy street, by Interstate 95, and by an exit ramp; cars and trucks fly by to destinations unknown at sixty-five miles per hour. Inside the forgotten plot crawl weeds and other overgrowth; the few graves that are marked have only metal plaques bearing numbers or dates. The last time I visited this plot someone had left a spray of lilies on one of the unmarked graves, a single splash of color in the unremitting gray. Surely historical archaeology, an esoteric enterprise at best, can have few more lofty goals than interpreting the lives of the Thomas Caseys of the world, according them some small measure of recognition for their unrewarded lives and forgotten deaths.

REFERENCES

Books, Articles, and Unpublished Manuscripts and Papers

Abercrombie, N., S. Hill, and B. S. Turner. 1980. *The Dominant Ideology Thesis*. London: G. Allen and Unwin.

Abu-Lughod, Lila. 1988. *Veiled Sentiments: Honor and Poetry in a Bedouin Society*. Berkeley: University of California Press.

———. 1990. The Romance of Resistance: Tracing Transformations of Power through Bedouin Women. *American Ethnologist* 17 (1): 41–55.

Adams, Virginia H., and Anne E. Tait. 1994. *Provisions Warehouse District National Register of Historic Places Evaluation, Kinsley and Harris Avenues, Providence County, Providence, Rhode Island*. Pawtucket, RI: PAL report no. 586-2, prepared for Vanasse Hangen Brustlin, Inc.

Adamson, Christopher R. 1984a. Hard Labor and Solitary Confinement: Effects of the Business Cycle and Labor Supply on Prison Discipline in the United States, 1790–1835. *Research in Law, Deviance and Social Control*, 4:19–56.

———. 1984b. Towards a Marxian Penology: Captive Criminal Populations as Economic Threats and Resources. *Social Problems* 4:435–58.

Anonymous. 1870. *Report of the Committee of Investigation on Charges against the Overseer of the Poor, Commissioners of the Town Asylum, Keeper of the Town Asylum, and General Treatment of the Poor in the Town of Smithfield (RCI)*. Central Falls, RI: privately printed.

Anonymous. 1877. *A Historical Sketch of the Jails and Prisons of Rhode Island, 1638–1877*. Providence: Angell, Burlingame.

Artemel, J. G., E. J. Flanagan, E. Crowell, and L. Akerson. 1984. *Providence Cove Lands Phase III Report*. Prepared by De Leuw, Cather/Parsons, Washington, DC, for the Federal Railroad Administration, Northeast Corridor Project, U.S. Department of Transportation, Washington, DC. Report on file at the Rhode Island Historical Preservation and Heritage Commission, Providence.

Baigell, Matthew. 1966. John Haviland in Philadelphia. *Journal of the Society of Architectural Historians* 25 (3): 197–208.

Barrett, John. 1987. Fields of Discourse: Reconstituting a Social Archaeology. *Critique of Anthropology* 7:5–16.

Bartlett, Irving H. 1954. *From Slave to Citizen: The Story of the Negro in Rhode Island*. Providence: Urban League of Greater Providence.

Bartlett, John Russell. 1867. *Memoirs of Rhode Island Officers Who Were Engaged in the Service of Their Country during the Great Rebellion of the South*. Providence: Sidney S. Rider & Brother.

Baugher, Sherene. 2001. Visible Charity: The Archaeology, Material Culture, and Landscape Design of New York City's Municipal Almshouse Complex. *International Journal of Historical Archaeology* 5 (2): 175–202.

Beaudry, Mary C., and Stephen A. Mrozowski, eds. 1987a. *Interdisciplinary Investigations of the Boott Mills, Lowell, Massachusetts*. Vol. 1, *Life at the Boarding Houses*. Cultural Resources Management Study No. 18, Division of Cultural Resources, North Atlantic Regional Office, National Park Service, U.S. Department of the Interior, Boston.

———. 1987b. *Interdisciplinary Investigations of the Boott Mills, Lowell, Massachusetts*. Vol. 2, *The Kirk Street Agents' House*. Cultural Resources Management Study No. 19, Division of Cultural Resources, North Atlantic Regional Office, National Park Service, U.S. Department of the Interior, Boston.

———. 1989. *Interdisciplinary Investigations of the Boott Mills, Lowell, Massachusetts*. Vol. 3, *The Boarding House System as a Way of Life*. Cultural Resources Management Study No. 21, Division of Cultural Resources, North Atlantic Regional Office, National Park Service, U.S. Department of the Interior, Boston.

Bell, Edward L. 1993. *Historical Archaeology at the Hudson Poor Farm Cemetery, Hudson, Massachusetts*. Occasional Publications in Archaeology and History No. 5, Massachusetts Historical Commission, Boston.

Bond, Kathleen H. 1987. ". . . That We May Purify Our Corporation by Discharging the Offenders": The Documentary Record of Social Control in the Boott Boardinghouses. In *Interdisciplinary Investigations of the Boott Mills, Lowell, Massachusetts*, vol. 2, *The Kirk Street Agents' House*, ed. Mary C. Beaudry and Stephen A. Mrozowski, 23–26. Cultural Resources Management Study No. 19, Division of Cultural Resources, North Atlantic Regional Office, National Park Service, U.S. Department of the Interior, Boston.

Bourdieu, Pierre. 1977. *Outline of a Theory of Practice*. Translated by R. Nice. Cambridge: Cambridge University Press.

———. 1984. *Distinction: A Social Critique of the Judgment of Taste*. London: Routledge/Kegan Paul.

Bowles, Samuel, and Richard Edwards. 1985. *Understanding Capitalism: Competition, Command and Change in the U.S. Economy*. New York: Harper & Row.

Bozovic, Miran. 1995. *Jeremy Bentham: The Panopticon Writings*. London and New York: Verso.

Braudel, Fernand. 1992. *Civilization and Capitalism*. Vol. 3, *The Wheels of Commerce*. Originally published in 1979. Berkeley: University of California Press.

Bruhn, Jutta-Annette. 1988. Providence Palaces: Public and Commercial Design. In *Thomas Alexander Tefft: American Architecture in Transition, 1845–1860*, ed. Kathleen A. Curran, 115–30. Providence: Brown University Department of Art.

Bukharin, N. I., and E. Preobrazhensky. 1969. *The ABC of Communism.* Originally published in 1922. London: Pelican Classics.

Burton, Jeffrey F. 1996. *Three Farewells to Manzanar: The Archeology of Manzanar National Historic Site, California.* Western Archeological and Conservation Center Publications in Archeology 67, National Park Service, Tucson, AZ.

Cady, J. H. 1957. *The Civic and Architectural Development of Providence, 1636–1950.* Providence: The Book Shop.

Carroll, Leo. 1988. *Hacks, Blacks and Cons: Race Relations in a Maximum Security Prison.* Originally published in 1974. Prospect Heights, IL: Waveland Press, Inc.

Cleaver, Eldridge. 1968. *Soul on Ice.* New York: Dell Books.

Comaroff, Jean. 1985. *Body of Power, Spirit of Resistance: The Culture and History of a South African People.* Chicago: University of Chicago Press.

Colvin, Mark. 1997. *Penitentiaries, Reformatories, and Chain Gangs: Social Theory and the History of Punishment in Nineteenth-Century America.* New York: St. Martin's Press.

Comaroff, John L., and Jean Comaroff. 1991. *Of Revelation and Revolution: Christianity, Colonialism, and Consciousness in South Africa.* Chicago: University of Chicago Press.

Conley, John A. 1980. Prisons, Production, and Profit: Reconsidering the Importance of Prison Industries. *Journal of Social History* 14:258–76.

———. 1981. Revising Conceptions about the Origins of Prisons: The Importance of Economic Considerations. *Social Science Quarterly* 62:247–58.

———. 1982. Economics and the Social Reality of Prisons. *Journal of Criminal Justice* 10:25–35.

Cook, Lauren J. 1991. The Uxbridge Poor Farm in the Documentary Record. In *Archaeological Investigations at the Uxbridge Almshouse Burial Ground in Uxbridge, Massachusetts*, ed. R. J. Elia and A. B. Wesolowsky, 40–81. Oxford: Tempus Reparatum.

Cotter, John L., Roger W. Moss, Bruce C. Gill, and Jiyul Kim. 1988. *The Walnut Street Prison Workshop.* Philadelphia: The Athenaeum of Philadelphia.

Cressey, Donald, ed. 1961. *The Prison: Studies in Institutional Organization.* New York: Holt, Rinehart and Winston.

Darvill, Timothy, Christopher Gerrard, and Bill Startin. 1993. Identifying and Protecting Historic Landscapes. *Antiquity* 67:563–74.

De Beaumont, Gustave, and Alexis de Tocqueville. 1979. *On the Penitentiary System in the United States and Its Application in France.* Carbondale: Southern Illinois Press.

De Cunzo, Lu Ann. 1995. Reform, Respite, Ritual: An Archaeology of Institutions: Magdalen Society of Philadelphia, 1800–1850. *Historical Archaeology* 29 (3): 1–168.

Delle, James A. 1998. *An Archaeology of Crisis: Analyzing Coffee Plantations in Jamaica's Blue Mountains.* New York: Plenum.

Dennehy, Patrick F. 1894. *The Convict's Story, and Other Poems Descriptive of Prison Life Written While in Prison.* Providence: privately published.

Escobar, Arturo. 1995. *Encountering Development: The Making and Unmaking of the Third World.* Princeton: Princeton University Press.

Etzioni, Amitai. 1961. *A Comparative Analysis of Complex Organizations.* New York: Free Press.

Evans, Robin. 1982. *The Fabrication of Virtue: English Prison Architecture, 1750–1840.* Cambridge: Cambridge University Press.

Faler, Paul G. 1981. *Mechanics and Manufacturers in the Early Industrial Revolution: Lynn, Massachusetts, 1780–1830.* Albany: State University of New York Press.

Field, Edward. 1902. *State of Rhode Island and Providence Plantations at the End of the Century: A History.* Vol. 3. Boston: Mason.

Fiske, John. 1996. *Media Matter: Race and Gender in U.S. Politics.* Minneapolis: University of Minnesota Press.

Foucault, Michel. 1970. *The Order of Things: An Archaeology of Human Sciences.* New York: Pantheon.

———. 1972. *The Archeology of Knowledge and the Discourse on Language.* Translated by Alan Sheridan. New York: Pantheon.

———. 1978. *History of Sexuality.* Translated by Michael Hurley. New York: Pantheon.

———. 1979. *Discipline and Punish: The Birth of the Prison.* Reprinted. Originally published in 1978. New York: Vintage Books.

———. 1980. *Power/Knowledge: Selected Interviews and Other Writings.* Edited and translated by Colin Gordon. New York: Pantheon.

———. 1988. *Madness and Civilization: A History of Insanity in the Age of Reason.* New York: Vintage Books U.S.A.

———. 1988. *Politics, Philosophy, Culture: Interviews and Other Writings, 1977–1984.* Edited by Lawrence Kritzman. New York: Routledge.

Garman, James C., and Paul A. Russo. 1995. *Phase Ic Archaeological Survey and Phase II Site Examinations of RI 1581 (The Rhode Island State Prison) and RI 1582 (The Roger Williams Foundry Complex)/Providence Place Mall and Garage/Providence, RI.* Pawtucket, RI: The Public Archaeology Laboratory, Inc. report no. 588, submitted to the Providence Place Group, LLC.

———. 1999. "A Disregard of Every Sentiment of Humanity": The Town Farm and Class Realignment in Nineteenth-Century Rural New England. *Historical Archaeology* 33 (1): 120–35.

Genovese, Eugene D. 1976. *Roll, Jordan, Roll: The World the Slaves Made.* New York: Vintage Books U.S.A.

Giallombardo, Rose. 1966. *Society of Women: A Study of a Women's Prison.* New York: John Wiley and Sons.

Giddens, Anthony. 1984. *The Constitution of Society: Outline of the Theory of Structuration.* Berkeley: University of California Press.

———. 1990. *The Consequences of Modernity.* Palo Alto: Stanford University Press.

Gramsci, Antonio. 1971. *Selections from the Prison Notebooks.* Translated by Q. Hoare and G. N. Smith. London: Lawrence and Wishart.

Greene, Richard A. 1963. Rhode Island Prisons, 1638–1848: A History. Master's thesis, University of Rhode Island.

Greene, Welcome Arnold. 1886. *The Providence Plantations for Two Hundred and Fifty Years: An Historical Review of the Foundation, Rise, and Progress of the City of Providence.* Providence: J. A. and R. A. Reid.

Gross, Laurence F. 1993. *The Course of Industrial Decline: The Boott Cotton Mills of Lowell, Massachusetts, 1835–1955.* Baltimore: Johns Hopkins University Press.

Hall, Stuart. 1986. The Problem of Ideology: Marxism without Guarantees. In *Stuart Hall: Critical Dialogues in Cultural Studies,* ed. David Morley and Kuan-Hsing Chen, 25–46. London: Routledge.

Hardy, Thomas. 1979. *Tess of the d'Urbervilles.* Originally published in 1891. New York and London: W. W. Norton & Co.

Harvey, David. 1985. *Consciousness and the Urban Experience.* Baltimore: Johns Hopkins University Press.

———. 1989. *The Condition of Post-Modernity.* London and New York: Basil Blackwell.

Hazard, Thomas R. 1851. *Report on the Poor and Insane in Rhode Island.* Providence: Joseph Knowles.

Hodder, Ian. 1986. *Reading the Past: Current Approaches to Interpretation in Archaeology.* Cambridge: Cambridge University Press.

Hood, J. Edward. 1996. Social Relations and the Cultural Landscape. In *Landscape Archaeology: Reading and Interpreting the American Historical Landscape,* ed. R. Yamin and K. Bescherer-Metheny, 120–45. Knoxville: University of Tennessee Press.

Howard, John. 1777. *The State of the Prisons in England and Wales, with Preliminary Observations, and an Account of Some Foreign Prisons.* Warrington, UK: William Eyres.

"Humanity." 1870. Town Asylum, or Poorhouse. *Providence Journal,* October 24, 1870.

Ignatieff, Michael. 1978. *A Just Measure of Pain: The Penitentiary in the Industrial Revolution, 1750–1850.* New York: Pantheon Books.

Jackson, George. 1970. *Soledad Brother: The Prison Letters of George Jackson.* New York: Coward-McCann.

Jamieson, Ross W. 2000. Doña Luisa and Her Two Houses. In *Lines That Divide: Historical Archaeologies of Race, Class, and Gender,* ed. J. A. Delle, S. A. Mrozowski, and R. Paynter, 142–67. Knoxville: University of Tennessee Press.

Johnson, Matthew. 1996. *An Archaeology of Capitalism.* Oxford: Basil Blackwell.

Johnston, Norman. 2000. *Forms of Constraint: A History of Prison Architecture.* Urbana and Chicago: University of Illinois Press.

Johnston, Norman, with Kenneth Finkel and Jeffrey A. Cohen. 1994. *Eastern State Penitentiary: Crucible of Good Intentions.* Philadelphia: Philadelphia Museum of Art.

Jones, Henry A. n.d. *The Dark Days of Social Welfare at the State Institutions at Howard, Rhode Island.* Providence: privately published.

Jordy, William A., and Christopher P. Monkhouse. 1982. Thomas Alexander Tefft: Addition to State Prison and County Jail. In *Buildings on Paper: Rhode Island Architectural Drawings, 1825–1945,* 168–69. Providence: Bell Gallery, List Art Center, Brown University.

Katz, Michael B. 1996. *In the Shadow of the Poorhouse: A Social History of Welfare in America.* Originally published in 1986. New York: Basic Books.

Larsen, Eric L. 1994. A Boardinghouse Madonna—Beyond the Aesthetics of a Portrait Created through Medicine Bottles. In *An Archaeology of Harpers Ferry's Commercial and Residential District,* ed. P. A. Shackel and S. E. Winter, 68–79. *Historical Archaeology* 28 (4): 68–79.

Lefebvre, Henri. 1991. *The Production of Space.* Translated by Donald Nicholson-Smith. Oxford: Basil Blackwell.

Leone, Mark P. 1973. Archaeology as the Science of Technology: Mormon Town Plans and Fences. In *Research and Theory in Current Archaeology,* ed. Charles Redman, 125–50. New York: Wiley.

———. 1984. Interpreting Ideology in Historical Archaeology: Using the Rules of Perspective in the William Paca Garden in Annapolis, Maryland. In *Ideology, Power, and Prehistory,* ed. D. Miller and C. Tilley, 25–35. Cambridge: Cambridge University Press.

———. 1988. The Georgian Order as the Order of Merchant Capitalism in Annapolis, Maryland. In *The Recovery of Meaning: Historical Archeology of the Eastern United States,* ed. M. P. Leone and P. B. Potter Jr., 235–61. Washington, DC: Smithsonian Institution Press.

———. 1995. A Historical Archaeology of Capitalism. *American Anthropologist* 97 (2): 251–68.

Leone, Mark P., and Constance A. Crosby. 1987. Epilogue: Middle-Range Theory in Historical Archaeology. In *Consumer Choice in Historical Archaeology,* ed. S. M. Spencer-Wood, 397–411. New York: Plenum.

Lewis, Orlando F. 1967. *The Development of American Prisons and Prison Customs, 1776–1845.* Originally published in 1922. Montclair, NJ: Patterson-Smith.

Linebaugh, Peter. 1992. *The London Hanged: Crime and Civil Society in the Eighteenth Century.* Cambridge: Cambridge University Press.

Little, Margaret Ruth. 1972. The Architecture of a Late, Lamented Genius: Thomas Alexander Tefft. Master's thesis, Brown University.

Mangan, Patricia Hart. 2000. Building Biographies: Spatial Changes in Domestic Structures during the Transition from Feudalism to Capitalism. In *Lines That Divide: Historical Archaeologies of Race, Class, and Gender,* ed. J. A. Delle, S. A. Mrozowski, and R. Paynter, 205–38. Knoxville: University of Tennessee Press.

Markus, Thomas. 1994. Can History Be a Guide to the Design of Prisons? In *Architecture of Incarceration,* ed. Iona Spens, 12–19. London: Academy Editions.

Marquardt, William H., and Carole L. Crumley. 1987. Theoretical Issues in the Analysis of Spatial Patterning. In *Regional Dynamics: Burgundian Landscapes in Historical Perspective,* ed. C. L. Crumley and W. H. Marquardt, 1–18. New York: Academic Press.

Mayne, Alan, and Tim Murray, eds. 2001. *The Archaeology of Urban Landscapes: Explorations in Slumland.* Cambridge: Cambridge University Press.

McBride, Kevin A., Mary G. Soulsby, and Bruce Clouette. 1991. *Combined Reports, Phase I and II Archaeological Surveys, Improvements to Route 7 (Douglas Pike) from Route I-295 to Providence Pike, Smithfield, Rhode Island.* Report prepared by the Public Archaeology Survey Team, Inc., for Garofalo and Associates, Inc., Providence.

McGowen, Randall. 1986. A Powerful Sympathy: Terror, the Prison, and Humanitarian Reform in Early Nineteenth-Century Britain. *Journal of British Studies* 25 (3): 312–34.

———. 1987. The Body and Punishment in Eighteenth-Century England. *Journal of Modern History* 59 (4): 651–79.

———. 1995. The Well-Ordered Prison: England, 1780–1865. In *The Oxford History of the Prison,* ed. N. Morris and D. J. Rothman, 79–109. Oxford: Oxford University Press.

McGuire, Randall H. 1992. *A Marxist Archaeology.* New York: Academic Press.

McKelvey, Blake. 1977. *American Prisons.* Originally published in 1936. Montclair, NJ: Patterson-Smith.

Melish, Joanne Pope. 1998. *Disowning Slavery: Gradual Emancipation and "Race" in New England, 1780–1860.* Ithaca: Cornell University Press.

Melossi, D., and M. Pavarini. 1981. *The Prison and the Factory: Origins of the Penitentiary System.* London: Macmillan.

Miller, Daniel, and Christopher Tilley, eds. 1984. *Ideology, Power and Prehistory*. Cambridge: Cambridge University Press.

Moakley, Maureen, and Elmer Cornwell. 2001. *Rhode Island Politics and Government*. Lincoln: University of Nebraska Press.

Mrozowski, Stephen A. 1991. Landscapes of Inequality. In *The Archaeology of Inequality*, ed. R. McGuire and R. Paynter, 79–101. Oxford: Basil Blackwell.

Mrozowski, Stephen A., James A. Delle, and Robert Paynter. 2000. Introduction. In *Lines That Divide: Historical Archaeologies of Race, Class, and Gender*, ed. J. A. Delle, S. A. Mrozowski, and R. Paynter, xi–xxxi. Knoxville: University of Tennessee Press.

Mrozowski, Stephen A., Grace H. Ziesing, and Mary C. Beaudry. 1996. *Living on the Boott: Historical Archaeology at the Boott Mills Boardinghouses, Lowell, Massachusetts*. Amherst: University of Massachusetts Press.

Nassaney, Michael S., and Marjorie R. Abel. 1993. The Political and Social Contexts of Cutlery Production in the Connecticut Valley. *Dialectical Anthropology* 18:247–89.

———. 1996. Historic Buildings and Labor Organization: Lessons from New England's Nineteenth-Century Cutlery Industry. Paper presented at the George Meany Memorial Archives symposium "Building History and Labor History," Silver Spring, MD.

———. 2000. Urban Spaces, Labor Organization, and Social Control: Lessons from New England's Nineteenth-Century Cutlery Industry. In *Lines That Divide: Historical Archaeologies of Race, Class, and Gender*, ed. J. A. Delle, S. A. Mrozowski, and R. Paynter, 276–306. Knoxville: University of Tennessee Press.

Nassaney, Michael S., and Robert Paynter. 1995. Spatiality and Social Relations. Paper presented at the Annual Conference on Historical and Underwater Archaeology, Washington, DC.

Nicolosi, Anthony S. 1989. The Newport Asylum for the Poor: A Successful Nineteenth-Century Institutional Response to Social Dependency. *Rhode Island History* 47 (1): 3–21.

Ong, Aihwa. 1987. *Spirits of Resistance and Capitalist Discipline: Factory Women in Malaysia*. Albany: State University of New York Press.

———. 1990. State vs. Islam: Malay Families, Women's Bodies and the Body Politic in West Malaysia. *American Ethnologist* 17 (2): 258–76.

Oshinsky, David M. 1996. *"Worse than Slavery": Parchman Farm and the Ordeal of Jim Crow Justice*. New York: Free Press.

Parmal, Pamela A. 1990. *Beauty in Hand: The Art of the Fan*. Providence: Museum of Art, Rhode Island School of Design.

Paynter, Robert. 1988. Steps to an Archaeology of Capitalism. In *The Recovery of Meaning: Historical Archeology of the Eastern United States*, ed. M. P. Leone and P. B. Potter Jr., 407–33. Washington, DC: Smithsonian Institution Press.

———. 1989. The Archaeology of Equality and Inequality. *Annual Review of Anthropology 1989*: 369–99.

Paynter, Robert, and Randall H. McGuire. 1991. The Archaeology of Inequality: Material Culture, Domination and Resistance. In *The Archaeology of Inequality*, ed. R. McGuire and R. Paynter, 1–27. Oxford: Basil Blackwell.

Perry, Amos. 1887. *Rhode Island State Census.* Providence: E. L. Freeman and Son, Printers to the State.

Petchesky, Rosalind P. 1993. At Hard Labor: Penal Confinement and Production in Nineteenth-Century America. In *Crime and Capitalism: Readings in Marxist Criminology*, ed. D. F. Greenberg, 595–611. Philadelphia: Temple University Press.

Peters, Edward M. 1995. Prison before the Prison: The Ancient and Medieval Worlds. In *The Oxford History of the Prison*, ed. N. Morris and D. J. Rothman, 79–109. Oxford: Oxford University Press.

Powell, Eric A. 2002. Tales from Storyville: Digging the "Sporting Life" in Old New Orleans. *Archaeology* 55 (6): 26–35.

Praetzellis, Mary, Adrian P. Praetzellis, and Marley R. Brown III. 1988. What Happened to the Silent Majority? Research Strategies for Studying Dominant Group Material Culture in Late Nineteenth-Century California. In *Documentary Archaeology in the New World*, ed. M. C. Beaudry, 192–202. Cambridge: Cambridge University Press.

Prisons and Prisoners: A Sketch of the Early Jails and of the Old State Prison. 1879. *Providence Journal*, January 20, 1–2.

Prude, Jonathan. 1983. *The Coming of Industrial Order: Town and Factory Life in Rural Massachusetts, 1810–1860.* Cambridge: Cambridge University Press.

———. 1985. Town-Factory Conflicts in Antebellum Rural Massachusetts. In *The Countryside in the Age of Capitalist Transformation*, ed. Steven Hahn and Jonathan Prude, 71–102. Chapel Hill: University of North Carolina Press.

Rothman, David J. 1971. *The Discovery of the Asylum: Social Order and Disorder in the New Republic.* Glenview, IL: Scott, Foresman and Company.

Rusche, Georg, and Otto Kirchheimer. 1968. *Punishment and Social Structure.* Originally published in 1939. New York: Russell and Russell.

Said, Edward. 1978. *Orientalism.* New York: Vintage Books.

———. 1983. *The World, The Text, and the Critic.* Cambridge: Harvard University Press.

Saitta, Dean J., Randall McGuire, and Philip Duke. 1999. Working and Striking in Southern Colorado. Paper presented at the Annual Conference on Historical and Underwater Archaeology, Salt Lake City, UT.

Sangren, Steven. 1995. "Power" against Ideology: A Critique of Foucauldian Usage. *Cultural Anthropology* 10 (1): 3–40.

Schmidt, Peter R., and Stephen A. Mrozowski. 1988. Documentary Insights into the Archaeology of Smuggling. In *Documentary Archaeology in the New World*, ed. M. C. Beaudry, 32–42. Cambridge: Cambridge University Press.

Scott, James C. 1985. *Weapons of the Weak: Everyday Forms of Peasant Resistance*. New Haven: Yale University Press.

———. 1990. *Domination and the Arts of Resistance: Hidden Transcripts*. New Haven: Yale University Press.

Seidel, John L. 1990. "China Glaze" Wares on Sites from the American Revolution: Pearlware before Wedgewood? *Historical Archaeology* 24 (1): 82–95.

Sellin, Thorsten. 1944. *Pioneering in Penology: The Amsterdam Houses of Correction in the Sixteenth and Seventeenth Centuries*. Philadelphia: University of Pennsylvania Press.

Semple, Janet. 1993. *Bentham's Prison: A Study of the Panopticon Penitentiary*. Oxford: Clarendon Press.

Shackel, Paul A. 1993. *Personal Discipline and Material Culture: An Archaeology of Annapolis, Maryland, 1695–1870*. Knoxville: University of Tennessee Press.

———. 2000. *Archaeology and Created Memory: Public History in a National Park*. New York: Kluwer Academic/Plenum Publishers.

Siracusa, Carl. 1979. *A Mechanical People: Perceptions of the Industrial Order in Massachusetts, 1815–1880*. Middletown, CT: Wesleyan University Press.

Soja, Edward W. 1989. *Postmodern Geographies: The Reassertion of Space in Critical Social Theory*. London: Verso.

———. 1997. *Thirdspace: Journeys to Los Angeles and Other Real-and-Imagined Places*. London: Basil Blackwell.

Spens, Iona, ed. 1994. *Architecture of Incarceration*. London: Academy Editions.

Spierenburg, Pieter. 1987. From Amsterdam to Auburn: An Explanation for the Rise of the Prison in Seventeenth-Century Holland and Nineteenth-Century America. *Journal of Social History* (Spring): 439–61.

———. 1991. *The Prison Experience: Disciplinary Institutions and Their Inmates in Early Modern Europe*. New Brunswick, NJ: Rutgers University Press.

———. 1995. The Body and the State: Early Modern Europe. In *The Oxford History of the Prison*, ed. N. Morris and D. J. Rothman, 49–78. Oxford: Oxford University Press.

Staples, William R. 1853. *History of the Criminal Law of Rhode Island*. Pamphlet published by order of the Rhode Island General Assembly, Providence.

Stachiw, Myron O. 2001. *The Early Architecture and Landscapes of the Narragansett Basin*. Privately published for the Annual Meeting of the Vernacular Architecture Forum.

Starbuck, David. 1984. The Shaker Concept of Household. *Man in the Northeast* 28:73–86.

Sweet, John Wood. 1995. Bodies Politic: Colonialism, Race, and the Emergence of the American North; Rhode Island 1730–1830. Ph.D. diss., Princeton University.

Takagi, Paul. 1993. The Walnut Street Jail: A Penal Reform to Centralize the Powers of the State. In *Crime and Capitalism: Readings in Marxist Criminology*, ed. D. F. Greenberg, 533–45. Philadelphia: Temple University Press.

Taussig, Michael T. 1980. *The Devil and Commodity Fetishism in South America*. Chapel Hill: University of North Carolina Press.

Teeters, Negley K. 1955. *The Cradle of the Penitentiary: The Walnut Street Jail at Philadelphia, 1773–1835*. Philadelphia: University of Pennsylvania Press.

Teeters, Negley K., and John D. Shearer. 1957. *The Prison at Philadelphia, Cherry Hill: The Separate System of Penal Discipline, 1829–1913*. New York: Columbia University Press.

Tilley, Christopher. 1990. Foucault: Towards an Archaeology of Archaeology. In *Reading Material Culture*, ed. Christopher Tilley, 281–347. London: Basil Blackwell.

Traven, B. 1962. *The Death Ship: The Story of an American Sailor*. Originally published in 1934. New York: Collier Books.

Upton, Dell. 1992. The City as Material Culture. In *The Art and Mystery of Historical Archaeology: Essays in Honor of James Deetz*, ed. A. E. Yentsch and M. C. Beaudry, 51–74. Boca Raton, FL: CRC Press.

Ward, David A., and Gene G. Kassebaum. 1965. *Women's Prison: Sex and Social Structure*. Chicago: Aldine Press.

Willis, Paul. 1977. *Learning to Labor: How Working Class Kids Get Working Class Jobs*. New York: Columbia University Press.

Wolf, Eric R. 1982. *Europe and the People without History*. Berkeley: University of California Press.

Woodhead, Henry, ed. 1991. *Echoes of Glory: Arms and Equipment of the Union*. New York: Time-Life Books.

Wriston, Barbara. 1940. The Architecture of Thomas Tefft. *Bulletin of the Museum of Art of the Rhode Island School of Design* 28: 37–45.

Yanni, Carla. 2003. The Linear Plan for Insane Asylums in the United States before 1866. *Journal of the Society of Architectural Historians* 62 (1): 24–49.

Zukin, Sharon. 1991. *Landscapes of Power: From Detroit to Disney World*. Berkeley: University of California Press.

ACTS, RECORDS, AND ARCHIVAL COLLECTIONS

An Act in Relation to Officers and Discipline of the State Prison. 1852. Sections 1, 5.

Acts and Resolves of the Rhode Island General Assembly (ARRIGA). 1834–78. On file at the Rhode Island State Archives, Providence.

Annual Reports of the Board of Inspectors of the Rhode Island State Prison (ARBI). 1839–78. On file at the Rhode Island State Archives, Providence.

Carlson, Kenneth S. 2002. State Prison Convicts, 1838–1880, Prisoners #1–1000. Compilation of inmate data on file at the Rhode Island State Archives, Providence.

Correspondence—Prisoners. Rhode Island State Prison and Providence County Jail Records 319B:1. Rhode Island State Archives, Providence.

Daybooks and Journals. Rhode Island State Prison and Providence County Jail Records 308/315D:3. Rhode Island State Archives, Providence.

First Report of the City Plan Commission. 1914. Rhode Island State Archives, Providence.

Francis, John Brown. Undated ephemera. Box 5, F 86, Rhode Island Historical Society, Providence.

Haviland, John. Papers. Special Collections, University of Pennsylvania Libraries.

Inspectors' Weekly Visits No. 1. Rhode Island Historical Society MS 231.1, Vol. 34. Rhode Island Historical Society, Providence.

Petitions to Governor/Prisoner's Pardons. General Treasurer's Records C 1184, 47C:1. Rhode Island State Archives, Providence, RI.

Preliminary Report of the Committee on Prison Industries. 1934. Rhode Island State House Library, Providence.

Prisoner Shop Time Books. Rhode Island State Prison and Providence County Jail Records 319A:2. Rhode Island State Archives, Providence.

Punishment—Discipline Books. Rhode Island State Prison and Providence County Jail Records 319C:2. Rhode Island State Archives, Providence.

Report of the Commission to Select and Purchase a Site and Erect Thereon a Building for the State Normal School (Normal School Commission). 1899. Report on file at the Rhode Island State Archives, Providence.

Report of the Committee Appointed upon the Subject of a State Prison (RCASSP). 1834. General Treasurer's Records C 0490, Box 70:B. Rhode Island State Archives, Providence.

Report of the Committee to Draw Up a Specification . . . for a State Prison (RCD-UASSP). 1835. General Treasurer's Records C 0490, Box 70:B. Rhode Island State Archives, Providence.

Report of the State Charities and Corrections Committee. 1883. Report on file at the Rhode Island State Archives, Providence.

Vote of the City of Providence about the Prison Lot. 1835. Manuscript docket (MSS 144 SS B22 F7), Rhode Island Historical Society, Providence.

Warden's Monthly Reports. Rhode Island State Prison and Providence County Jail Records 319A:1. Rhode Island State Archives, Providence.

INDEX

224

State House, Rhode Island, 198–201
surveillance, 14–15
"systematic soldiering," 174–75

Tefft, Thomas A.
    early career, 83
    project for City Hall and State House,
        105–6
    role in building Providence,104–6
    role in rebuilding the RISP, 85–86
Tilley, Thomas, 158–59
time off for good habits, 169–70
town farm system, 189–90
transportation to colonies, 35–36
trash pits, 108–9

Union Army, 2–3
    and the case of James O'Neil, 160–63
    and the case of Joseph McAdam,
        158–59
    Union Depot (Providence), 104–6
utopian communities, 26

Vermont State Prison, 124–25
Viall, Nelson
    choice of letterhead, 106–7
    and cronyism, 93–94
    directs move to new prison, 179
    early years, 2–5
    use of Dark Cell, 177

Walnut Street (Philadelphia)
    historical significance, 40
    implementation, 39–40
Wayland, Francis, 81
Woodbury, Augustus, 161–63
workshops
    exterior, 80–81
    initial construction, 86–87
    interior described, 81